Knowledge Processes in Globally Distributed Contexts

TECHNOLOGY, WORK AND GLOBALIZATION

Also in this series:

Knowledge Processes in Globally Distributed Contexts

Edited by

Julia Kotlarsky, Ilan Oshri
and
Paul C. van Fenema

HD
66
.K62
2008

Selection and editorial matter © Julia Kotlarsky, Ilan Oshri and
Paul C. van Fenema 2008

Individual chapters © contributors 2008

All rights reserved. No reproduction, copy or transmission of this
publication may be made without written permission.

No paragraph of this publication may be reproduced, copied or
transmitted save with written permission or in accordance with the
provisions of the Copyright, Designs and Patents Act 1988, or under the
terms of any licence permitting limited copying issued by the Copyright
Licensing Agency, 90 Tottenham Court Road, London W1T 4LP.

Any person who does any unauthorized act in relation to this publication
may be liable to criminal prosecution and civil claims for damages.

The authors have asserted their rights to be identified as the authors of
this work in accordance with the Copyright, Designs and Patents Act 1988.

First published 2008 by
PALGRAVE MACMILLAN
Houndmills, Basingstoke, Hampshire RG21 6XS and
175 Fifth Avenue, New York, N.Y. 10010
Companies and representatives throughout the world

PALGRAVE MACMILLAN is the global academic imprint of the Palgrave
Macmillan division of St. Martin's Press, LLC and of Palgrave Macmillan Ltd.
Macmillan® is a registered trademark in the United States, United
Kingdom and other countries. Palgrave is a registered trademark in the
European Union and other countries.

ISBN-13: 978–0–230–00731–4
ISBN-10: 0–230–00731–7

This book is printed on paper suitable for recycling and made from
fully managed and sustained forest sources. Logging, pulping and
manufacturing processes are expected to conform to the environmental
regulations of the country of origin.

A catalogue record for this book is available from the British Library.

Library of Congress Cataloging-in-Publication Data
Knowledge processes in globally distributed contexts / edited by Julia
    Kotlarsky, Ilan Oshri and Paul C. van Fenema.
        p.cm — (Technology, work and globalization)
    Includes index.
    ISBN 0–230–00731–7 (alk. paper)
    1. Virtual work teams. 2. Information technology—Management. 3.
    Knowledge management—Technological innovations. I. Kotlarsky,
    Julia. II. Oshri, Ilan. III. Fenema, Paul C. van.
    HD66.K62 2008
    658.4'038—dc22   2007052862

10   9   8   7   6   5   4   3   2   1
17 16 15 14 13 12 11 10 09 08

Printed and bound in Great Britain by
Cromwell Press Ltd, Trowbridge, Wiltshire

CONTENTS

University Libraries
Carnegie Mellon University
Pittsburgh, PA 15213-3890

List of Tables

LIST OF FIGURES

Notes on Contributors

Paul C. van Fenema is Associate Professor at the Netherlands Defence Academy, The Netherlands. He holds a PhD in Information Systems and Management from the Rotterdam School of Management at Erasmus University, The Netherlands. He has held positions at the Rotterdam School of Management and Florida International University. His research focuses on coordination and knowledge management in global information studies projects and high reliability organizations. His work has been widely published in books and journals.

Jos van Hillegersberg is Professor of Design and Implementation of Information Systems and Head of the Department of Information Systems and Change Management at the University of Twente, The Netherlands. He has published in the *Journal of Product Innovation Management*, *Information Systems*, the *Journal of Information Technology*, and many others.

Julia Kotlarsky is Associate Professor of Information Systems, Information Systems and Management Group, Warwick Business School, UK. She holds a PhD in Information Systems and Management from the Rotterdam School of Management Erasmus, The Netherlands. Her research interests revolve around managing knowledge, the social and technical aspects of globally distributed software development teams, and IT outsourcing. Kotlarsky has written on this subject and her work has been widely published in books and journals.

Kuldeep Kumar is Visiting Professor at the City University of Hong Kong, China. He is also the Professor of Information Studies (IS) at Florida International University, Miami (USA), and Professor of IS Research at Rotterdam School of Management Erasmus, The Netherlands. His research has been published in books and journals, such as *MIS Quarterly*, *Communications of the ACM*, *IEEE Transactions on Software Engineering*, *Information Systems*, and many others.

Katy J. Mason is Lecturer in Marketing and Strategic Management at the Lancaster University Management School, UK. She holds a PhD from

Warwick University, UK. Her research has focused on market orientation, the market-oriented supply chain, supply chain configuration typologies, and knowledge transfer and information flows across organizational boundaries. Her work has been published in *Industrial Marketing Management, Long Range Planning, Marketing Intelligence and Planning*, and the *Journal of Management Studies*.

Ilan Oshri is Associate Professor of Strategic Management, the Rotterdam School of Management Erasmus, The Netherlands. He holds a PhD in Strategic Management and Technological Innovations from Warwick Business School, UK. His main research interest lies in the area of learning, knowledge management and innovation in global teams. His work has been widely published in books and journals.

Vinay Tiwari is a PhD candidate at Rotterdam School of Management Erasmus University's research school ERIM. He received his BTech from IIT Kanpur, India, and his MPhil in Business Research (*cum laude*) from Rotterdam School of Management Erasmus University, The Netherlands. He previously worked within the Indian IT industry. His research interests concern issues of communication, and understanding and culture in distributed work, as well as intra- and interorganizational coordination.

Paul W. L. Vlaar, PhD *cum laude* Rotterdam School of Management Erasmus University, is Assistant Professor in the Department of Management and Organization of the Vrije Universiteit Amsterdam, The Netherlands. His work has been published in, amongst others, *Group and Organization Management* and *Organization Studies*. He has contributed to the *Handbook of Strategic Alliances* and *Research in Competence-Based Management*. His current research interests include the management and governance of interorganizational relationships, and issues of culture, understanding and communication in outsourcing and offshoring relations.

Leslie P. Willcocks is Head of the Information Systems and Innovation Group and Professor of Technology Work and Globalization at the London School of Economics and Political Science, UK. He holds a PhD from the University of Cambridge and is Visiting Professor at Erasmus and Melbourne Universities. He is also co-editor of the *Journal of Information Technology*. He has co-authored many books and over 150 refereed papers on information systems management, IT and business process outsourcing, IT-enabled change, IT evaluation, and social theory and philosophy for information systems.

INTRODUCTION

Globally distributed projects have always presented managers with major challenges. As the distances between parties involved in the joint development of new products and services have increased, management's struggle properly to design and execute global projects has also become more demanding, requiring managers to consider new ways to tackle managerial challenges. In this book we examine one particular challenge, namely the management of knowledge processes in globally distributed projects. The book, which is largely based on cases of information systems development, considers various knowledge processes that globally distributed teams often engage in during their software development and implementation projects.

As Peter Drucker has said, "Knowledge has to be improved, challenged, and increased constantly, or it vanishes." These knowledge processes represent the value an organization generates from engaging in, improving, and magnifying knowledge work by collaborating across distances, time zones, and cultures. But arriving at a successful approach to managing knowledge in a globally distributed context is not free of problems. So how do organizations create, share, transfer, and reuse knowledge within and across globally distributed teams? What can be learned from cases of leading companies that have successfully tackled this challenge?

In this book we deal with the various aspects involved in the knowledge work of globally distributed teams. We consider the diversity of team members around the world and their limited opportunities for real-time communication. Moreover, we examine their dependence on electronic media, rather than on face-to-face meetings we often take for granted in co-located teams, and their limited ability to understand who knows what within global teams.

We make an effort in this book to analyze and offer the most suitable practices that address such challenges from multiple angles. We consider various theoretical frameworks – such as transactive memory, coordination theory, a knowledge-based view of the firm – in explaining how knowledge and expertise is created, shared, transferred, coordinated, and reused in globally distributed contexts. We bring forward examples from leading organizations that have faced similar challenges and have introduced effective local and global practices. We report on their successes and conceptualize these learnings in frameworks that can be applied by other organizations.

In Chapter 1 we define the context of this book. We first discuss what we mean by distributed contexts and move on to consider knowledge sharing in globally distributed teams. In this chapter we discuss the notion of transactive memory, to convey the idea that knowledge sharing in globally distributed teams can be supported through a memory system in which counterparts are made aware of "who knows what". Chapter 2 goes deeper in developing this idea by considering knowledge transfer between onsite and offshore teams. We explain how a transactive memory system can be developed across distributed teams and how it can be extended beyond a co-located team. In Chapter 3 we look at the knowledge bases that professionals share to help them overcome the communication challenges associated with globally distributed work. Attention then shifts towards work coordination. We examine how coordination mechanisms impact on knowledge processes and enable distributed teams to face the challenge of coordinating distributed work processes (Chapter 4). In Chapter 5 we discuss how expertise is managed in distributed contexts. We advance the idea that expertise management consists of three processes: development, coordination, and integration. This chapter focuses on generic learning processes that take place in distributed contexts. Chapter 6, on the other hand, considers four specific learning processes that take place in an offshoring setting. Chapter 7 considers knowledge processes and aspects relating to the division of work in globally distributed teams. We examine the case of component-based design as a major challenge that globally distributed IS development teams face, and illustrate through two cases how such teams can benefit from knowledge reuse in spite of being globally distributed. Current work on collaboration across global teams is characterized by its complex and ambiguous nature. This calls for a detailed description and thorough understanding of the factors influencing the development of shared understanding across global distances, which is provided in Chapter 8. Furthermore, global teams depend on technology to improve and support collaboration. Chapter 9 describes how globally distributed teams use advanced e-collaboration technologies to support and automate knowledge work processes.

CHAPTER 1

Knowledge sharing, social ties and successful collaboration in globally distributed system development projects

Julia Kotlarsky and Ilan Oshri

> The biggest problem is a people problem: if people from different sites don't have the respect and trust for each other, they don't work well together. (Anthony, Chief Software Architect, LeCroy)

Introduction

Recent years have witnessed the globalization of many industries. Consequently, globally distributed collaborations and virtual teams have become increasingly common in many areas, for example in new product development (Malhotra *et al.*, 2001) and in Information Systems (IS) development (Sarker and Sahay, 2004; Herbsleb and Mockus, 2003; Carmel and Agarwal, 2002).

Managing dispersed development projects is far more challenging than co-located projects. However, ongoing innovations in Information and Communication Technology (ICT) make it possible to cooperate in a distributed mode. Indeed, recent research in the IS field has focused on ICT in the context of globally distributed IS development teams (Herbsleb *et al.*, 2002; Mockus and Herbsleb, 2002; Carmel, 1999). However, little is known about the social aspects associated with the management of globally distributed IS development projects and, in some studies, social aspects are perceived to be constraints on globally distributed collaboration (Sarker and Sahay, 2004; Evaristo, 2003; Jarvenpaa and Leidner, 1999). While other disciplines, such as organizational behaviour, have acknowledged the importance of social aspects, such as trust (Child, 2001; Storck, 2000), in global collaborations, evidence about the role that human and social aspects play in global collaborative work is still missing. To fill this gap, this chapter attempts to address the following question: *Do knowledge sharing and social ties contribute to successful collaboration in globally distributed IS development teams?*

The chapter begins with a discussion of the literature on globally distributed IS development projects. A review of past studies related to social ties, knowledge sharing, and successful collaboration in various contexts, such as co-located sites and global alliances, will be provided. Following this, the motivation for this research, and an identification of the gap in the literature, will be outlined. After an outline of the research methods applied, data drawn from SAP and LeCroy, two companies that have engaged in globally distributed IS development projects, will be set out. A qualitative presentation of these findings will be followed by a quantification of the research data, providing evidence for the importance of social ties and knowledge sharing to collaborative work in globally distributed IS development teams. Evidence regarding the mechanisms supporting the build-up of social ties observed in the companies studied will also be outlined. Finally, the implications for theory and practice are discussed.

Background

Globally distributed IS development projects consist of two or more teams working together to accomplish project goals from different geographical locations. In addition to geographical dispersion, globally distributed teams face time zone and cultural differences that may include, but are not limited to, different languages, national traditions, values, and norms of behaviour (Carmel, 1999).

Traditionally, the main focus of IS literature on globally distributed teams has been on technical aspects related to system development projects. Past research in the IS field suggests that the proper application of technical and operational mechanisms such as collaborative technologies, IS development tools and coordination mechanisms, is the key to successful system development projects (Herbsleb *et al.*, 2002;

Majchrzak *et al.*, 2000; Carmel, 1999). It has been claimed, for example, that a powerful ICT infrastructure is required to ensure connectivity and data transfer at high speed between remote sites (Carmel, 1999). Additionally, generic collaborative technologies (e.g. Groupware) are needed to enable remote colleagues to connect and communicate. The most commonly suggested collaborative technologies are email, chat (Instant Messaging), phone/teleconferencing, video-conferencing, intranet, group calendar, discussion lists, and electronic meeting systems (Herbsleb and Mockus, 2003; Smith and Blanck, 2002). Finally, in addition to generic collaborative technologies, a number of specific tools for software development have been suggested to support globally distributed teams. These include configuration and version management tools, document management systems, replicated databases, and CASE tools (Smith and Blanck, 2002; Carmel and Agarwal, 2002; Ebert and De Neve, 2001). Recent studies have focused on integrating development (e.g. Integrated Development Environment) with collaborative tools (e.g. email, Instant Messaging) in order to offer solutions that deal with breakdowns in communication and coordination among developers in dispersed development teams (Cheng *et al.*, 2004).

A related stream of studies has focused on issues pertaining to the geographical dispersion of work. Naturally, because of several constraints associated with globally distributed work, such as distance and time zone and cultural differences, traditional coordination and control mechanisms tend to be less effective in global development projects (Herbsleb and Mockus, 2003). Distance, for example, reduces the intensity of communications, in particular when people experience problems with media that cannot substitute face-to-face communications (Smith and Blanck, 2002). Cultural differences, expressed in different languages, values, working and communication habits, and implicit assumptions, are believed to be embedded in the collective knowledge of a specific culture (Baumard, 1999) and thus may cause misunderstanding and conflicts. Time zone differences reduce opportunities for real time collaboration, as response time increases considerably when working hours at remote locations do not overlap (Sarker and Sahay, 2004). Such challenges raise the question whether globally distributed work can benefit from other factors, human in nature, involved in dispersed projects. The following sections provide a review of the literature on the human and social aspects involved in collaborative work. We draw on studies from several disciplines in order to assess the extent to which human and social aspects have been considered as enablers for collaborative work in globally distributed projects.

Social aspects in globally distributed teams

A large number of factors that may contribute to collaborative work have been given consideration in earlier studies. Among the many socially related factors contributing to collaboration, past studies have considered formal and informal communications (Child, 2001; Dyer, 2001; Storck, 2000), trust (Arino et al., 2001; Child, 2001), motivation (Child, 2001), and social ties (Oshri et al., 2007; Storck, 2000; Child, 2001; Granovetter, 1973). The literature on IS development projects is far more limited in addressing the impact that human-related factors may have on IS projects in general, and successful collaboration in particular. It has been argued, for example, that informal communications play a critical role in coordination activities leading to successful collaboration in co-located IS development (Kraut and Streeler, 1995). As the size and complexity of IS development increases, the need to support informal communications also increases (Herbsleb and Moitra, 2001). Consequently, one of the central problems in distributed development projects is induced by time, cultural, and geographical distances that greatly reduce the amount of such communication. Nonetheless, past studies related to IS in the context of globally distributed teams have mainly raised concerns about managers' abilities to overcome geographical, time zone, and cultural differences. According to Smith and Blanck (2002: 294), for example, "an effective team depends on open, effective communication, which in turn depends on trust among members. Thus, trust is the foundation, but it is also the very quality that is most difficult to build at a distance."

Trust was defined by Child (2001: 275) as "the willingness of one person or group to relate to another in the belief that the other's action will be beneficial rather than detrimental, even though this cannot be guaranteed." Trust is more likely to be built if personal contact, frequent interactions, and socializing between teams and individuals are facilitated (Arino et al., 2001; Child, 2001).

Additional challenges to globally distributed work have been raised by Herbsleb and Mockus (2003). They claim that (i) distributed social networks are much smaller than same-site social networks; (ii) there is far less frequent communication in distributed social networks compared to same-site social networks; (iii) people find it much more difficult to identify distant colleagues with necessary expertise and to communicate effectively with them; and (iv) people at different sites are less likely to perceive themselves as part of the same team than people who are at the same site. Studies that have sought solutions to overcome the above challenges, often induced by the lack of personal interactions between remote teams, have suggested a division of labour and task between remote sites (e.g. Battin *et al.*, 2001; Grinter *et al.*, 1999). While it seems that the main challenge is to create rapport between members of the dispersed teams, the solutions proposed have been mainly in the field of technical and project procedures. *Rapport* is defined as "the quality of the relation or connection between interactants, marked by harmony, conformity, accord, and affinity" (Bernieri *et al.*, 1994: 113). Past research has indeed confirmed that rapport is the key to collaboration between project teams and individuals, though only in the context of co-located project sites (Gremler and Gwinner, 2000). Little is known about creating rapport between globally distributed teams.

To summarize, while past studies in the various disciplines have acknowledged the importance of social aspects in collaborative work, the studies that have focused on the IS field have tended to see such social aspects (e.g. trust and rapport) as very difficult to encourage or foster in the context of globally distributed projects.

Knowledge sharing in globally distributed teams

The importance of knowledge sharing for collaborative work has already been established in past studies (e.g. Hendriks, 1999; Goodman and Darr, 1998). Storck (2000), for example, claims that sharing knowledge is important to building trust and improving the effectiveness of group work. Herbsleb and Moitra (2001) reiterated such an observation, claiming that without an effective sharing of information, projects might suffer from coordination problems leading to unsuccessful collaborations.

Nonetheless, achieving an effective knowledge sharing process may encounter certain challenges, in particular when teams are faced with cultural, geographical, and time zone differences (Herbsleb and Mockus 2003; Kobitzsch *et al.*, 2001). Herbsleb *et al.* (2000: 3) described how one global IS development project was facing major challenges in identifying who knows what: "The difficulties of knowing who to contact about what, of initiating contact, and of communicating effectively across sites, led to a number of serious coordination problems."

There seemed to be a need to know whom to contact about what in this particular organization, something that is far more challenging in globally distributed teams. This organizational aspect, knowing who knows what, has been acknowledged as the key to knowledge sharing activities by several studies (Herbsleb and Mockus, 2003; Orlikowski, 2002). Faraj and Sproull (2000), for example, suggested that instead of sharing specialized knowledge, individuals should focus on knowing where expertise is located and needed. Such an approach towards knowledge sharing is also known as transactive memory. *Transactive memory* is defined as the set of knowledge possessed by group members coupled with an awareness of who knows what (Wegner, 1987). It has been claimed that the transactive memory may positively affect group performance and collaboration by quickly bringing the needed expertise to knowledge seekers (Faraj and Sproull, 2000; Storck, 2000). We will elaborate on the concept of transactive memory in distributed teams in Chapters 2 and 5.

Another socially constructed concept that was proposed as a connecting mechanism between individuals and teams is collective knowledge. Grant (1996) claims that collective knowledge comprises elements of knowledge that are common to all members of an organization. In the case of globally distributed system development projects, the "organization" involves all people participating in the project in remote locations. *Collective knowledge* is defined as "a knowledge of the unspoken, of the invisible structure of a situation, a certain wisdom" (Baumard, 1999: 66). Such a concept may entail the profound knowledge of an environment, of established rules, laws and, regulations. It may include language, other forms of symbolic communication and shared meaning (Grant, 1996). Building a sense of collective knowledge in co-located organizations would mean the development of a collective mind (Weick *et al.*, 1999; Weick and Roberts, 1993) through participation in tasks and social rituals (Orlikowski, 2002; Baumard, 1999; Orr, 1990).

To conclude, while globally distributed teams have employed a range of communication tools (e.g. Groupware applications comprising chat, email, discussion lists, and application sharing capabilities) which support the sharing of knowledge across remote sites, evidence from recent research suggests that the challenges involved in sharing knowledge across globally distributed teams are still widespread, and that breakdowns in sharing knowledge do occur. Indeed, technical solutions are important but are, however, not sufficient. This calls for further investigation of socially constructive elements involved in developing collective knowledge and transactive memory as complementary mechanisms to existing technical solutions.

Successful collaboration in information system projects

The word collaboration comes from the Latin words *com* (prefix "together") and *laborare* (verb "to work"). It means that two or more individuals work jointly on an intellectual endeavour (Webster, 1992). *Collaboration* is a complex, multidimensional process characterized by constructs such as coordination (Faraj and Sproull, 2000), communication (Weick and Roberts, 1993), meaning (Bechky, 2003), relationships (Gabarro, 1990), trust (Meyerson *et al.*, 1996), and structure (Adler and Borys, 1996; Scott, 1992).

The IS literature covers at length some factors that support successful collaboration. *Successful collaboration* is the process through which a specific outcome, such as a product or desired performance, is achieved through group effort. In this sense, successful collaboration is represented in this chapter as either product success or a desired performance of a distributed team (Hoegl and Gemuenden, 2001). Product success can be represented by various indicators, such as growth in sales, product delivery on time and within budget (Andres, 2002; Nellore and Balachandra, 2001), or short time-to-market (Datar *et al.*, 1997). In line with these indicators, *product success* is thus defined as the achievement of project objectives (Gallivan, 2001). This criterion for product success can either be objective, i.e. based on market or company data, or subjective, i.e. based on project participants' perception of product success.

A desired result of a distributed team can also be a people-related outcome (Hoegl and Gemuenden, 2001) which entails meeting the psychological needs of the members (Gallivan, 2001). Hoegl and Gemuenden, and Gallivan, for example, suggest that, in addition to performance objectives, teams must also work in a way that increases members' motivation to engage in future teamwork. There should be some level of personal satisfaction that motivates individuals and teams to continue their engagement in collaborative work despite geographical, time, and cultural differences. We perceive *personal satisfaction* as the outcome of a positive social experience. Such experience can, for example, be in the form of stress-free communication rituals between remote counterparts and collegial relationships between remote teams. Some factors that may foster people-related outcomes and thus may improve personal satisfaction are open and multiple informal communication channels (Hoegl and Gemuenden, 2001), the encouragement of interactions between parties involved in the development process (Nelson and Cooprider, 1996), and the cohesion of a team (Gallivan, 2001; Hoegl and Gemuenden, 2001). Naturally, geographical, cultural, and time-zone differences pose additional challenges to globally distributed teams to achieve successful collaboration, whether seen as a people-related outcome or as a product outcome.

The motivation for the research: The gap

By far, the solutions proposed to support globally distributed teams were technical in nature involving little attention to the human and social aspects involved in globally distributed work (Al-Mushayt *et al.*, 2001). Furthermore, in the few studies that focused on social aspects in globally distributed projects, these aspects were presented as concepts that added challenges to the coordinating of collaborative work because of cultural, geographical, and time-zone differences. Jarvenpaa and Leidner (1999), for example, indicated that lack of trust is likely to develop between globally distributed teams, while Carmel (1999) raised a concern about possible breakdowns in communications that may cause coordination problems because of language barriers, cultural differences, asymmetry in distribution of information among sites, and lack of team spirit.

While we accept the observation that insufficient trust and poor social relationships may act as barriers to successful collaboration in globally distributed teams, and sufficient trust and well-established social relationships may act as enablers to collaborative work, we also argue that there is a need to understand whether, and how, social aspects actually contribute to successful collaboration teams. The importance, and the contribution, of social aspects to collaborative work in globally distributed projects is neglected in the IS literature, and the little that is known about this area is mainly based on co-located project teams. To fill this gap, three concepts – social ties, knowledge sharing, and successful collaboration – will be studied in an attempt to address the following question: *Do knowledge sharing and social ties contribute to successful collaboration*

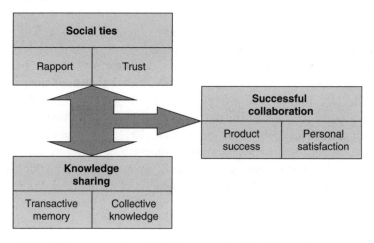

Figure 1.1　Main concepts and their categories in this study

in globally distributed IS development teams and, if so, through what mechanisms are social ties established and facilitated?

Figure 1.1 illustrates the three main concepts, social ties, knowledge sharing, and successful collaboration; and their categories, trust and rapport, transactive memory and collective knowledge, and product success and personal satisfaction, respectively. In addition, the importance of collaborative tools will be studied in order to assess their impact on successful collaboration in comparison to the contribution that social ties and knowledge sharing have made to successful collaborative work. Lastly, the mechanisms that support social ties will be explored in an attempt to explain how companies may create social ties between globally distributed team members.

About this research

An in-depth study of globally distributed software development projects is provided in this chapter. A qualitative, interpretive approach is adopted. In line with much past IS research (e.g. Palvia *et al.*, 2003), a case-study method was selected for this research. In this study, evidence was gathered from a variety of sources such as documentation, archival records, and interviews (Yin, 1994; Eisenhardt, 1989). Data were also triangulated through interviews with team counterparts in different locations and in cases where the interpretation of subjective evidence was questionable, such as in the case of successful collaboration. In addition, data analysis methods involved both the presentation of qualitative data in the form of statements made by interviewees as well as a quantification of data in the form of statement frequencies.

To correspond with the main interests of the research, only project teams at SAP and LeCroy that were globally distributed across at least two locations were considered for this study (see Company Background in the Appendix). Interviews were conducted at two remote sites per company: in India and Germany for SAP, and in Switzerland and the USA for LeCroy. Interviewees were chosen to include (i) counterparts working closely at remote locations; and (ii) diverse roles such as managers and developers. In total, ten interviews (five at each company) were conducted. Interviews lasted one hour and thirty minutes on average; they were recorded and fully transcribed. A semi-structured interview protocol was applied, to allow the researchers to clarify specific issues and follow up with questions.

Data analysis followed several steps. It relied on iterative reading of the data using the open-coding technique (Strauss and Corbin, 1998), sorting and refining themes emerging from the data based on the definitions of the categories with some level of diversity (Strauss and Corbin, 1998; Miles and Huberman, 1994), and linking these to categories and concepts.

Coding was done in Atlas.ti – packaged Qualitative Data Analysis (QDA) software. The QDA software facilitated the analysis process. In particular, it was used for coding, linking codes and text segments, documenting diversity in codes, creating memos, searching, editing and reorganizing, and visual representation of data and findings (Weitzman, 2000; Miles and Huberman, 1994).

Data were analyzed by the researchers independently. The interpretation of selective codes (those that seemed to have dual meaning), the consolidation of codes into categories, and the examination of empirical findings against the literature were done by both researchers together. In addition, feedback sessions with key informants in the case companies were organized and their comments were incorporated into the research findings. Such a data analysis approach is believed to enhance confidence in the findings (Eisenhardt, 1989).

Empirical results and analysis

In this section the results of two case studies carried out at SAP and LeCroy will be presented. Based on the empirical evidence presented below, we will argue that social ties and knowledge sharing contribute to successful collaboration in the companies studied. In principle, we claim, based on the data analyzed, that in globally distributed IS development teams, social ties and knowledge sharing improves collaboration. Furthermore, several organizational mechanisms supporting the build-up of social ties between remote sites are reported. In order to support the above claim, three levels of evidence will be outlined in the following section. The first level is an outline of statements made by interviewees associated with the concepts under investigation (i.e. social ties, knowledge sharing, and successful collaboration). The second level is the frequency of these statements. The third level will present the number of instances in which social ties, knowledge sharing, and collaborative tools are linked to successful collaboration.

Social ties in globally distributed teams: Evidence

Statements made by interviewees about rapport and trust are presented below. These statements were analyzed and associated with rapport and trust based on the definitions provided above.

Rapport:

LeCroy   "Most of the guys know each other very well – we try to make sure they interact, we increase the possibility that they really get to know each other." (Anthony)

SAP   "I need to have good relationships with the people I am working with . . . the better you know the people the easier it gets. I know Sudhir and Thomas, both of them I think by now quite well." (Christoph)

Trust:

LeCroy   "It makes a big difference, when the guys know each other but more importantly when the guys trust each other." (Anthony)

SAP   "The team-building exercise was a way to show that we care about remote locations. The end result of that exercise was that the entire team [globally distributed] feels more comfortable to work together. Now they know each other and trust each other better." (Stefan)

Knowledge sharing in globally distributed teams: Evidence

Statements made by interviewees about transactive memory and collective knowledge are presented below. These statements were analyzed and associated with rapport and trust based on the definitions provided above.

Transactive memory:

LeCroy   "When a problem occurs it is important for the team, instead of finding the bug, to find quickly who knows best about the failing component." (Gilles)

SAP   "What I did in the past was – this was in the very early phase of
          the project, I sent requests only to Sudhir and he would
          distribute the issues between people. But by now, after six
          months, I know quite well what everybody is doing. So after a
          time, you just know who's doing what." (Christoph)

Collective knowledge:

LeCroy   "How do you pick all the guys that we had – pure embedded
          programmers – and teach them all about Windows at the same
          time. Well, we all got together in the mountains of France. It
          was a real fun week with two purposes: one was to teach us all
          about this new technology. The other which was fairly equally
          important if not more important in some way – was to really try
          to build relationships between people." (Larry)
SAP   "It [team building] was a pretty good experience for myself:
          learning the culture and also how the team internally works. So
          my understanding of what you can expect from the team, and
          what you cannot expect, is very important for the project."
          (Stefan)

Successful collaboration in globally distributed teams: Evidence

Successful collaboration can be defined by various indicators. The very
perception of interviewees that a project team was collaborative is one
indication of such success. However, there may also be external indicators
of successful collaboration, such as project and product success. These
indicators can be either subjective or objective. Subjective evidence may
include statements made by interviewees about their perception of product
success, while objective evidence presents evidence in the form of sales,
growth, and industry recognition associated with the product. While
objective evidence should not be biased, one has to acknowledge that
some indicators may have been manipulated prior to presentation by the
company (e.g. sales figures). The perception of interviewees with regard
to product success and personal satisfaction, representing successful
collaboration, is presented below. These statements were analyzed and
associated with product success and personal satisfaction based on the
definitions provided above.

Product success:

LeCroy	Engineers described the Maui project as a component-based architecture, claiming that this new approach serves as a basis for future products because "we can take the bunch of different components and create different instruments . . . within a few months rather than in a few years." (Larry)
SAP	"We just went through a merger, so setting up a global project was not an easy task. Despite all the difficulties we managed to have a successful second software release in eight months." (Stefan)

Personal satisfaction:

LeCroy	"The job here is very demanding and challenging. I think that those who stay onboard are the engineers who share the same goal: to work on complex problems in cutting edge technologies. I think that the fact that we share this goal helps us to communicate well." (Gilles)
SAP	"The team building exercise from our side [Bangalore team] was more of a building of awareness about the whole team of Stefan, because he heads now all our team, so he needed to have a good picture of how the team composition is, what each individual is like or what different people are like." (Sudhir)

In addition, objective evidence, presented below, supports the perception of product success that was reported by interviewees.

Product and project success (objective evidence):

LeCroy
- LeCroy's WaveMaster 8600, the first release of the Maui Project, was announced as the Best Product of Year 2002 by *EDN*, a leading magazine for design engineers.
- While revenues in 2003 were down to $107.8m from $111.5m in 2002 because of the difficult economic environment, the WaveMaster had a positive impact on the financial results of year 2003: "Our high-end oscilloscope product orders grew by 7 per cent in the first quarter of fiscal 2003 over a comparable period in fiscal 2002. This success is due to the new WaveMaster

product line, including the introduction of the world's highest performance oscilloscope during the quarter, the WaveMaster 8600A." (Tom Reslewic, CEO, LeCroy, news release, October 16, 2002)

SAP
- According to JupiterResearch, a leading research and consulting company in emerging technologies, SAP Enterprise Portal is the third largest software solution, with 17 per cent of the US market in 2002. The studied collaboration project developed collaborative tools as one of the three main features of the SAP Enterprise Portal.
- The 2003 revenues for SAP Enterprise Portal were up by 5 per cent representing 13 per cent of SAP software sales (SAP's 2003 annual report).

Concept frequencies for social ties, knowledge sharing, collaborative tools, and successful collaboration

The above section presents a sample of statements made by interviewees from SAP and LeCroy with regard to social ties, knowledge sharing, and successful collaboration. This section presents a calculation of all statements made by interviewees at SAP and LeCroy in the context of social ties, knowledge sharing, collaborative tools, and successful collaboration. We refer to this calculation as concept frequencies. Fifty-one statements were made by interviewees from SAP, for example, with regard to knowledge sharing in globally distributed teams (see Table 1.1). In addition, "diversity in codes" was calculated. This represents the number of different codes grouped within one category. Under the category "trust", for example, three different codes were identified. In other words, "diversity in codes" represents the number of instances that a statement was found to be somehow different from another statement in the context of a particular category.

Our calculations show that 81 statements were made with regard to social ties, 72 statements concerning knowledge sharing, and 102 statements about collaborative tools. Within the concepts, a large number of statements were associated with rapport (71). These findings may suggest that interviewees have considered developing rapport with counterparts from remote sites to be an important element in collaborative work. The importance of social ties and knowledge sharing in successful collaboration will be further discussed in the following section.

Table 1.1 Concept frequencies for SAP and LeCroy based on number of statements

Concept	Categories in concept	Diversity in codes	Concept frequencies (number of statements per concept)		
			SAP	LeCroy	SUM
Social ties	Rapport	17	50	21	
	Trust	3	3	7	81
Knowledge sharing	Transactive memory	15	28	14	
	Collective knowledge	15	23	7	72
Collaborative tools	None	8	54	48	102
Successful collaboration	Product success	14	23	24	
	Personal satisfaction	19	45	28	120

The relationships between social ties, knowledge sharing, collaborative tools, and successful collaboration

To assess the importance of social ties and knowledge sharing for successful collaboration, a calculation was made of statements that represented explicit relationships between social ties, knowledge sharing, collaborative tools, and successful collaboration. These calculations are presented in Table 1.2 under the column "relationships with successful collaboration".

We can see from Table 1.2 that social ties (30 per cent) and knowledge sharing (43 per cent) were associated with successful collaboration, almost to the same extent or even further than collaborative tools (37 per cent). The significance of these findings can be further underlined by the observation that interviewees were asked a similar number of questions about human-related issues and for collaborative tools. Based on this evidence, we argue that our findings suggest that, in addition to technical solutions, human-related issues in the form of social ties and knowledge sharing were considered as the key to successful collaboration.

Table 1.2 Calculated values of relationships between concepts based on number of associated codes

Concepts	Concept Frequencies (count from Table 1.1)	Relationships with successful collaboration (statements %)
Social ties	81	**24** (30)
Knowledge Sharing	72	**31** (43)
Collaborative tools	102	**38** (37)

Organizational mechanisms supporting social ties in globally distributed teams

The analysis of the evidence collected at SAP and LeCroy suggests that there were two phases of activities that supported the build-up of social ties: (i) before Face to Face (F2F); and (ii) after F2F. In addition, the analysis of the empirical evidence suggests that there were some particular tools that the projects studied have applied. Table 1.3 outlines these activities and tools, and a calculation of the number of statements made with regard to a particular activity or tool is provided for each company. The highest frequency calculated is in bold letters.

Table 1.3 suggests that interviewees from SAP considered activities prior to a F2F meeting important for building social ties, i.e. rapport and trust, between members of the globally distributed team. In particular, a short visit to a remote location was mentioned as an important mechanism prior to a formal introduction of the team. Interviewees from LeCroy considered activities before F2F and after F2F as equally important for the build-up of social ties. Nonetheless, managers from LeCroy also considered an initial introduction activity before F2F as important for instituting social relationships. In terms of post-F2F activities, interviewees from both companies indicated the importance of open communication channels. A non-hierarchical communication approach was another mechanism contributing to social relationships. Lastly, the tools through which social relationships were created across different sites were mainly phone, email, and groupware applications. Nonetheless, interviewees also indicated that the quality of messages, meaning, the assurance that messages communicate the issue successfully and are understood and interpreted properly, is important for establishing social relationships between team members.

Table 1.3   Organizational mechanisms and activities supporting social ties in globally distributed teams

Mechanisms	Mechanism frequencies	
	SAP	LeCroy
Before Face to Face (F2F)	**88**	**30**
Promote initial (non-F2F) introduction (e.g. virtual F2F, *short visit to location,* set up virtual mini teams, advocate shared cyber spaces)	61	26
Reduce communication barriers (e.g. English courses, *set up contact person,* distribute newsletters and communication protocol)	27	4
After F2F	**35**	**34**
Routinize communications (e.g. regular reflection sessions, around the table discussions, project meetings, *visits to remote locations*)	14	9
Open communication channels (e.g. *direct communication channel,* centralized source of shared information)	18	15
Ensure message quality (e.g. detailed email, use phone, ensure understanding of message received, *use graphical representation*)	3	10
Tools	**62**	**58**
Various collaborative tools (e.g. *phone, email, Groupware tools,* knowledge repositories, teleconference, videoconference, online chat)	54	48
Practices (flexible working hours, standardized software packages)	8	10

So far, we have presented evidence about the importance of social aspects in globally distributed teams and the means through which social ties can be established. The following section will discuss the implications of this for research and practice.

Implications

Human and organizational aspects involved in system development projects are at the centre of this study. The cases of SAP and LeCroy have demonstrated the importance of some human aspects (e.g. social ties and knowledge sharing activities) and organizational aspects (e.g. tools and project procedures) in globally dispersed collaborative work. The implications for human and organizational aspects are both theoretical and practical.

Theoretical implications

From a theoretical perspective, this study suggests that more attention is needed to understand the relationships between social ties, knowledge sharing, and successful collaboration in globally distributed teams. As it stands, the IS literature tends to overemphasize the contribution of technical solutions and collaborative tools to the flow and sharing of information (e.g. Battin *et al.*, 2001; Ebert and De Neve, 2001), and in some cases to downplay the role of social aspects, such as rapport, in globally distributed collaborative work. We claim that collaborative work can also be understood from a social construction viewpoint in which the quality of the relation or connection between interactants in globally distributed teams can be enhanced through story telling (Orr, 1990) and participation in social rituals (Lave and Wenger, 1991). In this respect, the social practice is the primary activity, and collaboration is one of its characteristics. The learning involved in the manner in which people successfully collaborate is located within the social world. As part of the participation involved in a collaborative practice, members of a globally distributed project change locations and perspectives to create and sustain learning trajectories (Lave and Wenger, 1991: 36). We argue that collaboration is actually about renewing the set of relations between globally distributed project members through continuous participation and engagement. In this sense, collaborative tools are one mediator through which collaboration as a learned social practice is developed. The role that social interactions between remote counterparts play in reducing the perception of distance in remote communications and in establishing social capital will be elaborated in Chapters 3 and 4.

Practical implications

From a practical viewpoint, we argue that in order to achieve successful collaboration in globally distributed teams, companies need to introduce organizational mechanisms that create social spaces between team members. There is substantial support in research and practice, as for example in this study, for face-to-face meetings, suggesting that such meetings are important for teamwork and performance (Govindarajan and Gupta, 2001; Jarvenpaa *et al.*, 1998).

We argue that some activities should be planned both before and after face-to-face meetings, to ensure the participation and engagement of project members in collaborative work. We suggest, for example, that managers should facilitate social interaction prior to a F2F meeting, such as short visits to a remote location of key project-members, the introduction of a contact person to the virtual team, support for language courses, and the dissemination of clear communication procedures. These activities, often ignored prior to a F2F meeting in globally distributed teams, have been reported as the key to establishing social and human contact and supporting the build-up of rapport between counterparts from remote sites. Regular meetings, either virtual or in terms of short visits, after F2F meetings, will ensure participation of project members over time. We also suggest that a variety of communication tools be utilized to assist the maintenance of a high level of participation of project members and to enrich the quality of messaging involved in collaborative work, such as phone, videoconference media, and email.

Lastly, from a strategic viewpoint, management should demonstrate strong commitment to addressing human-related issues in IS globally distributed projects and should dedicate resources that ensure the renewal of social relationships, as was done at SAP and LeCroy.

Concluding remarks

In this chapter, the contribution of social ties and knowledge sharing to successful collaboration in distributed IS development teams has been explored. We conclude that, in addition to technical solutions, human-related issues in the form of social ties and knowledge sharing were reported as keys to successful collaboration. In particular, the importance of rapport and transactive memory was evident in the studied projects. Furthermore, organizational mechanisms that create and maintain social ties between dispersed team members were reported in detail.

The conclusions offered in this chapter are based on an in-depth study of two companies, by applying a qualitative, interpretive methodological lens. Additional methodological approaches may contribute to further understand the relationships between social ties, knowledge sharing, and successful collaboration in globally distributed teams. We propose that future studies should conduct a survey across the IS industry in which the causal relationships between these three main concepts will be further investigated.

Acknowledgement

Data collection in India was sponsored by a grant from the Netherlands Foundation for the Advancement of Tropical Research (WOTRO).

References

Adler, P. S. and Borys, B. (1996) "Two types of bureaucracies: enabling and coercive," *Administrative Science Quarterly*, 4161–89.

Al-Mushayt, O., Doherty, N. F., and King, M. (2001) "An Investigation into the Relative Success of Alternative Approaches to the Treatment of Organizational Issues in System Development Projects," *Organization Development Journal*, 19(1), 31–48.

Andres, H. P. (2002) "A Comparison of Face-to-Face and Virtual Software Development Teams," *Team Performance Management*, 8(1/2), 39–48.

Arino, A., De la Torre, J., and Ring, P. S. (2001) "Relational Quality: Managing Trust in Corporate Alliances," *California Management Review*, 44(1), 109–31.

Battin, R. D., Crocker, R., and Kreidler, J. (2001) "Leveraging Resources in Global Software Development," *IEEE Software* (March/April), 70–7.

Baumard, P. (1999) *Tacit Knowledge in Organizations*, SAGE Publications, London.

Bechky, B. A. (2003) "Sharing Meaning across Occupational Communities: The Transformation of Understanding on a Production Floor," *Organization Science*, 14(3), 312–30.

Bernieri, F. J., Davis, J. M., Rosenthal, R., and Knee, C. R. (1994) "Interactional Synchrony and Rapport: Measuring Synchrony in Displays Devoid of Sound and Facial Affect," *Personality and Social Psychology Bulletin*, 20, 303–11.

Carmel, E. (1999) *Global Software Teams: Collaborating Across Borders and Time Zones*, Prentice-Hall P T R, Upper Saddle River, NJ.

Carmel, E. and Agarwal, R. (2002) "The Maturation of Offshore Sourcing of Information Technology Work," *MIS Quarterly Executive*, 1(2), 65–77.

Cheng, L., DeSouza, C. R. B., Hupfer, S., Patterson, J., and Ross, S. (2004) "Building Collaboration into Ideas," *Queue*, 1(9), 40–50.

Child, J. (2001) "Trust – The Fundamental Bond in Global Collaboration", *Organizational Dynamics*, 29(4), 274–88.

Datar, S., Jordan, C., Kekre, S., and Srinivasan, K. (1997) "New Product Development Structures and Time-to-Market," *Management Science*, 43(4), 452–64.

Dyer, J. H. (2001) "How to Make Strategic Alliances Work", *MIT Sloan Management Review*, 42(4), 37–43.

Ebert, C. and De Neve, P. (2001) "Surviving Global Software Development," *IEEE Software* (March/April), 62–9.

Eisenhardt, K. M. (1989) "Building Theories from Case Study Research," *Academy of Management Review*, 14(4), 532–50.

Evaristo, R. (2003) "The Management of Distributed Projects across Cultures," *Journal of Global Information Management*, 11(4), 58–70.

Faraj, S. and Sproull, L. (2000) "Coordinating Expertise in Software Development Teams," *Management Science*, 46(12), 1554–68.

Gabarro, J. J. (1990) The Development of Working Relationships," in *Intellectual Teamwork: Social and Technological Foundations of Cooperative Work* (Eds, Galegher, J., Kraut, R. E., and Egido, C.) Lawrence Erlbaum Associates, Hillsdale, New Jersey, pp. 70–110.

Gallivan, M. J. (2001) "Striking a Balance between Trust and Control in a Virtual Organization: A Content Analysis of Open Source Software Case Studies," *Information Systems Journal*, 11(4), 227–304.

Goodman, P. S. and Darr, E. D. (1998) "Computer-Aided Systems and Communities: Mechanisms for Organizational Learning in Distributed Environments," *MIS Quarterly*, 22(4), 417–40.

Govindarajan, V. and Gupta, A. K. (2001) "Building an Effective Global Business Team," *MIT Sloan Management Review*, 42(4), 63–71.

Granovetter, M. S. (1973) "The Strength of Weak Ties," *American Journal of Sociology*, 78(6), 1360–80.

Grant, R. M. (1996) "Toward a Knowledge-Based Theory of the Firm," *Strategic Management Journal*, 17(Winter), 109–22.

Gremler, D. D. and Gwinner, K. P. (2000) "Customer–Employee Rapport in Service Relationships," *Journal of Service Research*, 3(1), 82–104.

Grinter, R. E., Herbsleb, J. D., and Perry, D. E. (1999) "The Geography of Coordination: Dealing with Distance in R&D Work," in *Proceedings of the International ACM SIGGROUP Conference on Supporting Group Work (Group 99)*, ACM Press, Phoenix, AZ.

Hendriks, P. (1999) "Why Share Knowledge? The Influence of ICT on the Motivation for Knowledge Sharing," *Knowledge and Process Management*, 6(2), 91–100.

Herbsleb, J. D., Atkins, D. L., Boyer, D. G., Handel, M., and Finholt, T. A. (2002) "Introducing Instant Messaging and Chat into the Workplace," in *Proceedings of the Conference on Computer–Human Interaction*, Minneapolis, MN, pp. 171–8.

Herbsleb, J. D., Mockus, A., Finholt, T. A., and Grinter, R. E. (2000). "Distance Dependencies, and Delay in Global Collaboration," Conference on Computer Supported Cooperative Work, Philadelphia, Pennsylvania, US.

Herbsleb, J. D. and Mockus, A. (2003) "An Empirical Study of Speed and Communication in Globally-Distributed Software Development," *IEEE Transactions on Software Engineering*, 29(6), 1–14.

Herbsleb, J. D. and Moitra, D. (2001) "Global Software Development," *IEEE Software* (March–April), 16–20.

Hoegl, M. and Gemuenden, H. G. (2001) "Teamwork Quality and the Success of Innovative Projects: A Theoretical Concept and Empirical Evidence," *Organization Science*, 12(4), 435–49.

Jarvenpaa, S. L., Knoll, K., and Leidner, D. E. (1998) "Is Anybody out There? Antecedents of Trust in Global Virtual Teams," *Journal of Management Information Systems*, 14(4), 29–64.

Jarvenpaa, S. L. and Leidner, D. E. (1999) "Communication and Trust in Global Virtual Teams," *Organization Science*, 10(6), 791–815.

Kobitzsch, W., Rombach, D., and Feldmann, R. L. (2001) "Outsourcing in India," *IEEE Software* (March/April), 78–86.

Kraut, R. E. and Streeler, L. A. (1995) "Coordination in Software Development," *Communications of the ACM*, 38(3), 69–81.

Lave, J. and Wenger, E. (1991) *Situated Learning Legitimate Peripheral Participation*, Cambridge University Press, Cambridge.

Majchrzak, A., Rice, R. E., King. N., Malhotra, A., and Ba, S. (2000) "Computer-Mediated Inter-Organizational Knowledge-Sharing: Insights from a Virtual Team Innovating Using a Collaborative Tool," *Information Resources Management Journal*, 13(1), 44–54.

Malhotra, A., Majchrzak, A., Carman, R. and Lott, V. (2001) "Radical Innovation without Collocation: A Case Study at Boeing-Rocketdyne," *MIS Quarterly*, 25(2), 229–49.

Meyerson, D., Weick, K. E. and Kramer, R. M. (1996) "Swift Trust and Temporary Groups," in *Trust in Organizations: Frontiers of Theory and Research* (Eds, Kramer, R. M. and Tyler, T. R.) Sage, Thousand Oaks, CA.

Miles, M. B. and Huberman, A. M. (1994) *Qualitative Data Analysis: An Expanded Sourcebook* (2nd edn), Sage, Thousand Oaks, CA.

Mockus, A. and Herbsleb, J. D. (2002) "Expertise Browser: A Quantitative Approach to Identifying Expertise," in *Proceedings of the International Conference on Software Engineering*, Orlando, FL, pp. 503–12.

Nellore, R. and Balachandra, R. (2001) "Factors Influencing Success in Integrated Product Development Projects," *IEEE Transactions on Engineering Management*, 48(2), 164–74.

Nelson, K. M. and Cooprider, J. G. (1996) "The Contribution of Shared Knowledge to IS Group Performance," *MIS Quarterly*, 20(4), 409–32.

Orlikowski, W. J. (2002) "Knowing in Practice: Enacting a Collective Capability in Distributed Organizing," *Organization Science*, 13(3), 249–73.

Orr, J. (1990) "Sharing Knowledge Celebrating Identity: Community Memory in a Service Culture," in *Collective Remembering* (Eds, Middleton, D. and Edwards, D.) Sage, London.

Oshri, I., Kotlarsky, J., and Willcocks, L. P. (2007) "Global Software Development: Exploring Socialization in Distributed Strategic Projects," *Journal of Strategic Information Systems*, 16(1), 25–49.

Palvia, P., Mao, E., Salam, A. F., and Soliman, K. S. (2003) "Management Information System Research: What's there in a Methodology?" *Communications of the Association for Information Systems*, 11, 289–309.

Sarker, S. and Sahay, S. (2004) "Implications of Space and Time for Distributed Work: An Interpretive Study of US–Norwegian System Development Teams," *European Journal of Information Systems*, 13(1), 3–20.

Scott, W. R. (1992) *Organizations: Rational, Natural, and Open Systems*, Prentice-Hall, Englewood Cliffs, New Jersey.

Smith, P. G. and Blanck, E. L. (2002) "From Experience: Leading Dispersed Teams," *The Journal of Product Innovation Management*, 19(4), 294–304.

Storck, J. (2000) "Knowledge diffusion through 'strategic communities'," *Sloan Management Review*, 41(2), 63–74.

Strauss, A. L. and Corbin, J. M. (1998) *Basics of Qualitative Research* (2nd edn), Sage, Thousand Oaks, CA.

Webster (1992) *Webster's Dictionary*, Oxford University Press, Oxford.

Wegner, D. M. (1987) "Transactive Memory: A Contemporary Analysis of the Group Mind," in *Theories of Group Behaviour* (Eds, Mullen, G. and Goethals, G.) Springer Verlag, New York.

Weick, K. E. and Roberts, K. H. (1993) "Collective Mind in Organisations: Heedful Interrelating on Flight Desks," *Administrative Science Quarterly*, 38(3), 357–82.

Weick, K. E., Sutcliffe, K. M., and Obstfeld, D. (1999) "Organizing for High Reliability: Processes of Collective Mindfulness," in *Research in Organizational Behaviour* (Eds, Straw, B. and Cumings, L. L.) JAI Press, Greenwich, CT.

Weitzman, E. A. (2000) "Software and Qualitative Research," in *Handbook of Qualitative Research* (Eds, Denzin, N. K. and Lincoln, Y. S.) (2nd edn), Sage, Thousand Oaks, CA, pp. 803–20.

Yin, R. K. (1994) *Case Study Research: Design and Methods*, Sage, Newbury Park, CA.

CHAPTER 2

Knowledge transfer in globally distributed teams: The role of transactive memory

Ilan Oshri, Paul C. van Fenema, and Julia Kotlarsky

Introduction

Knowledge transfer has become a key issue for globally distributed work, such as global software development projects (e.g. Kotlarsky and Oshri, 2005), global business process outsourcing (e.g. Feeny *et al.*, 2005), and infrastructure management (e.g. Beulen *et al.*, 2005). In these novel organizational forms, success depends on the rapid transfer of business and technological knowledge from and to offshore facilities. This transfer of knowledge may improve knowledge integration across various sites and products, and may contribute to successfully coordinating complex projects (Grant, 1996).

Globally distributed projects, consisting of two or more teams working together from different geographical locations to accomplish project goals, face major challenges in transferring knowledge across remote sites. For example, these teams confront cultural differences that may include, but are not limited to, different languages, national traditions, values, and norms of behaviour (Carmel, 1999; Carmel and Agarwal, 2002). To overcome geographical distances and time-zone differences such teams mainly collaborate through Information and Communication Technology (ICT), and occasionally meet face to face to discuss project matters.

Nonetheless, over the past decade, studies have demonstrated repeatedly that, despite advances in technologies, ICTs do not prevent breakdowns in the transfer of knowledge across distributed sites (e.g. Cramton, 2001). While ICTs are critical for knowledge transfer processes in distributed teams, a neighbouring stream of studies within the IS field has considered human-related factors, such as trust (Jarvenpaa and Leidner,

1999; Ridings *et al.*, 2002) and interpersonal ties (Ahuja and Galvin, 2003; Kanawattanachai and Yoo, 2002), which may act as facilitators for knowledge transfer between remote counterparts.

In line with such advances in the IS field, scholars have increasingly considered the concept of the transactive memory as an enhancer of knowledge transfer (Nevo and Wand, 2005). The encoding, storing, and retrieving processes involved in a transactive memory system (TMS) (Wegner *et al.*, 1985) could support the transfer of knowledge between individuals (Nevo and Wand, 2005). While the concept of transactive memory has been studied in the context of traditional organizational forms and co-located teams, little is known about the process through which a TMS in globally distributed teams could be created and could support knowledge transfer between remote sites. The few studies that have indeed explored the concept of transactive memory in virtual teams have highlighted the importance of it for team performance (e.g. Yoo and Kanawattanachai, 2001) without addressing the broader challenge of knowledge transfer.

To contribute toward a filling of this gap, this chapter explores how remote counterparts encode, store, and retrieve information about the location of knowledge to support knowledge transfer between dispersed sites. In particular, this chapter will address the following questions: *How does transactive memory enable knowledge transfer in globally distributed teams?* And: *Through what mechanisms can a TMS be created and maintained?* In order to understand knowledge transfer in globally distributed teams from a transactive memory perspective, we first explore knowledge transfer challenges, and the development and use of a TMS in dispersed teams. This conceptual contribution is followed by an in-depth case study of global software development projects. The chapter concludes by providing theoretical and practical implications and suggestions for future research.

The challenges of knowledge transfer in globally distributed teams

Globally distributed teams – both within and between organizational boundaries – represent a new organizational form that has emerged in conjunction with the globalization of socio-economic processes. Such teams have replaced the traditional single-site hierarchy and the functional department structure for various reasons. For one, companies in developed nations have outsourced parts of their IT services and business processes to developing nations (Carmel and Agarwal, 2002; Currie and Willcocks, 1998). Short-cycle development and the launch of new products and software for global markets has required expertise from a range of geographical areas (Desouza and Evaristo, 2004). Following this trend, the transfer of knowledge has become a key challenge for global teams attempting to deliver products and services adjusted to local markets and yet aiming to standardize expertise and business and technological operations on an international scale (Sole and Edmondson, 2002). Indeed, this growing trend of outsourcing has increased the exchange of information and knowledge between knowledge workers located both offshore and onsite during different stages of product and service lifecycles.

Knowledge transfer is the process through which one organization (or unit) identifies and learns specific knowledge that resides in another organization (or unit), and reapplies this knowledge in other contexts (Hansen et al., 1999). On the individual level, Cutler (1989) has previously observed that knowledge transfer is indeed a process by which the knowledge of one actor is acquired and reapplied by another. While the literature has so far provided various explanations as to how knowledge is transferred between individuals – e.g. through knowledge codification and socialization processes (Nonaka, 1994) – several studies have expressed concern with regard to the transferability of knowledge between remote counterparts and dispersed teams, prompted by a number of factors.

First, the diversity of local contexts may exacerbate the stickiness of information (von Hippel, 1994) and hamper the transfer of contextual knowledge between remote sites (Cramton, 2001). Second, remote counterparts often adopt unique local routines for working, training, and learning (Desouza and Evaristo, 2004). These unique routines may obstruct the development of shared understanding of practices and knowledge across remote sites. Third, differences in skills, expertise, technical infrastructure, and development tools and methodologies further raise the barriers for knowledge transfer between remote sites. And finally, time-zone differences can reduce the window for real time interactions (Boland and Citurs, 2001), thus limiting opportunities for remote team-members to discuss, debate, and explain diverse opinions and perspectives.

Indeed, while co-located teams may develop various memory systems that support knowledge transfer, globally distributed teams often face challenges in developing such memory systems that may provide support for the transfer of contextual and embedded knowledge. The following section discusses the concept of transactive memory and aspects relating to how such a memory system may act as an enabler of knowledge transfer in globally distributed teams.

Transactive memory: The concept

The concept of transactive memory was briefly discussed in Chapter 1. In this chapter we seek to extend the discussion and offer a link to knowledge processes. A TMS has been defined as the combination of individual memory systems and communications (also referred to as "transactions") between individuals. The group-level TMS is constituted by individuals using each other as a memory source. Transactions between individuals link their memory systems; through a series of processes (i.e. encoding, storing, and retrieving), knowledge is exchanged. Individuals encode information for storing and retrieval, similar to a librarian entering details of a new book in the particular library system before putting it on the shelves. Through encoding, knowledge is categorized (i.e. assigned labels that reflect the subjects of the knowledge) for systematically storing the location of the knowledge, but not the knowledge itself. Then, individuals store this information internally (building their own memory), or externally (storing it in artifacts or indirectly in other people's memories). And lastly, information about the location of the knowledge or expertise is retrieved when someone else asks for it (Nevo and Wand, 2005). Retrieval thus consists of two interconnected subprocesses: person A asks person B for information; person B retrieves the information. As Nevo and Wand (2005: 551) put it: "knowledge is encoded, stored and retrieved through various transactions between individuals" (see Figure 2.1). Wegner (1995) explains that for a TMS to work, three corresponding aspects to encoding, storing, and retrieving should be considered. These aspects, which accommodate interactions between multiple actors, are:

1. Directory updating: where actors keep information about "who knows what" up-to-date
2. Information allocation: where actors decide in whose memory to store new information that arrives in the transactive memory system, and
3. Retrieval coordination: where actors use a set of guidelines to determine in which order other actors should be consulted for the missing information.

A common assumption in the knowledge management literature is that the type of knowledge involved in a transaction (i.e. explicit or tacit) matches the type of knowledge management approach to capturing, storing, and reapplying it (i.e. codified or personalized). Correspondingly, the literature distinguishes between codified (e.g. Hansen *et al.*, 1999) and personalized memory systems (e.g. Blackler, 1995). Similarly, based on

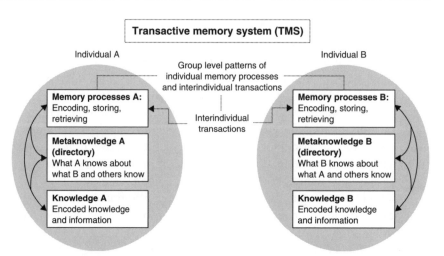

Figure 2.1   The concept of a transactive memory system
Source: After Wegner (1987).

the work of Hansen *et al*. (1999), DeSouza and Evaristo (2004: 87) discuss the differences between the codification-based and personalization-based knowledge approaches. With the codification approach, individual knowledge is "made centrally available to members of the organization via databases and data warehouses". The personalization knowledge approach, on the other hand, "recognizes the tacit dimension of knowledge and assumes that knowledge is shared mainly through direct person-to-person contacts." Similarly, the directories that point to where knowledge and expertise reside can either be codified (e.g. information systems and technologies) or personalized (e.g. personal memory or other people's memories). In other words, transactions between individuals take place through the use of various codified (e.g. databases) and personalized (e.g. theirs or other people's memory) directories. Such a TMS can be further developed and renewed through a constant update of these codified and personalized directories.

In line with such an approach, the following section addresses the challenges associated with knowledge transfer in globally distributed contexts from a transactive memory perspective.

Knowledge transfer through transactive memory: The challenges

A TMS may offer various benefits to both teams and individuals. Through the development of a TMS and the awareness of "who knows what", the performance of a team can be improved (Moreland and Myaskovsky, 2000; Faraj and Sproull, 2000). More specifically, a TMS may enhance specialization and division of labour. Teams and individuals could develop expertise in their own areas while being aware of the existence of expertise elsewhere (Majchrzak and Malhotra, 2005). In addition, the literature asserts the positive association of a TMS with team learning, speed to market, new product success (Akgun *et al.*, 2005), and an efficient coordination of expertise in teams through the development of similar labels and categories for encoding and retrieving information (Majchrzak and Malhotra, 2005; Nevo and Wand, 2005; Faraj and Sproull, 2000).

The development of a TMS can be facilitated through various activities. Past studies have illustrated this by studying the close relationships between couples (Wegner *et al.*, 1991). More recently, research has proposed that training activities contribute to the development of a TMS (Moreland and Argote, 2003). In co-located teams, the development of a TMS within a team seems achievable through sporadic training sessions and continuous problem-solving activities (Majchrzak and Malhotra, 2005; Yoo and Kanawattanachai, 2001).

However, several studies have raised concerns that developing a TMS may face significant challenges in distributed contexts (e.g. Majchrzak and Malhotra, 2005). For one, globally distributed teams often experience changes in membership that negatively affect the long-term development of a TMS (Ancona *et al.*, 2002). Furthermore, in many distributed settings, team members do not have any prior experience of working together. Their distributed mode of operation decreases communications and increases the possibilities for conflict (Armstrong and Cole, 1995), misunderstanding, and breakdowns in communication (Cramton, 2001; Chudoba *et al.*, 2005). In teams that do not carry out joint training or arrange face-to-face meetings (Yoo and Kanawattanachai, 2001); the development of shared understanding is even more challenging because members of such teams do not stand on "common ground" (Cramton, 2001). These challenges faced by distributed teams may hamper individuals' efforts to successfully maintain a system in which personalized directories are created and maintained. Furthermore, developing and updating a codified directory of information may be hampered by the adoption of different routines and methodologies across dispersed teams (DeSouza, 2003) and by difficulties to standardize work practices across remote locations. This problem results in fewer opportunities to access knowledge by remote counterparts.

Table 2.1 reviews the meaning of encoding, storing, and retrieving processes in the context of codified and personalized directories in globally distributed teams. We have developed these definitions and

Table 2.1 Transactive memory processes, codified and personalized directories in globally distributed teams

Memory process in a TMS	Types of directories in a TMS	
	Codified directories	**Personalized directories**
Encoding		
Having a shared "cataloging" system	Creating a shared system to categorize information. This can be effectively achieved by developing a set of rules of how to label the subject and location of the expertise	Creating a shared understanding of context and work-related processes, terminology, and language
Storing		
The way in which the information is organized in physical locations and in the memories of dispersed team members	Storing information about the subject and location of the knowledge. This can be achieved by creating pointers to the location of knowledge in an expertise directory Storing capabilities include up-to-date records of available documents and expertise	Storing information about "who knows what" and "who is doing what" in individuals memories
Retrieving		
(i) Knowing where and in what form information is stored in the dispersed team (ii) Being able to find required information through determining the location of information, and, sometimes, "the combination or interplay of items coming from multiple locations"	Developing capabilities to find information necessary to coordinate expertise Includes search capabilities (e.g. keyword-based) for effective and efficient search and retrieval processes	Developing interpersonal channels through which individuals can search for information about who has expertise and in which areas, and where this expertise resides

Source: After Wegner (1987).

observations based on the existing literature of globally distributed teams, knowledge management, and transactive memory, as discussed above.

We will use transactive memory processes and definitions, as presented in Table 2.1, to explore how one software vendor transferred knowledge between onsite and offshore teams.

About this research

To analyze the role of transactive memory in knowledge transfer between members of dispersed teams our primary case-selection criterion was to find globally distributed projects that were actively involved in knowledge transfer. Two projects from TATA Consultancy Services (TCS) were selected and studied in depth in the context of transactive memory. The projects faced complex and challenging knowledge-transfer situations, as remote counterparts needed to transfer knowledge while codeveloping and implementing the TCS Quartz financial platform for Scandia and Dresdner banks.

Evidence was collected from interviews, project documentation and observations (Yin, 1994; Eisenhardt, 1989). Interviews were conducted at two remote sites: in India and Switzerland (for the Scandia bank), and in India and the USA (for the Dresdner bank). Interviewees were chosen to include (i) counterparts working closely at remote locations and (ii) diverse roles such as managers and developers. In total, 14 interviews were conducted. Each one lasted on average 1.5 hours; and they were recorded and transcribed in full. A semi-structured interview protocol was applied, to allow the researchers to clarify specific issues and to follow up with questions.

Data analysis relied on iterative reading of the data using open-coding techniques (Strauss and Corbin, 1998), to sort and refine themes emerging from the data (Miles and Huberman, 1994). In particular, six themes that represent the concept of *transactive memory* were carefully studied: *encoding*, *storing*, and *retrieving processes*. Each process was examined in relation to *codified* and *personalized directories*. Statements that were found to correspond with these six themes were selected, coded, and analyzed using Atlas.ti – Qualitative Data Analysis software (Miles and Huberman, 1994; Weitzman, 2000).

The first step in our data analysis aimed to examine *how transactive memory enables knowledge transfer in globally distributed teams* (the first part of the research question). It involved reading through the interview transcripts and collected documents, then (i) coding statements that illustrate different elements of a TMS, according to definitions presented in Table 2.1, and (ii) marking evidence of knowledge transfer. During this stage chunks of text (paragraphs or sentences) describing (i) elements of a TMS and (ii) evidence of knowledge transfer were coded. Next, statements (i.e. codes) illustrating elements of a TMS were grouped into the six above-mentioned categories that represent the six elements of a TMS.

In addressing the second part of the research question – *through what mechanisms a TMS can be created and maintained* – we analyzed statements in each of these six categories to identify specific organizational mechanisms that enabled TCS to develop and maintain a TMS for knowledge transfer in globally distributed teams.

The Quartz project: Knowledge transfer in a globally distributed team

To explore the role of transactive memory in knowledge transfer the analysis will be organized around knowledge transfer challenges during encoding, storing, and retrieving processes and the role that transactive memory has played in overcoming these challenges. Some background information about TCS and the organization of the onsite and offshore teams can found in the Appendix.

The need for knowledge transfer

The philosophy TCS followed in dividing the work between the onsite and offshore sites was, whenever possible, to send work offshore to take advantage of the cost, quality, and availability of offshore personnel. As one interviewee explained, the onsite team was sending requirements offshore "because the expertise and major source code are here [offshore, in Gurgaon], and mainly because of the expertise, it is quicker and easier to work here." However, the majority of activities required close interactions with customer representatives through the onsite team. Activities during the initial project phases that required direct customer contact and access to the customer's site, such as user requirements and release management, were done onsite. Activities that required involvement of the client and close interactions among the TCS developers were conducted in a mixed onsite–offshore mode. Overall, the majority of the activities required ongoing bi-directional knowledge transfer between onsite and offshore teams. The only activities that were undertaken independently at the offshore location were coding and unit testing. Table 2.2 illustrates the knowledge transfer flows and challenges per project phase as described by the TCS engineers. Knowledge transfer challenges are identified (C1, C2, etc.) for further analysis.

In the next section, we focus on some specific knowledge transfer challenges (from Table 2.2) to illustrate the way engineers at TCS dealt with these through the creation, use, and updating of codified and personalized directories. We discuss knowledge transfer processes by examining encoding, storing, and retrieving processes.

Knowledge transfer: Encoding and updating codified and personalized directories

To overcome knowledge transfer challenges, TCS had developed a memory system that ensured the flow of knowledge between the client, onsite, and offshore teams. To achieve effectiveness from this memory system, encoding of the knowledge and updating of directories took place. This was done through a set of rules and standards (for codified directories) and by propagating common terminology, language, and concepts that team members use on a daily basis (for personalized directories). The encoding process supported the transfer of knowledge between onsite and offshore by creating a catalog of pointers to knowledge holders and knowledge seekers.

For example, one particular challenge is to transfer knowledge about customer requirements from onsite to offshore team (C2 in Table 2.2). In overcoming this challenge, onsite team members first codified customer requirements by summarizing them in writing; and following this, the team used a template document (e.g. Business Requirement Overview) to describe these requirements. More importantly, this template also encoded the subject and the location of this document. As members of the offshore teams were familiar with these templates and the Quartz terminology, they could locate the document, interpret customer requirements defined onsite (C2), and act upon them. One manager said: "We have set procedures for defining the requirements. If people follow the procedures, then the things become very easy to interpret or understand."

Table 2.2 Knowledge transfer during project phases

Project phases	Knowledge transfer from onsite (Zurich, San Francisco) to offshore (Gurgaon, Bombay)	Knowledge transfer from offshore (Gurgaon, Bombay) to onshore (Zurich, San Francisco)	Knowledge transfer challenges
Requirement definition	Customer requirements		• Onsite team needs to capture all customer requirements (C1) • Offshore team should be able to understand correctly customer requirements as documented by the onsite team, i.e. definition and interpretation of requirements should be consistent between onsite and offshore teams (C2) • Offshore team members need to know who to contact onsite for different requirements if clarifications are required (C3)
Analysis and prototyping	Customer feedback on prototype design	Prototype design	• Onsite team should understand the prototype created offshore and be able to show and explain it to the customer, with minimum guidelines from the offshore team (C4)
High-level design	Modified and signed specifications	Specifications	• Offshore team should be able to understand correctly customer feedback communicated in writing or verbally by the onsite team (C5) • Offshore team members need to know who to contact onsite for different issues that require clarifications (C6) • Onsite team should be able to interpret product specifications created by the offshore team and understand how to address customer requirements (C7)
Construction (Quartz configuration, coding, and unit testing)	n/a	n/a	• Offshore team should be able to identify quickly modifications made by the onsite team and interpret them correctly (C8) • Few challenges as construction is carried out mostly offshore

Integration and system testing	Actual system components and guidelines for integration and testing	• Onsite team should be able to understand the functionality of the system components guidelines for system integration, with minimum guidelines for integration and testing (C9)
		• Members of the onsite team may ask for clarifications and/or help with debugging from the offshore team: they need to know who to contact offshore for different issues (in particular, who wrote codes for different system components) (C10)
	Change requests	• Offshore team members should be notified about new Change Requests (C11)
		• Members of the onsite team should be able to track the status of the changes they requested (C12)
	Changes to the system and guidelines for their implementation	• Onsite team members should be notified when change requests have been implemented (C13)
		• Offshore team members should know who to contact onsite, if clarifications are required and/or when changes have been completed (C14)
		• Onsite team members should be able to understand the essence of the change and what aspects of the system may be affected by the change (C15)
Release management (system roll-out and user training)	Roll-out guidelines and training material	• Onsite team should be able to understand roll-out guidelines and how to use training material, with minimum guidelines and clarifications from the offshore team (C16)
	Questions, requests	• Onsite team members should know who to contact for different issues/ system components when they (or customers) have questions (C17)
	Clarifications, modifications	• Onsite team should be able to identify quickly modifications done by the offshore team and know how to implement them (C18)

Similarly, during high-level design, to transfer knowledge from offshore to onsite about the prototype created offshore (C4), and to enable the onsite team to explain product specifications to the customer (C7), the offshore team encoded the subject and location of this knowledge using Business Requirement Specification templates and High Level Design Document templates. Onsite team members were familiar with these templates (the encoding scheme the templates are based on) and could easily locate the knowledge, understand the specifications created offshore, and explain these to the customer. Furthermore, these documents specified the subject, and the name of the expert and his or her location, so that when a remote counterpart needed clarifications about this matter, he or she could easily locate the expert through this codified directory.

The use of standard templates to capture and transfer knowledge from onsite to offshore locations has created a cataloging system that served as a codified directory in which pointers to where information resides have been mapped out. Among the templates that were stored in this cataloging system were (i) procedural standards, such as the Quartz Implementation Methodology for the Quartz system, and (ii) documentation standards that include (but are not limited to): the Project Documentation Set (Business Requirements Overview, Business Requirements Specifications, High Level Design Document, DB Design Document, Module Test Specifications, and Product Acceptance Testing Specifications), and the User Documentation Set (Online Help, User's Manual, Installation Manual, Operations Manual). The update of this directory took place each time new information was placed in this directory. For example, when the customer wanted to add new functionality to the prototype design, the onsite team captured this request in Business Requirement Overview template (C5) and created a new entry to the codified directory. This new entry updated the codified directory for both onsite and offshore teams.

Knowledge transfer challenges were also overcome through personalized directories by linking knowledge seekers with knowledge holders. For example, the requirement definition stage posed two knowledge transfer challenges (C2 and C3 in Table 2.2) of which the overcoming may also depend on the existence of updated personalized directories among members of the onsite and offshore teams. Properly understanding customer requirements (C2) and knowing who to contact at the onsite team with queries (C3) required the offshore team to develop an understanding of the onsite team composition and the respective area of expertise per individual. Personalized directories as such offered an alternative route to the codified directory to transfer knowledge between onsite and offshore teams. Put simply, the constant interactions between onsite and offshore team members created and updated directories that were based on personal memory or other people's memory and that categorized personal experiences (what person A knows) and assigned "labels" as to what other people know (what A knows about B) and what they know about what other people know (what A knows about what B knows about C). To arrive at such a personalized directory system and to support the development of common patterns for encoding personal knowledge about oneself and other people's knowledge, TCS introduced various activities to encourage interactions between remote counterparts and facilitate shared experiences and shared understanding of the design and the use of common terminology and language. As a first step toward bringing people together and developing a shared understanding of the product, a joint Quartz training programme was introduced, compulsory for all employees joining the Quartz group. This programme included introductory training during which new employees received an overview session of the Quartz platform and its components, learned about standard Quartz implementation methodologies, and were introduced to the terminology used in this project. In addition, newcomers learned the basics of the programming language which was used to develop the Quartz platform. This training provided the basis for common encoding of information in personalized and codified directories that, in turn, improved understanding and created a basis for efficient knowledge transfer between future remote counterparts. For example, as one team leader described it: "We all speak Quartz language. It is a loss for us if somebody leaves Quartz because for somebody new it will take time to learn Quartz".

Additional training programmes were introduced in later stages of the project during which engineers were encouraged to develop their own expertise in one functional area of Quartz. This facilitated the development of mini-teams: though not co-located, each team still shared a specialized functional area and a similar understanding of that particular function. Furthermore, as stated earlier, some team members were rotated between onsite and offshore locations to increase face-to-face interactions between remote counterparts and to promote learning and the development of shared expertise between dispersed teams.

For members of globally distributed teams, updating personalized directories involves updating "what they know" and "what they know about what others know". In terms of updating "what they know", this had mainly relied on individuals encoding new experiences (e.g. about new product functionality) in their memory using "labels" based on the Quartz terminology, standards, and values. Because of the lack of face-to-face and informal interactions between onsite and offshore teams, updating "what they know about what others know" had mainly relied on regular teleconferences and short visits to remote locations by project leaders and some team members.

Knowledge transfer: Allocating and storing information through codified and personalized directories

While the encoding process is important to overcome knowledge challenges through the development of a cataloging system, the storing process is imperative for knowledge transfer between onsite and offshore teams because of the risks involved in passing information between onsite and offshore. In such knowledge exchanges there is a risk that information will be lost or dispersed in several locations. The storing process, in this regard, ensures the consistent allocation of information according to specific rules (e.g. information organization based on project stages) or according to expertise (information transfer based on area of expertise). For example, feedback provided by the customer about the prototype design should be captured by the onsite team and transferred to the offshore team (C5 in Table 2.2). In this process, the TCS onsite team codified the feedback provided by the customer. Indeed, to ensure a consistent storing process, most of the documents used by the Quartz team to capture and codify knowledge were in a digital format and were available from one central location. To transfer this knowledge to the expert offshore, two storing processes were possible. First, the member of the onsite team relied on his or her personalized directory to allocate the appropriate expert in the offshore team who should receive this information. The second storing process involved a codified directory, in the form of a database (e.g. project repository), which served as an intermediary holder for the knowledge prior to it being retrieved by the offshore expert. The codified knowledge was stored in the intermediary location, labelled according to the subject matter and the location of the expertise involved, until the offshore team accessed this object and retrieved the information. Often, the transfer of knowledge was enacted through the use of both personalized and codified directories; i.e. storing the codified knowledge in an intermediary location, and placing a call to the offshore expert, so that the effectiveness of the memory system was improved.

To ensure that members of the Quartz project used these documents in a consistent manner, i.e. could access, modify, and store documents created by either the offshore or onsite teams, TCS have standardized the tools and methods used across remote locations. One manager explained:

> In a distributed development environment, we need to identify clearly the quality processes to be followed and ensure commonality in the compliance of such processes. For example, common processes and tools for bug tracking, configuration management, release management, impact analysis, change management.

Indeed, through the standardization of tools and methods, TCS ensured the compatibility and the "integratability" of files, components, and applications developed and used at remote locations. Such standardization supported the storing process because understanding "who is the expert" and "to whom this knowledge should be allocated" was commonly communicated and understood. Indeed, when an offshore team transferred knowledge about system components to the onsite team during the integration, the onsite team, we have learned, encountered almost no problems in taking over the integration, with minimum guidelines required from the offshore team (C9). The codified directory was constantly updated since the source code and various project documents were replaced by the new versions, creating new labels and pointers to knowledge holders within the team.

Knowledge transfer also benefited from the application of personalized directories during the storing process. In this regard, members of the onsite and offshore teams enhanced their acquaintance with the pool of expertise available within the project through a division of work based on expertise. One engineer described this process:

> We [onsite and offshore teams] work in parallel: we send them the source code and they integrate it into the infrastructure before delivering it to the client ... I'll check out our source code and send the code to the onsite team to work on it. Then they send the changed code back to me and I'll check it in.

One manager reiterated this point: "Between us [offshore] and our onsite team we say 'we'll do this portion of the job because we have more competent people here who can look at this part, and then you can look at that portion of the job'."

Through this systematic approach to the division of work, TCS ensured that knowledge is stored in dedicated storage locations (personal memories of individual team members). Activities generating new knowledge and developing new expertise were allocated to specific team members based on their present expertise or management's attempt to develop new expertise in the particular area. By basing the division of work on expertise, TCS encouraged individuals to interact and establish links with other remote counterparts who shared a similar functional specialization. In addition the company utilized "Centres of Excellence" in various functional areas and technologies to disseminate expertise and bring expertise to where and when these were needed. Through such mechanisms, remote counterparts developed an understanding of the area of expertise in each remote location, which in turn assisted them to trace experts during the knowledge transfer process. Indeed, members of a dispersed project contacted remote counterparts to inform them about changes and share with them "experiences" related to the design process. In this regard, members of onsite and offshore teams used their counterparts as "storage" for personalized experiences, in which each member "stored" in his or her memory experiences relating to the area of expertise that the entire team had accumulated during the project. One manager explained: "Each and every team member is aware of nearly all the things which are happening, the whole team has a basic knowledge about everything."

Through frequent interactions between onsite and offshore teams, remote counterparts continuously updated information in their personal directories about what others know and what others do, which enabled remote team members to know whom to contact during knowledge transfer processes.

Knowledge transfer: Coordinating the retrieval process through codified and personalized directories

To deal with some of the knowledge transfer challenges described in Table 2.2, the retrieval of knowledge required the application of search mechanisms to locate who held the knowledge and where, using codified and personalized directories. Such a retrieval process can successfully be achieved when the information is previously encoded and stored properly. For example, during integration and system testing, members of the onsite team may need to ask for clarifications and get help from the offshore team. In this specific project, the TCS onsite team needed to know whom to contact (C10). To overcome this knowledge transfer challenge, the onsite team could search the codified directory for experts who were involved in developing this particular code. This information was stored in the codified directory as part of the encoding and storing processes.

In addition, a central project repository was implemented to streamline the retrieval of information between onsite and offshore locations. For example, we have learned that during integration and system testing, an onsite team placed Change Requests into a web-based system (C11). These Change Requests were automatically assigned to the offshore team who notified by email about additional customer requirements. The offshore team retrieved this information through the Change Request system and implemented the change. Following this, the offshore team logged the solution and made the changes implemented accessible to the onsite team (C13). During the critical stages of system integration, this retrieval process allowed the transfer of critical information between onsite and offshore teams, based on the labels created in the encoding and storing processes, during the critical stages of system integration.

Nonetheless, in some situations, when help from remote counterparts was urgently needed (e.g. C10: debugging during acceptance testing), remote team members mainly relied on their own knowledge of "who knows what" recorded in their personalized directories to speed up the knowledge transfer process. The utilization of personalized directories for retrieving processes was mainly promoted through the coordination and integration of expertise across the various sites. In addition to familiarizing remote counterparts with the existing expertise in other locations and developing an expertise-based system for the division of labour, TCS invested in various mechanisms such as Centres of Excellence and a computerized-expertise system that allowed for searching for specific expertise among all TCS employees and that brought expertise together when it was needed. In this regard, the retrieval of personalized knowledge and the notion of personalized directories had evolved through expertise coordination and integration activities. Aspects that were critical for coordinating expertise revolved around time-zone differences and the notion of knowing "who is doing what". Indeed, members of the Quartz team indicated that it was common to contact remote counterparts at any time of the day. Flexible working hours even further supported person-to-person interactions for information retrieval, despite time-zone differences. For example, one manager illustrated their communication patterns: "Within Quartz we can actually call up anybody whom we know at any point in time to get some assistance, even if we don't know somebody, if he's recommended by someone else, then we can call up and get assistance immediately."

Bringing in the required knowledge to solve problems quickly also relied on the expertise-based division of labour that TCS had implemented across its onsite and offshore locations. Other mechanisms were put in place to coordinate the retrieval of information and to update personalized directories. For example, the management introduced various meetings and review sessions to familiarize and refresh the memory of team members with regard to "who is working on what". One interviewee described the implications of this approach: "It's not that only one person can do a job, otherwise, if one person doesn't come in, we won't be able to work without him/her. So we try to overcome this by making each and every team member aware of nearly all the things which are happening."

Lastly, onsite and offshore teams maintained a high degree of comm-unication by phone, up to three or four times a day, which further assisted in keeping updated the notion of "who is working on what". Issues discussed during these conference calls, as observed, revolved around progress updates, handover of work from one team to another when a working day had ended, and clarifications with regard to changes and design problems. One engineer, describing the implications for transferring expertise within the team, explained that:

> When a project is being established, proper ground work includes that everything should be conveyed and project information is shared among team members. ... Each and every team member is aware of nearly all the things which are happening, the whole team has a basic knowledge about what others do.

As a result of these communications, interviewees claimed that they developed a better understanding of the team composition in a remote site and the areas of specialties that each member covered. This promoted knowledge transfer at various stages of the project.

Discussion

In current IS research, transactive memory is gaining ground as a powerful analytical concept (e.g. Yoo and Kanawattanachai, 2001; Akgun *et al.*, 2005). However, the implications for knowledge transfer have hardly been explored, particularly in the context of distributed teams. Therefore, the objective of this chapter was to investigate *how transactive memory enables knowledge transfer in globally distributed teams*, and *through what mechanisms a TMS can be created and maintained*. Through a transactive memory perspective, we studied knowledge transfer between offshore teams in India and onsite teams in Western Europe and the US.

Indeed, as Table 2.2 conveys, globally distributed teams involved in offshoring activities face various knowledge transfer challenges. Furthermore, the transfer of knowledge between the customer, onsite, and offshore teams almost always involves the codification of the knowledge prior to transferring it. This approach to knowledge, as described in the case above, is an attempt to overcome geographical distances between onsite and offshore teams and to enable the transfer of work from more costly onsite locations to the cost-effective offshore locations. However, such a codification of knowledge may increase the misunderstandings and errors involved in the transfer of knowledge because of local contexts, routines, and different skill and expertise levels between the customer, onsite, and offshore teams. The Quartz case suggests that the standardized routines propagated by TCS assisted in creating memory systems that constantly update codified and personalized directories, enabling directory sharing regardless of the physical location of the teams, and offering multiple channels effectively to retrieve information when needed (Wegner, 1995). More specifically, standards, guidelines, and templates were developed to enable systematic encoding of the subject and location of the information to be exchanged between these teams. This information was allocated to individuals through an intermediary object (e.g. project repository and tools) that, in turn, supported the transfer of codified knowledge between onsite and offshore teams. While common methods for storing enabled compatibility and exchangeability of codified knowledge, regardless of the geographical location and local contexts, search capabilities and the use of messaging to inform individuals about the relevant information available in knowledge bases were central in supporting the retrieval of codified knowledge.

The development of personalized directories, on the other hand, relied on individuals' knowledge of who knows what, and their engagement in interpersonal processes disclosing personal knowledge bases to others. Indeed, the Quartz project teams developed patterns for encoding, storing, and retrieving knowledge in the sense of a common language (Barinaga, 2002) and common patterns of communication. These were initially built through socialization and training. During later phases of the projects, the personalized directories were further developed through the division of work based on expertise, job rotations, and regular communications.

From a social constructionist viewpoint (e.g. Lave and Wenger, 1991), the Quartz's personalized directories mainly relied on the continuous development, management, and coordination of expertise that supported encoding, storing, and retrieving processes. Similarly, Orr (1990) has demonstrated how collective expertise could be developed through storytelling in a co-located environment. In this regard, personalized directories, that are "developed communally, over time, in interactions among individuals in the group" and that "exist more or less complete in the head of each group member who has been completely socialized in the group" (Leonard and Sensiper, 1998: 121), may offer opportunities to remote counterparts to develop, manage, and coordinate the collective expertise of the entire team through encoding, storing, and retrieving activities.

First, in the Quartz case, the encoding of project and product knowledge facilitated the development of collective expertise. Indeed, the initial Quartz training programme for the entire global team facilitated the development of common terminology and understanding related to product development, project management, and collaborative processes. Through these training activities, members of the Quartz project team negotiated the meanings of various technical and administrative aspects involved in the project, devising a procedure for future engagement (Wegner, 1987). In a later stage, short relocations and daily communications between onsite and offshore sites offered new opportunities to renegotiate procedures and redefine the terminology used by the team.

Second, the storing of knowledge enabled the management of collective expertise. This was mainly achieved through an expertise-based division of work. This approach to division of work resulted in the creation of multiple distributed teams consisting of like-minded experts who remotely collaborated on a particular aspect of the project (Evaristo and van Fenema, 1999). As part of their personal development, and through their participation in problem-solving activities, members of these expertise-based distributed teams relayed stories to remote counterparts (Lave and Wenger, 1991). By negotiating the meaning of these stories, an understanding of "what A knows about what B (i.e. a counterpart) knows" emerged for A. This understanding assisted members of the expertise-based distributed teams to locate the most appropriate members, who share the same meaning and context, for future "storing" activities. In this way, members of the distributed team manage their knowledge of the expertise available within the team.

And third, through the retrieval of the knowledge the coordination of collective expertise within the distributed team is made possible. In retrieving knowledge, members of the team coordinated the transfer of knowledge needed for problem-solving. Indeed, retrieving information requires knowing "where expertise lies" (Faraj and Sproull, 2000). The development of the metaknowledge described above supported members of the expertise-based distributed teams when they (re)approached counterparts to "retrieve" knowledge. The retrieval of knowledge was largely enabled by the shared meaning and context that these teams developed throughout the project, supported by virtual and face-to-face meetings, and short visits. These ideas as to how collective expertise is managed is further developed in Chapter 5.

We further argue that the three transactive memory processes; i.e. encoding, storing, and retrieving, play different roles in knowledge transfer. First, the development of collective expertise, i.e. encoding, acts as a process for defining the procedure through which knowledge will be transferred. During the encoding, parties negotiate the meaning of knowledge (i.e. the subject and location of the knowledge) following either a codified, standardized approach or by relying on an embedded routine developed within the organization. Second, the management of expertise, i.e. storing, creates a pointer to the location where the knowledge is stored and from which it can later be transferred. In this regard, creating a pointer involves the actual storing activity during which A and B (following Figure 2.1) attach particular labels to the knowledge stored within A, B, or elsewhere. These labels – including for instance contextual information – make it possible to negotiate and clarify the meaning of this information, and its subsequent retrieval from its place of storage. And third, the coordination of expertise, i.e. retrieval, concerns the integration of knowledge by bringing together experts through search mechanisms and interpersonal contacts. For knowledge transfer to take place, teams rely, on the one hand, on the procedures and shared meanings established through encoding processes, and, on the other hand, on interpretation and the use of labels attached to the transferred knowledge during the storing process. The coordination of expertise – and thus knowledge transfer – can be supported by relying either on the codified or personalized directories or both.

The question that we may pose at this juncture is: To what extent do personalized or codified directories matter to knowledge transfer? We claim that it would be wrong that either of these memory systems would be perceived as "better" or "worse" for knowledge transfer. In line with Cook and Brown's (1999) observation on epistemologies of knowledge, we argue that codified and personalized directories are best seen as two complementary, rather than competing, memory systems (Sorensen and Lundh-Snis, 2001). Furthermore, the findings of this study provide insights into how the two types of directories interact. They do not operate in isolation or as substitutes. Absence of the codified directories would deprive the teams of shared methods for encoding, storing, and retrieving information, which may strain the personalized directories beyond feasibility. Leaving out the personalized directories, on the other hand, for instance due to high personnel turnover rates, would leave the project with independently working individuals who would find it difficult to agree on collaboration standards (Cramton, 2001).

These insights lead to a conceptual question: How to theorize the interplay of codified and personalized directories? We suggest that groups develop metaroutines (Moorman and Miner, 1998) that interlink the two types of directories. In this regard, there is a "generative dance" (Cook and Brown, 1999) between these two memory systems that contributes to the transfer of knowledge between A and B. The codified directories depend on interpersonal "norming" processes for defining standards, templates, and procedures. The personalized directories extend the codified system by offering additional avenues in cases when documents provide incomplete knowledge about a task. In these cases, individuals know whom to contact and how to retrieve information. Evidently, the development and use of a TMS may change over time. During initial phases of the project, rudimentary parameters of transactive memory are defined (e.g. which sites and individuals are responsible for which tasks and knowledge domains). These are extended and refined when people work together over prolonged periods of time, renegotiating meanings and regenerating learning around the knowledge transfer process.

In terms of the organizational mechanisms that create and maintain a TMS in a distributed context, we claim, based on the case reported above, that a TMS can be developed and maintained in order to support knowledge transfer through the propagation of certain rules and standardized work routines that can overcome differences in local contexts, skill levels, and work routines. While such standardization also derives from an increased standardization in software development, evidence from the Quartz case suggests that TCS capitalize on this recent trend to offer remote counterparts a memory system through which knowledge can be exchanged. For example, the standardized templates that were used by the onsite team to capture customer knowledge were designed with the thought in mind that these would also be a pointer to where this knowledge resides. Other organizational mechanisms directed at offering remote counterparts opportunities to expand their personalized directories were also implemented. The rotation of team members, the expertise-based division of work that encouraged interactions between onsite and offshore teams, and frequent teleconferences, are only some of the mechanisms supporting the development of a TMS as an enabler for knowledge transfer. Table 2.3 outlines these organizational mechanisms based on the three main processes in a TMS.

Table 2.3 Organizational mechanisms and processes supporting the development of a TMS in globally distributed teams

	Codified directories	**Personalized directories**
Encoding/ updating directories	• Standard document templates (for product deliverables and process phases) • "Glossary of terms" to include unique (e.g. product-specific) terminology	• Rotation of onsite and offshore team members • Joint training programs • Team building exercises • Social activities
Storing/ allocation information	• Central project repository • Standardization of tools and methods across locations • Centralization of tools on the central server, Web access	• Expertise-based division of work • Creating complementary documentation for software components (includes the name of the developer)
Retrieval coordination	• Standard process procedures (to include pointers to the location of information) • Keywords-based search capabilities • Tools that enable automated notification of changes and requests (e.g. Software Configuration Management and Change Management tools)	• Systematic and frequent communications using email, tele- and video-conferencing • Technologies that enable reachability when on the move and out of working hours (e.g. mobile phones, pagers, PDAs)

Implications

What implications does this study have for research and practice? From a theoretical perspective, this study advances understanding of knowledge transfer in distributed contexts and offers linkages to the concept of transactive memory. While the literature on knowledge transfer is extensive, little is known about the challenges involved in transferring knowledge between the customer representatives, and onsite and offshore vendor teams. In addressing this gap, this chapter has outlined specific knowledge-transfer challenges involved in the Quartz implementation project, and explored through the lens of transactive memory how these teams transferred knowledge and overcame different local contexts, work routines, and expertise levels. Indeed, the few studies that had explored the concept of transactive memory in distributed teams provided little insight, if any, into the possibilities to improve knowledge-transfer processes through the development of a TMS. In particular, past research paid little attention to the possibility that transactive memory might act as an enabler of knowledge transfer in distributed teams. In addressing this gap, this study has illustrated how transactive memory supports knowledge transfer between onsite and offshore locations. Furthermore, by unpacking the concept of transactive memory and presenting two types of directories, namely, codified and personalized, this study extends the discussion about the elements that constitute a TMS in an organization. For instance, we extend the IS literature, which so far has somewhat downplayed the role of personalized directories and has often focused on codified directories in the context of distributed environments. In exploring the way knowledge was transferred between onsite and offsite locations, an array of processes and mechanisms associated with the personalized directories emerged. Furthermore, by offering a link to the development, management, and coordination of collective expertise, this study emphasizes the role that collective expertise plays in knowledge transfer processes.

From a practical viewpoint, we argue that in order to enable the transfer of knowledge between remote sites, organizations should consider the mechanisms reported above that support the development, management, and coordination of collective expertise, and enable the transfer of knowledge between onsite and offshore teams. In doing so, managers should consider two key aspects with respect to work division. First, they should attempt to select project members based on their shared histories of collaboration in their respective area of expertise. In doing so, remote counterparts know each other, have already developed a metaknowledge relating to their counterparts and have established procedures for engagement. Such teams will tend to focus on renegotiating and (re)clarifying meaning about knowledge transfer procedures and contexts. Such a staffing approach is likely to speed up the development of the TMS, as procedures, codified routines, and social ties have already been established. Second, an expertise-based division of work should be considered when members of the team have worked with each other before and have developed shared histories. Teams that do not have shared histories, however, may benefit from a division of work that is based on geographical location for a period of time, which enables this team to establish procedures, standards, and templates from the development of its codified directories, before changing to an expertise-based division of work approach.

References

Ahuja, M. K. and Galvin, J. E. (2003) "Socialization in Virtual Groups," *Journal of Management*, 29(2), 161–85.

Akgun, A. E., Byrne, J., Keskin, H., Lynn, G. S., and Imamoglu, S. Z. (2005) "Knowledge Networks in New Product Development Projects: A Transactive Memory Perspective," *Information & Management*, 42(8), 1105–20.

Ancona, D., Bresman, H. and Kaeufer, K. (2002) "The Comparative Advantage of X-Teams," *MIT Sloan Management Review*, 43(3), 33–9.

Armstrong, D. J. and Cole, P. (1995) "Managing Distances and Differences in Geographically Distributed Work Groups," in *Diversity in Work Teams: Research Paradigms for a Changing Workplace* (Eds, Jackson, S. E., and Ruderman, M. N.) American Psychological Association, Washington, DC, pp. 187–215.

Barinaga, E. (2002) *Levelling Vagueness: A Study of Cultural Diversity in an International Project Group*, PhD Thesis, Stockholm School of Economics, Stockholm, Sweden.

Beulen, E., van Fenema, P. C., and Currie, W. (2005) "From Application Outsourcing to Infrastructure Management: Extending the Offshore Outsourcing Portfolio," *European Management Journal*, 25(April).

Blackler, F. (1995) "Knowledge, Knowledge Work and Organizations: An Overview and Interpretation," *Organisation Studies*, 16(6), 1201–41.

Boland, R. J. and Citurs, A. (2001) "Work as the Making of Time and Space," *SPROUTS: Working Papers on Information Environments, Systems and Organizations, http://sprouts.case.edu/2002/020101.pdf*.

Carmel, E. (1999) *Global Software Teams: Collaborating Across Borders and Time Zones*, Prentice Hall P T R, Upper Saddle River, NJ.

Carmel, E. and Agarwal, R. (2002) "The Maturation of Offshore Sourcing of Information Technology Work," *MIS Quarterly Executive*, 1(2), 65–77.

Chudoba, K. M., Wynn, E., Lu, M., and Watson-Manheim, M. B. (2005) "How Virtual are We? Measuring Virtuality and Understanding its Impact in a Global Organization," *Information Systems Journal*, 15(4), 279–306.

Cook, S. and Brown, J. (1999) "Bridging Epistemologies: The Generative Dance Between Organizational Knowledge and Organization Knowing," *Organization Science*, 10(4), 381–400.

Cramton, C. D. (2001) "The Mutual Knowledge Problem and Its Consequences for Dispersed Collaboration," *Organization Science*, 12(3), 346–71.

Currie, W. L. and Willcocks, L. P. (1998) "Analysing Four Types of IT Sourcing Decisions in the Context of Scale, Client/Supplier Interdependency and Risk Mitigation," *Information Systems Journal*, 8(2), 119–43.

Cutler, R. S. (1989) "A Comparison of Japanese and U.S. High-technology Transfer Practices," *IEEE Transactions on Engineering Management*, 36(1), 17–24.

DeSouza, K. (2003) "Facilitating Tacit Knowledge Exchange," *Communications of the ACM*, 46(6), 85–8.

DeSouza, K. C. and Evaristo, J. R. (2004) "Managing Knowledge in Distributed Projects," *Communications of the ACM*, 47(4), 87–91.

Eisenhardt, K. M. (1989) "Building Theories from Case Study Research," *Academy of Management Review*, 14(4), 532–50.

Evaristo, R. and van Fenema, P. C. (1999) "A Typology of Project Management: Emergence and Evolution of New Forms," *International Journal of Project Management*, 17(5), 275–81.

Faraj, S. and Sproull, L. (2000) "Coordinating Expertise in Software Development Teams," *Management Science*, 46(12), 1554–68.

Feeny, D., Lacity, M., and Willcocks, L. P. (2005) "Taking the Measure of Outsourcing Providers," *MIT Sloan Management Review*, 46(3), 41–8.

Grant, R. M. (1996) "Toward a Knowledge-based Theory of the Firm," *Strategic Management Journal*, 17(Winter), 109–22.

Hansen, M. T., Nohria, N., and Tierney, T. (1999) "What's Your Strategy for Managing Knowledge?" *Harvard Business Review*, 77(2), 106–16.

Jarvenpaa, S. L. and Leidner, D. E. (1999) "Communication and Trust in Global Virtual Teams," *Organization Science*, 10(5), 791–815.

Kanawattanachai, P. and Yoo, Y. (2002) "Dynamic Nature of Trust in Virtual Teams," *Journal of Strategic Information Systems*, 11(3–4), 187–213.

Kotlarsky, J. and Oshri, I. (2005) "Social Ties, Knowledge Sharing and Successful Collaboration in Globally Distributed System Development Projects," *European Journal of Information Systems*, 14(1), 37–48.

Lave, J. and Wenger, E. (1991) *Situated Learning Legitimate Peripheral Participation*, Cambridge University Press, Cambridge.

Leonard, D. and Sensiper, S. (1998) "The Role of Tacit Knowledge in Group Innovation," *California Management Review*, 40(3), 112–32.

Majchrzak, A. and Malhotra, A. (2005) "Virtual Workspace Technology Use and Knowledge-Sharing Effectiveness in Distributed Teams: The Influence of a Team's Transactive Memory," *Knowledge Management Knowledge Base, http://knowledgemanagement.ittoolbox.com/documents/document.asp?i=3164.*

Miles, M. B. and Huberman, A. M. (1994) *Qualitative Data Analysis: an expanded sourcebook*, Sage, London.

Moorman, C. and Miner, A. (1998) "Organizational Improvisation and Organizational Memory," *Academy of Management Review*, 23(4), 698–723.

Moreland, R. L. and Argote, L. (2003) "Transactive Memory in Dynamic Organizations," in *Leading and Managing People in the Dynamic Organization* (Eds, Peterson, R. and Mannix, E.) Erlbaum, Mahwah, NJ, pp. 135–62.

Moreland, R. L. and Myaskovsky, L. (2000) "Exploring the Performance Benefits of Groups Training: Transactive Memory or Improved Communication?" *Organizational Behavior and Human Decision Processes*, 82(1), 117–33.

Nevo, D. and Wand, Y. (2005) "Organizational Memory Information Systems: A Transactive Memory Approach," *Decision Support Systems*, 39(4), 549–62.

Nonaka, I. (1994) "A Dynamic Theory of Organizational Knowledge Creation," *Organization Science*, 5, 14–37.

Orr, J. (1990) "Sharing Knowledge Celebrating Identity: Community Memory in a Service Culture" in *Collective Remembering* (Ed., Edwards, D. M.) Sage, London.

Ridings, C., Gefen, D., and Arinze, B. (2002) "Some Antecedents and Effects of Trust in Virtual Communities," *Journal of Strategic Information Systems*, 11(3–4), 271–95.

Sole, D. and Edmondson, A. (2002) "Bridging Knowledge Gaps: Learning in Geographically Dispersed Cross-Functional Development Teams," in *The Strategic Management of Intellectual Capital and Organizational Knowledge* (Eds, Choo, C. W. and Bontis, N.) Oxford University Press, New York, 587–604.

Sorensen, C. and Lundh-Snis, U. (2001) "Innovation through Knowledge Codification," *Journal of Information Technology*, 16(2), 83–97.

Strauss, A. L. and Corbin, J. M. (1998) *Basics of Qualitative Research*, Sage Publications, Thousand Oaks, CA.

von Hippel, E. (1994) "'Sticky Information' and the Locus of Problem Solving: Implications for Innovation," *Management Science*, 40(4), 429–39.

Wegner, D. M. (1987) "Transactive Memory: A Contemporary Analysis of the Group Mind," in *Theories of Group Behavior* (Eds, Mullen, G. and Goethals, G.) Springer Verlag, New York.

Wegner, D. M. (1995) "A Computer Network Model of Human Transactive Memory," *Social Cognition*, 13, 319–39.

Wegner, D. M., Giuliano, T., and Hertel, P. (1985) "Cognitive Interdependence in Close Relationships," in *Compatible and Incompatible Relationships* (Ed., Ickes, W. J.) Springer-Verlag, New York, pp. 253–76.

Wegner, D. M., Raymond, P. and Erber, R. (1991) "Transactive Memory in Close Relationships," *Journal of Personality and Social Psychology*, 6(6), 923–9.

Weitzman, E. A. (2000) "Software and Qualitative Research" in *Handbook of Qualitative Research* (Eds, Denzin, N. K. and Lincoln, Y. S.) Sage, Thousand Oaks, CA, 803–20.

Yin, R. K. (1994) *Case Study Research: Design and Methods*, Sage, Newbury Park, CA.

Yoo, Y. and Kanawattanachai, P. (2001) "Developments of Transactive Memory Systems and Collective Mind in Virtual Teams," *International Journal of Organizational Analysis*, 9(2), 187–208.

CHAPTER 3

Bridging gaps in globally dispersed collaboration: Developing knowledge bases

Julia Kotlarsky and Paul C. van Fenema

Introduction

Globally distributed collaboration and virtual teams are becoming increasingly common in areas such as aerospace (Malhotra *et al.*, 2001) and software development (Carmel, 1999). There are a number of economic and technical trends that accelerate the growth of globally distributed projects and the creation of distributed or virtual teams. For economic and financial considerations, many companies are switching to offshore outsourcing of products and services. For instance, in the software and electronics industries offshore outsourcing of development (for software) and manufacturing (for electronics) is very common. Outsourcing of services such as call centers to English-speaking developing countries is becoming increasingly popular. On the technological side, ongoing innovations in information and communication technologies make it possible to cooperate in a distributed mode.

However, despite growing experience in the area of globally distributed collaboration and teams (King, 2006), research on this topic remains segmented and focused on different aspects of distributed collaboration and deferring levels of analysis. Literature on global collaboration is mainly focused on the constraints associated with geographical dispersion, that is with distance and time zone differences (Cramton, 2001; Jarvenpaa *et al.*, 1998; Meadows, 1996). These lead to breakdowns in coordination and communication. Distance leads to reduced communications, or to people experiencing problems with media that cannot substitute for face-to-face communications, as they lack richness and interactivity.

Time zone differences reduce opportunities for real time collaboration (Carmel and Tjia, 2005).

However, research shows that sometimes people do not seem to suffer from these problems and are successful despite geographical dispersion (Aron and Singh, 2005; Majchrzak *et al.*, 2000). If people can deal with the constraints, this means that they can work remotely while being as productive as co-located teams (or even more productive). In the literature on dispersed or virtual teams various findings have been described, yet an overarching explanatory analysis is missing. Roughly speaking, most studies can be classified into two streams: pessimistic and optimistic. Researchers in the pessimistic tradition have found support for the proposition that collaboration suffers from dispersion (Cramton, 2001; Kraut and Galegher, 1990). The optimistic stream of research provides anecdotal and empirical evidence of projects where people were not hindered by constraints (distance and time zone differences), or, if they were, were able to use these advantageously (Carmel, 1999). More research is needed to explain this difference.

The objective of this chapter, therefore, is to help practitioners and researchers understand the different perceptions of dealing with the constraints and their impact. We introduce a theoretical framework that extends Channel Expansion Theory by exploring the role of knowledge bases for communication in the context of globally distributed work. We report on an in-depth case study on a globally distributed team where people did not perceive space and time as constraints when working remotely. Sometimes, they even used time differences as an advantage to work around the clock. Chapter 4 moves beyond communications and offers another lens to understand coordination in distributed teams, this time from a knowledge-based perspective.

Theoretical background

Pessimistic and optimistic perspectives on constraints in distributed collaboration

Research on geographically distributed collaboration started in the early 1990s when email and computing became widespread (Turoff *et al.*, 1993; Abel, 1990). One could categorize this work into pessimistic and optimistic perspectives on the basis of the two main consequences of geographical dispersion: distance and time zone differences. First, much of this research points to the constraints people face when they work remotely. Due to the absence of face-to-face meetings, they lack communication richness and interactivity (Kraut and Galegher, 1990). Distance means that people can be easily excluded from meetings, as research on a dispersed meeting preceding the Challenger space shuttle disaster shows (Vaughan, 1997). Collaboration across great distance also implies that people are located in different time zones (Carmel, 1999). This further limits opportunities for exchange as local working hours do not overlap across sites (Jarvenpaa *et al.*, 1998; Meadows, 1996).

However, a second stream of research adopts a more optimistic perspective on the "constraints" associated with dispersed collaboration. A classic case of highly successful dispersed collaboration was the Apollo 13 lunar mission. After the crew experienced technical problems in space, their counterparts in Houston worked with them on understanding and resolving the causes of malfunctioning (Cooper, 1972). Much later, the optimistic viewpoint emerged in professional publications in which people proclaimed the "death of distance" (Cairncross, 2001). The proliferation of novel technologies like Groupware, email, and videoconferencing would enable boundaryless collaboration (Mohrman *et al.*, 2003; Davenport and Pearlson, 1998), and *ad hoc* virtual teams to operate with minimal trust (Meyerson *et al.*, 1996). A few academic studies suggest that people do collaborate over distances without being too constrained. Researchers have found that dispersed teams could successfully develop new products (Malhotra *et al.*, 2001) and exchange information in communities (Goodman and Darr, 1998). Some studies found instances of both successful and less successful distributed collaboration, suggesting support for both the optimistic and pessimistic theories (Jarvenpaa and Leidner, 1998). Boland and Citurs (2001) investigated a dispersed project with team members in the US, Europe, and India:

> Communication with the first shift Indian team appeared to be more difficult for the American team. This difficulty was sometimes attributed to the lack of overlapping standard work times. Another factor possibly contributing to the perceived difference in ease of communication between the first and second shift Indian contractor team was that two of the second shift contractors had worked "onshore" in America as part of the American team during part of the project. Thus, the American team members felt that those contractors had a better grasp of the project objectives and vision for the e-catalog system than those that had not been "onshore." (Boland and Citurs, 2001: 14)

According to the pessimistic stream of research, the Americans should have experienced (*ceteris paribus*) the same problems with the two shifts of Indians as they faced similar constraints. Yet the fact that some of the Indians had been onshore changed the impact of space and time constraints.

Though these differing findings have been brought to light, an explanatory analysis is still missing. Most studies have focused on understanding particular settings without theorizing on a metacontextual level (Ciborra and Patriotta, 1996). In this chapter we present a theoretical explanation of the phenomenon, illustrated by empirical evidence. For the conceptual part of our study, we turn to a debate in the area of electronic communications theory. This debate shows similarities with the optimistic–pessimistic discussion. This stream of research started with Media Richness Theory, which claims that perceived richness is an objective property of electronic media. This position has been challenged by more recent work on social communications theories (Carlson and Zmud, 1999; Ngwenyama and Lee, 1997; Markus, 1994). We now elaborate on the clash of these perspectives, before presenting a research framework.

The debate on the impact of perceived media richness

Media Richness Theory (MRT) – also referred to as Information Richness Theory (Lee, 1994) – considers perceived richness of electronic media to be an inherent property of the media (Daft and Lengel, 1986). The theory emerged in the early 1980s in the tradition of contingency and information processing theory (Trevino *et al.*, 1987; Daft and Lengel, 1986; Daft and Macintosh, 1981). Its central claim is that communication media differ in their capacity to process rich information (Daft and Macintosh, 1981). The richness of a medium depends on its capacity to provide immediate feedback, the number of cues and channels used, personalization, and language variety (Daft and Lengel, 1986: 560). The richest medium is face-to-face communication, which provides immediate feedback, multiple cues, and the opportunity to use natural language. Shifting to (electronic) media reduces this richness as people experience different levels of cue transmission and interactivity. A continuum is proposed, that ranges from rich media (telephone, personal documents for communications) to lean ones (impersonal documentation, forms) (Trevino *et al.*, 1990). Richness is a property of electronic media. According to MRT, people select a medium by matching the objective properties of various media with their information processing needs. Individuals working on complex, uncertain tasks require high levels of information processing, and they are expected to choose rich media.

Researchers have recently shown that perceived richness depends on the social context in which media are used (Carlson and Zmud, 1999; Ngwenyama and Lee, 1997; Lee, 1994; Markus, 1994; Fulk *et al.*, 1992). They criticize MRT for theorizing on the individual level, while communication media are used to connect people, meaning that theories are required which incorporate the social context. In contrast with MRT, perceived richness of a message is no longer considered a property of the medium.

Two studies elaborate on this alternative view to MRT. First, Markus (1994) shows that the use of email – a lean medium according to MRT – depends not only on individual choice. Using social definition and critical mass theory, she argues that media use is gradually institutionalized in an organization, and reinforced through collective norms and social control (Ngwenyama and Lee, 1997; Markus, 1994). Second, Carlson and Zmud (1999) developed Channel Expansion Theory (CET) as an alternative to MRT, providing an alternative explanatory model that relates perception of media richness to four categories of experience (knowledge bases): experience with the channel; experience with the messaging topic; experience with the organizational context; and experience with communication co-participants (*ibid.*). More experience in these categories equips people with "knowledge bases that may be used to more effectively encode and decode rich messages on a channel" (*ibid.*: 155). Knowledge bases cause people to perceive channels as rich, since they are able to exploit minimal cues.

Research framework

We adopt the MRT–CET debate as a theory to explain the paradoxical findings relating to distributed collaboration. Our reason for using the debate is twofold. First, empirical research suggests that space and time "constraints" do not have the same impact on collaboration in different situations. Second, from a content point of view, people bridge distance and asynchronous working hours using electronic media (Majchrzak *et al.*, 2000). The central role of these media suggests the application of results from mediated communications theory.

We therefore propose that distance and time zone differences are not objective constraints with the same impact in different situations. Their potentially constraining impact correlates with the four knowledge bases

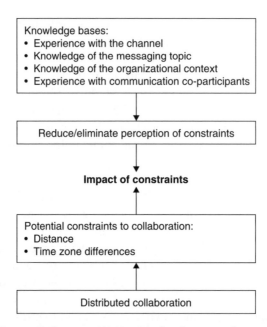

Figure 3.1   Research framework: Knowledge bases and constraints

proposed by Carlson and Zmud (1999). They suggest that the more experience people have of (i) the technology they use, (ii) the messaging topic (task) they deal with, (iii) the organizational context in which they operate, and (iv) their remote counterparts the less they experience distance and time zone differences as constraining. More experience may even lead to advantageous use of "constraints": some organizations are capable of running non-stop workflows that follow the sun (Carmel, 1999). Figure 3.1 presents the research framework that represents the above-mentioned proposition in a schematic way. This was used as the basis for our empirical investigation of the Maui project at LeCroy.

About this research

Data collection at LeCroy was driven by the categories of the four types of experience bases as defined above; the two potential constraints are the spatial and temporal. The categories guided data collection and served as a basis for analysis. We conducted semi-structured, open-ended, individual, face-to-face interviews that lasted about 1.5 hours each. We interviewed project and team managers, and software engineers who interacted on a daily basis with counterparts at remote locations. Interviews were taped and transcribed. In addition, one of the authors engaged in direct observations during site visits – five days at the New York office, and one day at the Geneva office – collected documents, and had informal conversations.

Empirical investigation involved several rounds of data collection, which included visits of the first author to both distributed locations, and feedback sessions. Data collection covers a period of more than one year – from November, 2001 until January, 2003. Additional information about LeCroy can be found in the Appendix.

Lecroy's Maui project and space and time constraints

Since the mid 1980s, the software for the LeCroy oscilloscopes has partly been developed in Geneva, and partly in New York (initially there were about five or six people in both cities). These two teams interacted frequently. Andrea explained:

> We have always interacted. From the original interactions – it was with punch cards, it was tapes or floppy disks that were sent in-between the two sites. For sending software guys used to use the teletype terminal – this is going back a long time. From there on it just progressed and then we got an email and we started work with email and then we threw out all modems and we got the WAN between the two. So the interactions, I would say, they just become closer and closer. And now we use MSN Messenger from Microsoft – every member of the software development group, they appear on the list. So for having a chat with someone, wherever they may be in the world in the given time, you just need to double click on their name and start typing a line.

The LeCroy software team did not perceive remote collaboration as a problem. As we will illustrate, geographical distance and time differences were not perceived as gaps.

Firstly, distance. This was not a major obstacle: "I would say there is not any difference of communications between two workers in the same location and two workers in the different locations" (Gilles).

Team members were separated by *geographical distance*: the software team was distributed between three locations:

1. New York (US): head office with 13 software engineers
2. Geneva (Switzerland): 14 software engineers
3. Maine (US): main software architect (1 person).

Potentially, physical separation could create constraints for teamwork (Kraut and Galegher, 1990). However, for the LeCroy software team geographical distance caused limited inconvenience – only when physical presence was required: "for an important meeting, people get on the plane and fly over for a meeting, but that is an extreme." For example, new development of a product part generally started with a meeting in one place involving all key players.

Geographical distance was perceived as a gap when there was a need to travel to remote locations: as costs in terms of travel time and the complexity of travel arrangements. Otherwise, and on a regular basis, team members communicated remotely using various types of media. For them geographical distance between New York and Geneva was perceived as comparable to the distance between people working in different offices or different buildings. They worked in a similar way to neighbouring offices, and those across the Atlantic, for instance, doing code reviews using Net Meeting:

> I have even seen it within this building, which is really interesting – you see two guys in almost the next cubical to each other – they do a code review: sitting next to each other, but they are sitting at *their* desks and looking at *their own* screen working through the code. So, it is actually an interesting tool, and people are used to doing code reviews across the ocean or up to Maine. So that the code reviewers will go through designed documents that way [using Net Meeting]. (Larry)

Gilles explained about his experience of working with remote counterparts: "for example when I control his machine, it doesn't respond as fast as I am straight on the computer. So it is a technical delay in terms of seconds, but the understanding is absolutely identical remotely or just on site."

Secondly, time differences were perceived as offering advantages: "we use the fact that we are not working together to allow us to work around the clock" (Gilles). There is a six-hour time difference between the US East coast (UTC –5; New York and Maine are in the same time zone) and Switzerland (UTC +1): see Table 3.1.

Table 3.1 Comparing time zones, US east coast and Switzerland

	Time zone UTC-5	Time zone UTC-4	Time zone UTC-3	Time zone UTC-2	Time zone UTC-1	Time zone UTC	Time zone UTC+1
	Maine and New York						Switzerland
No overlap							6 AM
						6 AM	7 AM
					6 AM	7 AM	8 AM
				6 AM	7 AM	8 AM	9 AM
			6 AM	7 AM	8 AM	9 AM	10 AM
		6 AM	7 AM	8 AM	9 AM	10 AM	11 AM
Normal overlap	6 AM	7 AM	8 AM	9 AM	10 AM	11 AM	12 noon
	7 AM	8 AM	9 AM	10 AM	11 AM	12 noon	1 PM
	8 AM	9 AM	10 AM	11 AM	12 noon	1 PM	2 PM
	9 AM	10 AM	11 AM	12 noon	1 PM	2 PM	3 PM
	10 AM	11 AM	12 noon	1 PM	2 PM	3 PM	4 PM
	11 AM	12 noon	1 PM	2 PM	3 PM	4 PM	5 PM
	12 noon	1 PM	2 PM	3 PM	4 PM	5 PM	6 PM
	1 PM	2 PM	3 PM	4 PM	5 PM	6 PM	7 PM

(Continued)

Table 3.1 (Continued)

	Time zone UTC-5	Time zone UTC-4	Time zone UTC-3	Time zone UTC-2	Time zone UTC-1	Time zone UTC	Time zone UTC+1
	Maine and New York						Switzerland
Extension	2 PM	3 PM	4 PM	5 PM	6 PM	7 PM	8 PM
	3 PM	4 PM	5 PM	6 PM	7 PM	8 PM	9 PM
	4 PM	5 PM	6 PM	7 PM	8 PM	9 PM	10 PM
	5 PM	6 PM	7 PM	8 PM	9 PM	10 PM	11 PM
	6 PM	7 PM	8 PM	9 PM	10 PM	11 PM	12 midnight
	7 PM	8 PM	9 PM	10 PM	11 PM	12 midnight	1 AM
	8 PM	9 PM	10 PM	11 PM	12 midnight	1 AM	2 AM
No overlap	9 PM	10 PM	11 PM	12 midnight	1 AM	2 AM	3 AM
	10 PM	11 PM	12 midnight	1 AM	2 AM	3 AM	4 AM
	11 PM	12 midnight	1 AM	2 AM	3 AM	4 AM	5 AM
	12 midnight	1 AM	2 AM	3 AM	4 AM	5 AM	
	1 AM	2 AM	3 AM	4 AM	5 AM		
	2 AM	3 AM	4 AM	5 AM			
	3 AM	4 AM	5 AM				
	4 AM	5 AM					
	5 AM						

Despite this six-hour difference, "generally we have quite an overlap", Anthony Cake said, because the first developer who started working in New York was in the office at about 6 a.m. (which is noon Geneva time): see "normal overlap" in Table 3.1. And in times when LeCroy is close to a product launch (date) or a significant milestone, developers in Geneva stayed in the office until midnight, so there were only a few hours when working hours in the two locations did not overlap: see "no overlap" and "extension" rows in Table 3.1. Anthony summarized this: "Generally it doesn't really matter, it is not a big advantage, not a big disadvantage. I would not say that time differences are a disadvantage and close to a release or big milestone they can be a big advantage. Because problems, bug fixing can be passed on from time zone to time zone." Gilles says: "Of course we know that with Geneva, we have to work in the morning. And they have to work with us [with New York] in the day-afternoon. But after that constraint, I don't see any."

Results of our empirical investigation show that well-developed experience bases help to overcome potential gaps and problems in dispersed collaboration.

The Maui project and four knowledge bases

1   Experience with the channel

Remote team members used a variety of media and technologies for communicating. Generally, within the software team, *MSN Messenger* was used for online chatting. Every member of the software development group appeared on the list: "So for having a chat with someone, wherever they may be in the world in the given time, you just need to double click on their name and start typing a line" (Anthony). "It is about typing a question and if it is just a one line or two lines response – it is immediate, never matter where they are in the world – whether they are in the next cubical or whether they are in the next country, they use that system" (Larry). But, generally, if it was more than a couple of lines of response, then they picked up the *phone*, and talked to each another. "And stuff that doesn't need an immediate answer or things that happens outside of the overlapping time period, that all happens by *email*" (Anthony).

Net Meeting was used for application/desktop sharing; it allowed developers to share the control of the computer remotely. Software developers in LeCroy made extensive use of Net Meeting for code reviews and when somebody needed help with debugging problems:

> If someone has a problem in Geneva: he finds where the code is failing and he wants to show me the code and the condition (under which) it is failing – then we use Net Meeting to show me the code. So I control his computer to see what happens wrong, what is the problem, and I get results right on my screen. (Gilles)

Typically, in such situations, developers used Net Meeting to see what was happening (the code) and at the same time they used the phone (or the voice chat capability of Net Meeting) to discuss the problem.

Larry and Anthony also used Net Meeting frequently when designing a new feature or user interface: "We have been working in *Visual Studio* when laying out a dialog for a product via Net Meeting, when Anthony will be in Geneva and I'll be here [in New York]", Larry explained.

Another communication medium used was *Video Conference*. It was used on a regular basis (at least once a week) for meetings between all software managers.

2   Experience with the messaging topic

Experience with the messaging topic encompasses two types in our study. First, *task* experience (the content of activities that need to be done), and, second, experience with *tools* (that are not communication media) used to accomplish tasks. For the LeCroy software team, *task* involved an understanding of what components to build and how they were supposed to work; *tools* refer to technologies, software development tools, and the principles used to develop software (components).

At the LeCroy software team, development of similar experiences was facilitated. For instance, when new technology (Microsoft COM) was introduced, Larry and Anthony organized a conference in the Alps where they took all the software developers from New York and Geneva for a joint introductory course: "We all got together in the mountains of France and it was a real fun week, and it had two purposes: one was to teach us all this new technology. The other which was equally important if not more important in some ways – was to really try to build relationships between people" (Larry).

Furthermore, to develop experience in new topics (new technology and new product), people who had most experience were chosen: "there were guys who wrote the original code 15 years ago. So they were also the natural guys to work on the next generation, or defining the next generation" (Anthony). These people had developed the new component-based Maui platform. They knew the most about it and became a source of the experiences for others. Team members often contacted them. This facilitated the creation of similar experiences for other team members: Gilles and Jon in Maine know the basics and have a global view of the system; they, therefore, spent about half a day "just speaking and helping other guys to solve their problems". These communications could be via MSN Messenger, Net Meeting, telephone, or emails. "Half a day I would say. But this is just for us two – the guy in Maine and myself", Gilles said.

Jon has got a cable modem and, as Anthony explained:

> He is online most of the day with either someone from New York or someone in Geneva talking. Because he is one of the architects of the system, he gets all the guys in Geneva when he wakes up in the morning; they have questions for him and they get on the line with him, and then in the afternoon he has guys in New York who get online.

Microsoft COM technology was adopted for the new development. It was new and very different from the technology used for earlier products. Therefore, after the Maui platform was developed, a guide was created so that everybody could learn about it: the environment and tools used to develop products. The guide served as a reference framework for everybody. It facilitated creating shared experiences of the tasks:

> We developed Maui. Maui is really a software platform, I guess. This document here is Maui software developers guide, this is a kind of "getting started guide" for new engineers coming on board with Maui. Because one of the problems we had is that our old system was a heavily embedded system based on embedded operating systems and embedded compilers. And moving those developers into Maui [i.e.] using tools like Visual C, things like Rational Rose for the UML diagrams, just when everything changed, everything that we used and lived in for years changed. So this guide, this bible, is explaining how to move into this new development environment. (Anthony)

Similar experiences of remote team members with software development tools were created by *standardization* and *centralization* of the tools used for task accomplishment. *Standardization* of tools used at all remote locations helped remote team members to develop similar experiences with software development tools. Everyone working with Maui uses the same methods and procedures, protocols and tools: *"All are identical, absolutely identical.* We have one Version Control System, at least for Maui, which is located in Geneva, it is on the network, so everyone can get to it. The Lotus Notes system we use is on servers in NY and in Geneva. And they are replicated, so they are identical essentially. But everything is the same. Everyone working with Maui uses the tools which are on this list" (Anthony).

Centralization of tools in one location ensures one single environment for all remote locations. The tools include a Version Control System, and a component interdependencies manager called COMProjMgr. For the LeCroy software team, there were no "local" tools as such – all tools are located at one central place. This helped to develop similar experiences of working with tools:

> The Version Control System – Per Force – exists in Geneva and guys access it here the same way over LAN so the only difference there is: from here it takes a little longer to access it, speed is slower. It doesn't matter where you are in the world, you still can access the same single Version Control System. (Anthony)

COMProjMgr is a tool created in-house to manage interdependencies between components: "COMProjMgr manages the entire project. So I don't have to build every component locally – if someone changes the hardcopy component and they put it back – it will be rebuilt on the server and then in the morning I can import that component and just use it" (Larry). Standardization and centralization ensured commonality of experiences and equal distribution of knowledge.

3   Experience of the organizational context

At LeCroy, we found that experience of the organizational context comprises having similar goals, knowing the organizational culture, knowing about remote sites, and feeling part of the organization (not only of the local team).

Understanding the goals and having similar goals is a driving motivation to collaborate and shape organizational context. Gilles described the type of work software developers were involved in:

> It is very interesting and at the same time very demanding, because we have to stay at the top edge of the technology. Which is not the case

for all other companies. Here it is really one part to have to keep in mind. And because of that – because it is demanding – the workers who stayed, are interested in working on really complex problems, this is kind of the same goal. Because we have the same goal it does help with the communication and the relationships. (Gilles)

Cross-pollination implied that people from the one group spend a significant amount of time in the other group (other location) and *vice versa*. It helped to *get to know the organizational culture and to develop deep understanding of remote sites.* One of the interviewees stressed the importance of cross-pollination by giving an example of unsuccessful collaboration of the LeCroy hardware team. Initially the team was distributed between New York and Geneva as well: "I think, part of the problem is – there was no kind of cross-pollination. There was nobody from the NY group who spent a significant amount of time in Geneva group or *vice versa*. So there were already two separate groups. How to explain, they just didn't get on. Really didn't have any respect for each other" (anonymous, at his request).

In the software team, one of the advantages was that a couple of members of the Geneva software group originally worked in New York. Anthony started there in 1986. Another senior person – Martin, Chief Scientist currently based in Geneva – worked in New York for many years. (He has been at the company since the late 1970s.) Anthony shared his viewpoint: "To take people with experience, I think, working in the group, and then move them into another group, is a good way to seed the other group, to make sure that everything works together."

Remote team members have similar experiences of an organizational context if there is one single context represented in a single unified team, and not several teams each "marinating" in its own local context. Therefore *feeling part of the organization* and being "plugged into organizations" helped in creating a similar organizational context experience for remote team members. Among the developers in Geneva "there is a natural feeling that they are kind of unplugged from the rest of the company. Because it is! It is an outpost." In order to handle this feeling, letting people know what was going on in the company, what everyone else was working on – was a big help. "Really, it helps everyone to feel we are working as a team and that they are part of the LeCroy team", Anthony observed. Frequent visits by Larry to Geneva (four to five times a year) helped to maintain a team environment between the New York and the Geneva group.

Frequent interaction of team members and visits of managers and team members to remote locations helped to *get more knowledge about remote sites*. Larry explained:

> I am back and forth all the time, and Anthony as well. But occasionally, we do have people coming from Geneva here or from here going to Geneva for a week or two and we even have a few cases where we put someone over. We have one guy right now who is spending a year here from Geneva. And that is really useful sharing experiences and stuff.

Long-term employment helps to develop in-depth experience of the LeCroy organizational context:

> Because the work here is very interesting but at the same time very demanding and we have to innovate and to do some research – part of our job is also research – people who want to work hard tend to stay and people who don't want to really work hard – tend to leave. That's why maybe you see not too many young people here. (Gilles)

4   Experience with communication co-participants

Finally, experience with communication co-participants covers some knowledge about remote counterparts, and also the relationships between them. Experience can be based on working together – knowing working habits, areas of expertise, and communication style. Experience and relationships can be more personal, and include trust, knowing how a counterpart thinks and reacts in certain situations. "I think because we started to know each other better, we know each others' feelings better, so now even before asking him a question we know how he is going to start to think", Gilles said about his experience of working from Geneva with Jon, who was working from Maine.

The more interpersonal a relationship between counterparts was, the more extensively experience with communication co-participants was developed. This implied that people knew about each other. Therefore, building relationships and sharing knowledge between remote counterparts was very important. Managers of LeCroy software team realized that. Anthony explained: "The biggest problem is a people problem, or people from different sites. It happened that people do not respect and trust each other, they [people] don't work well together. But in most cases that is not really an issue any more."

Knowing this, managers tried to facilitate interactions and create relationships between remote counterparts: "We try to make sure they interact, we increase the possibility that they really get to know each other. We had this software convention – we had the course up in the Alps where we tried to get all of the software team together" (Anthony). As Larry explained:

> The course had two purposes: one was to teach us all this new technology. The other, which was equally important if not more important in some ways, was to really try to build relationships between people because what we found over the years is – whenever people had worked face-to-face or even if it was only for a few days – the fact that you could put someone's face to it – made it that much easier for someone to pick up the phone and ask the question than if it was just a name. (Larry)

Talking about the importance of experience with communication counterparts and its influence on success of remote collaboration, Anthony said:

> It makes a big difference, when the guys know each other. And more importantly – when the guys trust each other and they know what the others' capabilities are. I think that makes a huge difference. It is because there are very clever guys in the group. And when you get fairly clever guys talking to each other, there needs to be certain degree of trust, I guess respect is maybe a better word, for each other. And where that is lacking, there is really a communication problem. But when there is a lot of trust and respect, people get on very well, they are very productive. (Anthony)

It was a challenging task to create relationships between remote counterparts. Being in one place, in the same environment, was much more effective. According to Anthony

> Meeting has got a lot to do with it. In fact, I would say that someone's most valuable time spent meeting is probably in the local bar than in the meeting room. Because most of getting to know each other, getting respect, happens over a few beers. And that develops into all kinds of professional things; I think that's a very important thing. And that is one of the ideas behind the conference in the Alps, to get people in an environment where there was plenty time for that. It was pretty important. (Anthony)

In this section we have provided empirical evidence that illustrates the impact of space and time constraints. We have shown that well-developed experience bases help to overcome potential gaps and problems in dispersed collaboration. We have presented and analyzed each of the four knowledge bases in the case-study company, and discussed the importance of these experiences for successful distributed collaboration.

Conclusion

This chapter provides a theoretical explanation for the phenomenon of the impact of space and time constraints in distributed collaboration by applying electronic communication theory. Using recent debates in an adjacent field of study, it has allowed insights into the paradoxical findings on distributed collaboration.

Implications for practitioners

Globalization and economic acceleration introduce constraints that increasingly determine current organizational practices. The findings of this chapter are significant for practice. So far, pessimistic and optimistic research outputs have sent confusing signals to practitioners. This chapter explains the reasons for the existence of space and time constraints in distributed collaboration and provides guidelines for how to eliminate these constraints. The impact of the four types of experience on the perception of constraints points toward several important lessons for practitioners involved in, or responsible for, distributed collaboration. First, select people with experience bases to participate in distributed collaboration. Second, invest in the development of the four knowledge bases. Third, try to reduce loss of experience in organizations by reducing turnover and aiming for long-term employment. The more extreme potential constraints are (for instance extremely short time to market, or zero time overlap if people work between sites in different continents), the more important it is to invest in the development and maintenance of experience bases. Thus, potential constraints and knowledge bases should be matched. Chapter 4 elaborates on the role of experience in the context of knowledge management processes and Chapter 9 on the role of experience in e-coordination activities. Also discussed will be the importance of experience in establishing social capital.

Implications for researchers

This chapter represents a shift in thinking from the development of contrasting views on distributed collaboration toward the explanation of the conditions under which each stream of research provides valuable results. Our study confirms that knowledge bases impact on the perception of constraints, and implies that more research is needed on the nature of constraints and how people deal with them dynamically over time. This seems an important research direction in today's time- and resource-pressed economic climate. More research is also required to understand and operationalize how knowledge bases impact on distributed collaboration processes. We would argue that knowledge bases have the following effects. First, they enable anticipation of a counterpart's behaviour and task-related expectations, e.g. information needs. This reduces communications aimed at organizing collaboration. Second, knowledge bases enrich communications, leading to communications that become more meaningful and efficient ("half a word is enough"). These improvements economize communication processes and free up attention to novel experiences.

References

Abel, M. (1990) "Experiences in an Exploratory Distributed Organization" in *Intellectual Teamwork: Social and Technological Foundations of Cooperative Work* (Eds, Galegher, J., Kraut, R. E., and Egido, C.) Lawrence Erlbaum, Hillsdale, NJ.

Aron, R. and Singh, J. V. (2005) "Getting Offshoring Right," *Harvard Business Review*, 83(12), 135–43.

Boland, R. J. and Citurs, A. (2001) "Work as the making of Time and Space," vol. 2, Winter. http:/weatherhead.cwru.edu/sprouts/2002/020101.pdf Sprouts: Working Papers on Information Environments, Systems and Organizations.

Cairncross, F. (2001) *The Death of Distance*, Harvard Business School Press, Boston, MA.

Carlson, J. R. and Zmud, R. W. (1999) "Channel Expansion Theory and the Experiential Nature of Media Richness Perceptions," *Academy of Management Journal*, 42(2), 153–70.

Carmel, E. (1999) *Global Software Teams: Collaborating Across Borders and Time Zones*. Englewood Cliffs, NJ: Prentice Hall.

Carmel, E. and Tjia, P. (2005) *Offshoring Information Technology Sourcing and Outsourcing to a Global Workforce*, Cambridge University Press, Cambridge.

Ciborra, C. U. and Patriotta, G. (1996) "Groupware and Teamwork in New Product Development: The Case of a Consumer Goods Multinational," in *Groupware & Teamwork: Invisible Aid or Technical Hindrance?* (Eds, Ciborra, C. U., Orlikowski, W. K., Failla, A., Patriotta, G., Bikson, T. K., Suetens, N. T., and Wynn, E.) John Wiley, Chichester.

Cooper, H. S. F. Jr (1972) *Thirteen – The Apollo Flight that Failed*, The John Hopkins University Press, Baltimore.

Cramton, C. D. (2001) "The Mutual Knowledge Problem and Its Consequences for Dispersed Collaboration," *Organization Science*, 12(3), 346–71.

Daft, R. L. and Lengel, R. H. (1986) "Organizational Information Requirements, Media Richness and Structural Design," *Management Science*, 32(5), 554–71.

Daft, R. L. and Macintosh, N. B. (1981) "A Tentative Exploration into the Amount and Equivocality in Organizational Work Units," *Administrative Science Quarterly*, 26, 207–24.

Davenport, T. H. and Pearlson, K. (1998) "Two Cheers for the Virtual Office," *Sloan Management Review* (Summer), 51–65.

Fulk, J., Schmitz, J., and Steinfield, C. W. (1992) "A Social Influence Model of Technology Use," in *Organizations and Communication Technology* (Eds, Fulk, J. and Steinfield, C.) Sage, Newbury Park, CA, 117–40.

Goodman, P. S. and Darr, E. D. (1998) "Computer-Aided Systems and Communities: Mechanisms for Organizational Learning in Distributed Environments," *MIS Quarterly* (December), 417–40.

Jarvenpaa, S. L., Knoll, K., and Leidner, D. E. (1998) "Is Anybody Out there? Antecedents of Trust in Global Virtual Teams," *Journal of MIS*, 14(4), 29–64.

Jarvenpaa, S. L. and Leidner, D. E. (1998) "Communication and Trust in Global Virtual Teams," *Journal of Computer-Mediated Communication*, 3(4), http://www.ascusc.org/jcmc.

King, W. R. (2006) "Offshoring Decision Time is at Hand," *Information Systems Management*, 23(3), 102–3.

Kraut, R. E. and Galegher, J. (1990) "Patterns of Contact and Communication in Scientific Research Collaboration," in *Intellectual Teamwork: Social and Technological Foundations of Cooperative Work* (Eds, Galegher, J., Kraut, R. E., and Egido, C.) Lawrence Erlbaum Associates, Hillsdale, NJ.

Lee, A. S. (1994) "Electronic Mail as a Medium for Rich Communication: An Empirical Investigation Using Hermeneutic Interpretation," *MIS Quarterly*, 18(2), 143–57.

Majchrzak, A., Rice, R. E., King, N., Malhotra, A., and Ba, S. (2000) "Technology Adaptation: The Case of a Computer-Supported Inter-organizational Virtual Team," *MIS Quarterly*, 24(4), 569–600.

Malhotra, A., Majchrzak, A., Carman, R., and Lott, V. (2001) "Radical Innovation Without Collocation: A Case Study at Boeing-Rocketdyne," *MIS Quarterly*, 25(2), 229–49.

Markus, M. L. (1994) "Electronic Mail as the Medium of Managerial Choice," *Organization Science*, 5(4), 502–27.

Meadows, C. J. (1996) "Globework: Creating Technology with International Teams," PhD Thesis, Harvard University, Boston.

Meyerson, D., Weick, K. E., and Kramer, R. M. (1996) "Swift Trust and Temporary Groups," in *Trust in Organizations: Frontiers of Theory and Research* (Eds, Kramer, R. M. and Tyler, T. R.) Sage, Thousand Oaks, CA.

Mohrman, S. A., Klein, J. A., and Finegold, D. (2003) "Managing the Global New Product Development Network," in *Virtual Teams That Work: Creating Conditions for Virtual Team Effectiveness* (Eds, Gibson, C. B. and Cohen, S. G.) Jossey-Bas, San Francisco.

Ngwenyama, O. K. and Lee, A. S. (1997) "Communication Richness in Electronic Mail: A Critical Social Theory and the Contextuality of Meaning," *MIS Quarterly*, 21(2), 145–67.

Trevino, L. K., Daft, R. L., and Lengel, R. H. (1990) "Understanding Managers' Media Choices: A Symbolic Interactionist Perspective," in *Organizations and Communication Technology* (Eds, Fulk, J. and Steinfield, C.) Sage, Newbury Park, CA, pp. 71–94.

Trevino, L. K., Lengel, R. H., and Daft, R. L. (1987) "Media Symbolism, Media Richness, and Media Choice in Organizations: A Symbolic Interactionist Perspective," *Communication Research*, 14(5), 553–74.

Turoff, M., Hiltz, S. R., Bahgat, A. N. F., and Rana, A. R. (1993) "Distributed Group Support Systems," *MIS Quarterly*, 17(4), 399–417.

Vaughan, D. (1997) "The Trickle-down Effect: Policy Decisions, Risky Work, and the *Challenger* Tragedy," *California Management Review*, 39(2), 80–102.

CHAPTER 4

Developing a knowledge-based perspective on coordination: The case of global software projects

Julia Kotlarsky, Paul C. van Fenema, and Leslie P. Willcocks

Introduction

Coordination, defined as the achievement of concerted action (Goodhue and Thompson, 1995), underpins the development and delivery of products and services, and continues to attract attention in current research (Quinn and Dutton, 2005; Gittell and Weiss, 2004; Bechky, 2003). Current coordination theory is commonly built on an information processing perspective (Galbraith, 1973). According to this approach, differentiation of work translates into task dependencies which are resolved through coordination mechanisms (Crowston, 1997). Mechanisms bring varying information processing capacity to organizations (Mintzberg, 1979). Examples include standards (low information capacity) and mutual adjustment (high information capacity). Matching information processing needs and capacity is required for effective coordination (van de Ven *et al.*, 1976). While this information-based perspective on coordination has been dominant and useful, its assumptions combined with recent developments in organization theory have made a revision necessary.

Since the mid 1990s organizational economists (e.g. Grant, 1996; Spender and Grant, 1996) and knowledge management scholars (e.g. Nonaka, 1994) have worked on a knowledge-based perspective on organizations. Here the previous assumption that individuals are information processing entities is extended to one in which they are considered as intelligent, learning, reflexive, creative, and communicative knowledge workers (Giddens, 1991). This shift becomes particularly pressing as organizations tend to become more knowledge-intense and globally distributed. Coordination, from this emerging knowledge angle, is perceived as a problem of sharing, integrating (Grant, 1996), creating (Kogut and Zander, 1996), transforming (Bechky, 2003), and transferring knowledge (Szulanski, 1996; von Hippel, 1994). However, at present, it seems too early for a strong knowledge-based perspective on coordination. The knowledge-based perspective has received most attention from, first, organizational economists who revised the theory of the firm (Kogut and Zander, 1996). These researchers tend to focus on knowledge-based coordination as something that differentiates firms from other governing modes, such as the market. Second, knowledge management researchers have paid most attention to knowledge as a dependent variable in their theorizing, leaving coordination as a peripheral spin-off effect. And third, researchers have proposed that transactive memory, mental models, and frames support coordination (Akgun *et al.*, 2005; Levesque *et al.*, 2001; Faraj and Sproull, 2000). However, the mechanics of how these cognitive similarities and linkages lead to coordination remain unclear. While Chapter 3 explored the role of knowledge bases for communication, the objective of this chapter is to move further and offer the beginnings of a knowledge-based perspective on coordination. Specifically, we seek to answer the following research question: *How do coordination mechanisms contribute to knowledge processes so that coordination is achieved?* After elaborating on our research context and conceptual underpinnings, we present findings from our empirical research on globally distributed software development projects. We analyze the role of coordination mechanisms in supporting knowledge processes in this organizational form that is becoming increasingly common nowadays.

Research context: Globally distributed software development projects

These projects consist of two or more teams working together to accomplish project goals from different geographical locations (Carmel, 1999). Difficulties recorded include distance, time-zone, and cultural differences that may include but are not limited to different language, values and traditions, norms and values of behaviour (Kumar *et al.*, 2005; Walsham, 2002).

Most researchers agree that global distribution of knowledge work impacts on coordination practices. A growing number of studies have investigated specific areas and reported problems such as coordination breakdowns (Barkhi *et al.*, 2006; Herbsleb and Mockus, 2003; Carmel, 1999), lack of understanding of a counterpart's context (Orlikowski, 2002) and different competencies in language (Sarker and Sahay, 2004). Other studies show global work distribution exacerbating the chance of misunderstandings (Olson and Olson, 2004; Battin *et al.*, 2001), lack of trust (Jarvenpaa *et al.*, 1998), asymmetry in distribution of information among sites (Carmel, 1999), and difficulty in collaborating due to different skills and training, and mismatches in Information Technology (IT) infrastructure (Sarker and Sahay, 2004). The practices recommended to overcome these difficulties mainly focus on (i) intersite coordination through division of work that minimizes cross-site communication and synchronization (Ebert and De Neve, 2001; Mockus and Weiss, 2001) and (ii) technologies that support collaboration in a distributed environment (Cheng *et al.*, 2003/4; Smith and Blanck, 2002).

Studies focusing on global software team performance point to the importance of knowledge sharing in building trust and improving effectiveness, while at the same time they recognize the additional complexity in sharing knowledge across geographically dispersed sites, not least because of the sheer amount of so much knowledge (Kotlarsky and Oshri, 2005; Orlikowski, 2002). Following Wegner (1987), Faraj and Sproull (2000) found that transactive memory is important in globally distributed software teams: instead of sharing specialized knowledge, individuals should focus on knowing where expertise is located and needed. A need to know "whom to contact about what" in global teams has been reported in several studies in this area (e.g. Akgun *et al.*, 2005; Kotlarsky and Oshri, 2005; Majchrzak and Malhotra, 2004).

Despite the fact that most of the problems reported in global software projects are fundamentally to do with information and knowledge, overall, past research has stressed the importance of coordination mechanisms and technologies, and has focused much less on the role of knowledge sharing and social aspects in global software projects. One has to go to a different literature, such as organization studies, to work up strong links with such issues. These considerations lead to the need to understand how coordination, knowledge, technical, social, work-based, and organization design factors can be related among themselves and form a more comprehensive heuristic and explanatory model. This is addressed in the next section, and is grounded in a critique of an extensive, relevant literature.

Theoretical background

Coordination mechanisms

Since the development and delivery of products and services exceeds the capacities of individuals, work is divided and coordinated in organizations. Literature, both historically and to this day, distinguishes various categories of coordination mechanisms (Gittell and Weiss, 2004; Goodhue and Thompson, 1995; McCann and Galbraith, 1981). While the names of these mechanisms have changed, they usually include ones emphasizing the formal, structural dimension of organizations, and those based on the social and informal dimensions, i.e. interpersonal adjustment and feedback (Donnellon *et al.*, 1986; van de Ven *et al.*, 1976). Following this literature, one could distinguish the following categories of coordination mechanisms: organization design mechanisms, work-based mechanisms, technology-based mechanisms, and social mechanisms. These mechanisms are usually considered in terms of their information processing properties:

- *Organization design mechanisms* encompass formal role structures such as hierarchies, linking pins, teams, and direct contacts (Galbraith, 1973). These structures can be considered as "mental traces" that are enacted and modified in practice (Orlikowski, 1992). The objective of organization design is to accomplish the integration of differentiated tasks. Professionals and units with unique tasks must work together to integrate knowledge and achieve a common output (Grant, 1996). How their accomplishments are linked at a general level is determined by the role to which people and units are assigned, and how these roles are linked. Information processing theorists suggest that direct forms of design (direct contacts, teams) have higher information processing capacity than indirect forms (hierarchy, liaisons) (Galbraith, 1973). The former is more suited to complex, uncertain tasks that may involve diversely skilled professionals.
- *Work-based mechanisms* concern the specific structuring of tasks to be accomplished by an organization. Examples include plans, specifications, standards, categorization systems (Bowker and Starr, 1999), and representations of work-in-progress, such as prototypes (von Hippel, 1994) and design documents. Research suggests that people tend to rely more on work-based practices if tasks are complex (e.g. discussing a complex prototype of a new car), if communication opportunities are limited (e.g. remote communications), if many people are involved, and if achieving common understanding is highly important.

- *Technology-based mechanisms* are defined here in terms of Information Systems (Gittell and Weiss, 2004). These support coordination by enabling information capturing, processing, storage, and exchange (e.g. electronic media, Groupware, shared databases). As coordination practice, technologies automate and informate organizations (Zuboff, 1988). Automating implies that technology replaces humans for accomplishing coordinating tasks (e.g. a traffic-light system). In the project management this may include automated scheduling, automated file version control, and automated notification when tasks are finished. Informating relies more on human involvement in the coordination process. In this role, technologies enable people to communicate asynchronously and possibly remotely.
- *Social (interpersonal) mechanisms* involve communication activities, working relationships, and social cognition: (1) Communication has been traditionally recognized as a mode for adaptive coordination (van de Ven *et al.*, 1976). When people encounter novel circumstances or counterparts, they must communicate in order to make sense and establish a shared understanding (Donnellon *et al.*, 1986). (2) Working relationships enhance the accuracy of expectations concerning a counterpart's thoughts, activities, and expectations. This promotes coordination and communication efficiency (Gabarro, 1990). (3) Social cognition refers to the frames and mental models people have in common because of similar experiences (Cramton, 2001; Krauss and Fussell, 1990). The coherence of individuals' functionings becomes more likely when these social practices occur. Organizations select and deploy them particularly when they work on novel or tightly linked tasks, or when people from different functional areas have to cooperate (Dougherty, 1992).

Matching information processing needs and capacity is required for effective coordination (van de Ven *et al.*, 1976). Information processing need varies with contingent factors such as diversity, work unit size, and task uncertainty (*ibid.*; van Fenema, 2002). Typically these mechanisms are considered as complementary. For example, often work-based mechanisms such as plans and specifications are made available for all teams members in a project repository and made accessible on the Web.

Toward a knowledge-based perspective on coordination

While this information-based perspective on coordination has been dominant and useful, it was developed in the 1960s and 1970s, a period in which organizational processes were relatively simple, and organizational literature hardly paid attention to knowledge management. Over the past decades, organizational processes have become more complex and knowledge intense, and they therefore require more awareness and capability in the area of knowledge management. Scholars in the area of information management, information theory, computer science, and sociology continue debating the definitions of, and relationships between, knowledge and information. While the two concepts refer to different entities, they appear closely related as they can be placed on a data-information-knowledge continuum (Liew, 2007): information refers to the data (i.e. raw unorganized facts) represented in a meaningful way to the user to allow some form of analysis, knowledge takes more environmental aspects into consideration and requires human experience and judgment.

Knowledge, has been defined as "information combined with experience, context, interpretation, and reflection. It is a high-value form of information that is ready to apply to decisions and actions" (Davenport *et al.*, 1998: 43). Thus, knowledge differs from, and seems to exceed, information. Suppose that a person has information on the design of a complex IS or technical installation. This does not imply that he or she knows the background of the system and the process for building or maintaining it. The ability to interpret data on an object in a meaningful manner does not imply possession of knowledge.

Following Davenport and Prusak (2000) as cited in Liew (Liew, 2007): "knowledge is a fluid mix of framed experience, values, contextual information, and expert insights that provides a framework for evaluating and incorporating new experiences and information." Therefore, information and knowledge are closely related.

Knowledge changes the meaningfulness of data to an individual (see Carlson and Zmud, 1999; Boland, 1991). The meaningfulness of data thus depends on knowledge: "one person's knowledge is often another's raw data. What a vice president for marketing, production, or finance thinks he knows is just data to the chief executive officer's staff. What a scientist thinks he knows about the merits of a flu vaccine or the safety of a nuclear reactor is just data for presidential policy and politics. Data or knowledge are just types of information content – of greater or lesser value, of greater or lesser cost" (Oettinger, 1999). Knowledge work depends on meaningful interaction amongst experts. The increasing knowledge intensity of work has spurred research on knowledge-based perspectives on organizations and the coordination of knowledge processes (e.g. Faraj and Sproull, 2000; Grant, 1996). In Information System Development (ISD) projects, knowledge of a business context, applications, infrastructure, and project management is transferred, combined, and integrated to achieve collective understanding of the emerging system (Crowston and Kammerer, 1998).

In order to understand how knowledge-intense work is coordinated, we must extend the information processing perspective. After all, typical information processing issues such as who does what and when seem inadequate to understand the complexity of coordinating knowledge processes. Yet current literature on coordination hardly pays attention to knowledge management, except for research on expertise coordination (Faraj and Sproull, 2000). The literature on knowledge management, on the other hand, addresses knowledge processes without considering coordination as a dependent variable. To fill this gap, this chapter takes a knowledge-based view on coordination. Table 4.1 compares this view with an information processing perspective.

Column one shows common dimensions of coordination theory: work, work division, task dependencies, aspects of coordination, and workers. We suggest that an information processing researcher tends to emphasize pragmatic dimensions of coordination (e.g. who does what?) that are commonly perceived in task environments where knowledge require-ments of work are well known and much of the work has been structured (e.g. traffic lights). A knowledge management researcher focuses on individuals' understandings and how these interrelate (Bigley and Roberts, 2001). Specifically, coordinating the work from knowledge workers involves synchronizing, adapting, and fine-tuning processes of knowledge sharing, integrating, creating, transforming, and transferring knowledge, and is not merely a problem of processing information that represents work. The knowledge-based perspective suggests that coordina-tion is less about scheduling and fitting pre-defined task-accomplishments, but more about interrelating the efforts of knowledgeable professionals in a concerted manner, i.e. to achieve order (Lorand, 2000).

Adopting the categories of coordination mechanisms mentioned earlier (organization design mechanisms, work-based mechanisms, technology-based mechanisms, and social mechanisms), we now examine how these mechanisms shape knowledge processes and lead to coordination.

Research model: A knowledge-based perspective on coordination

Moving to a knowledge-based perspective, coordination becomes a challenge of developing concerted action in the sense of interrelating

Table 4.1 Comparing information processing and knowledge-based perspectives on coordination

Dimensions	Assumptions of an *information processing* perspective on coordination	Assumptions of a *knowledge-based* perspective on coordination
Work, work division, task dependencies	• Larger task outcome and processes are known • Subtasks are defined and assigned to individuals • Task dependencies are known • Interpretations of tasks are unequivocal	• Larger tasks are known only in intention and broad terms, not in detail • Emphasis on knowledge specialization and knowledge-based contribution of individuals rather than task and work division
Coordination challenge	• Coordination of *activities* • Who does what, when, in cooperation with whom? • After answering relatively straightforward "tip of the iceberg" questions, coordination can be achieved • These questions require information processing	• Coordination of *experts' thoughts* • How do individuals interpret work? • How can they understand what others think? • How can they interrelate their understandings and work toward coordinated processes and outcomes? • These challenges require knowledge processes
Role of coordination mechanisms	• Selection and use of coordination mechanisms is straightforward, and will lead to coordination • Coordination mechanisms have primarily a role as enablers of information processing for addressing the coordination challenge	• Coordination mechanisms enable coordination through their influence on knowledge processes • Coordination mechanisms promote building social capital, facilitating knowledge flows, making knowledge explicit, and amplifying knowledge
Workers	• Accomplish physical activities or simple routine services • Process information for coordinating tasks with others	• Accomplish knowledge processes for knowledge outputs • Process information and knowledge for coordinating tasks with others

interpretations, expectations, and possible action trajectories. When coordination is considered from a knowledge point of view, the four coordination mechanisms discussed above gain further depth in the sense of their role in knowledge processes. Key questions – as part of our overall research objective – become *How do these mechanisms contribute to knowledge processes?* and *What must happen to knowledge in order to achieve coordination?* Organizations must do something with their (potential) knowledge resources in order to coordinate activities that are performed in different time–space configurations and across a variety of units, teams, and communities (Brown and Duguid, 2001). If they do not, their performance suffers from knowledge asymmetries, knowledge that remains "stuck" to particular sites (von Hippel, 1994), and unrealized potential of knowledge creation and collective creativity (Grant, 1996; Kogut and Zander, 1996). Coordination mechanisms thus become knowledge management instruments, with a focus on their contribution to the coherence of knowledge processes and activities, i.e. to achieving a coordinated outcome. As shown in our research model (Figure 4.1), we conceptualize for each category of coordination mechanisms their impact on knowledge processes and thus ultimately on a coordinated outcome.

First, organization design mechanisms *facilitate knowledge flows* by providing a structure through which knowledge workers can channel their expertise. To achieve coordination, knowledge must flow, be connected, and different perspectives must be confronted (Boland and Tenkasi, 1995). Organization design clarifies who is supposed to know what and who is supposed to communicate with whom. It therefore economizes knowledge flows.

Second, work-based mechanisms that capture knowledge are important for *making knowledge explicit*, as they enable activity replication and commonality (Adler, 1995). Hence, we reconsider the explicitation–internalization cycles proposed in Nonaka *et al.*'s SECI (Socialization, Externalization, Combination, Internalization) model in the light of achieving coordination. The use of work-based mechanisms implies that knowledge and expectations are made explicit and thus are known and useful to other people working at different sites or at different times (i.e. with limited communication opportunities).

Third, in dispersed organizations, knowledge must be rapidly disseminated by means of technology-based mechanisms. Knowledge-intense multinationals and service firms *amplify their knowledge management processes* using intranets, knowledge databases, and Groupware (Majchrzak *et al.*, 2000; Hendriks, 1999; Ciborra *et al.*, 1996). While IS processes data and information, to knowledge workers within the same community and organization these constitute pieces of knowledge that trigger new thoughts and enable coordinated action (Ngwenyama and Lee, 1997).

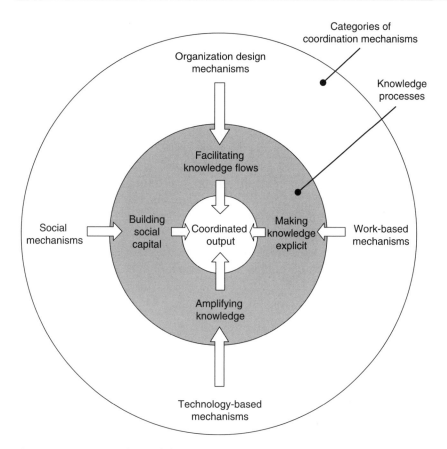

Figure 4.1   Research model

And fourth, social mechanisms *establish social capital* in the sense of relationships (Gabarro, 1990), and of knowledge of who knows and does what, i.e. transactive memory (Faraj and Sproull, 2000; Moreland, 1999). Individuals are not just information processors, but knowledge workers who negotiate points of view (Brown and Duguid, 2001), and transform their understandings (Bechky, 2003) to generate innovative outputs. In this context, they have relational needs that are relevant for coordinating their work.

Our research framework presented in Figure 4.1 suggests that four types of coordination mechanisms impact on knowledge processes. By considering this knowledge dimension of the mechanisms, we can better understand how coordination is achieved. We now examine how this perspective could improve our understanding of achieving coordination in practice.

About this research

To analyze the role of coordination mechanisms in supporting knowledge processes we compare two cases, one of which is successful (i.e. a coordinated outcome is achieved) and another one which is unsuccessful (i.e. failed to achieve a coordinated outcome). The nature of success and failure is therefore assessed according to whether an organization succeeded or failed at producing a coordinated outcome (i.e. completing the project) through the use of (one or more) coordination mechanisms (Nidumolu, 1996, 1995). (Coordinated outcome implies product success which is one of the measures of successful collaboration, as discussed in Chapter 1.) Based on this criterion we selected one successful project at SAP and one project that failed at Baan. By comparing coordination mechanisms used to facilitate knowledge processes in the successful and unsuccessful cases, we could draw conclusions about the role of knowledge processes in achieving coordination and demonstrate how the proposed research model (Figure 4.1) can be applied in practice.

Evidence was collected from interviews, documentation, and observation. Interviews were conducted at two remote sites per company: in India and Germany for SAP; in India and the Netherlands for Baan. Interviewees were chosen to include (i) counterparts working closely at remote locations, and (ii) diverse roles such as managers and developers. In total, 19 interviews in two companies were conducted. Interviews lasted on average 1.5 hours; they were recorded and fully transcribed. A semi-structured interview protocol was applied, to allow the researchers to clarify specific issues and follow up with questions. Data analysis followed several steps. It relied on iterative reading of the data using open-coding techniques (Strauss and Corbin, 1998), and sorting and refining themes emerging from the data with some degree of diversity (Miles and Huberman, 1994). In particular, four themes that represent the concept *coordination* were carefully studied: *coordination by organization design, work-based coordination, technology-based coordination*, and *social coordination*. Statements that were found to correspond with mechanisms that support these four types of coordination were selected, coded, and analyzed using Atlas.ti – Qualitative Data Analysis software (*ibid.*).

Analysis and results

In this section the results of two case studies carried out at SAP and Baan are presented. Additional information about these two companies can be found in the Appendix. Based on the empirical evidence presented below, we explore how the use of coordination mechanisms facilitates knowledge processes between globally dispersed teams and enables remote counterparts to share and integrate their knowledge, which results in achieving coordination when they work toward knowledge-intense innovative outcomes. In order to support the above claim, empirical evidence illustrated by statements made by interviewees will be outlined in the following section. A presentation of the cases follows the analysis process described above and aims to illustrate the knowledge dimension of the coordination mechanisms (i.e. how these impact on knowledge processes and on achieving a coordinated outcome).

SAP case: Analysis

In September, 2001, when the collaborative tools project started, key players (managers and architects) and team members from remote locations did not know each other. Some of the team members had previous experience of working in a globally distributed environment, but not necessarily with Indian, German, or American cultures. For the majority of key players and team members this cross-cultural setting was new. Furthermore, at the beginning of the project, there was a knowledge gap between individuals involved in the project:

> People have different profiles: here [in Bangalore], the maximum experience is five years. But if you take these three colleagues traveling to the team-building exercise [Stefan, Christoph, and Thomas], the two of them have about 12–15 years of experience, and the minimum experience here [in Bangalore] is about two and a half years, so that's a huge experience gap that they have to bridge. (Sudhir)

From the very beginning managers of the KM Collaboration group realized the importance of sharing and coordination of knowledge across dispersed locations and put a lot of effort in setting up and facilitating the knowledge process. In this section four types of coordination practices employed to facilitate knowledge processes between globally dispersed team members are discussed and illustrated using quotations made by interviewees.

Coordination by organization design

The organization design of KM Collaboration group aimed to facilitate knowledge flows in order to reduce existing knowledge gaps and prevent knowledge and information gaps in the future. In particular, a clear division of technical versus "social" supervision (i.e. management of local teams) between the technical architects located in Walldorf and the local development manager aimed to ensure the quality of the product and effective team management. The local development manager of each team was responsible for team management: he divided specific assignments (tasks) between team members and resolved social issues. The development manager and team members belonged to the same culture. This made it easier for the development manager to understand and deal with the team members. Furthermore, mini-teams were created and reporting channels across the globe were established. For example, Christoph and Martin (development architects located in Walldorf) served as technical contact persons for the remote teams: Christoph was a contact person for the Bangalore team (which together constituted one mini-team), and Martin was a contact person for the Palo Alto team (another mini-team). The architects provided technical supervision for the assigned remote team, and were responsible for technical issues and the quality of software developed by this team. Creating cross-continental mini-teams was helpful in shaping communication patterns, providing clarity and, as a result, facilitating knowledge-sharing processes between the head office in Walldorf and remote sites.

Moreover, direct communications were encouraged in the KM Collaboration group to facilitate knowledge sharing. After the key players visited the Bangalore site and got to know remote team members personally, centralized communications (via Sudhir) were replaced by direct communications. Christoph explained:

> From a code perspective, what I did before I met all of them [the team in Bangalore] in person, was to send all things to Sudhir and he was the one to distribute it within the team, and this has changed now. I address most of the things directly to the team members . . . . Quick and direct communications, as far as possible, is the most important thing. "Direct" means: do not communicate through other people but with the people directly. If you have one contact person who

distributes all the information, you lose some amount of information, just because you do not reach the right people. (Christoph)

Work-based coordination

Work-based coordination was aimed to capture knowledge and make it explicit and accessible for all team members despite their geographical location. It was achieved through division of work and creating common knowledge about software development tools and procedures.

First, work was divided feature-wise, providing dispersed teams with full ownership of and responsibility for an entire block of functionality: "You are responsible for what you have taken up" (Stefan). This approach aimed to reduce knowledge dependencies in the newly formed global team, reducing possibilities for misunderstandings and conflicts. Moreover, it was important, in particular for offshore teams, to have full ownership of their work. It gave them a feeling of being valuable and the motivation to collaborate and share knowledge in the future.

Second, to ensure consistency in the methods and tools used by dispersed teams and to facilitate common understanding of the evolving product, the managers of KM Collaboration group decided to standardize tools and methods across dispersed locations: "We use all the same tools, so there is no difference. We even use the same Word templates [templates with project activities and related documents], so even the specifications look more or less the same" (Christoph). A sharing of knowledge being embedded into the standards facilitates coordination across dispersed locations, as people from remote locations perform interrelated tasks coherently.

Technology-based coordination

A variety of technologies were used to communicate, coordinate, and share knowledge over distance, amplifying the knowledge sharing of the SAP global team. Technologies enabled remote team members to share explicit knowledge resources and increased the speed and flexibility of knowledge sharing by making it independent of place and time (remote/ asynchronous collaboration). Therefore, technologies were very important for the integration of knowledge across dispersed locations: for achieving a common understanding between remote counterparts, ensuring consistency in the evolving product, and coordinating of tasks between teams and individual team members. Furthermore, technologies were used to facilitate the reuse of knowledge and software components across locations, which could reduce time-to-market of new product versions. For example, videoconferences (VC) that involved members from all remote teams were used to identify opportunities for reuse:

> The team in Walldorf should be aware of what is being developed in Bangalore or Palo Alto, so that we don't reinvent the wheel again and again. So we communicate about things that are being done, and whether there is something reusable which we are developing, or have they developed something which somebody else can use. Then you are not rewriting the whole product again and again. Maybe they can just use our available package, make some changes according to what they need, and use it. For things like that we need to interact with each other. (Akhilesh)

The quotation above illustrates how technologies can increase the efficiency of knowledge processes (by avoiding reinventing the wheel).

Internet and Web technologies enabled the centralization of technologies under a single environment accessible from all remote locations. This was important to ensure that everybody was working with the same, most up-to-date, versions. For example, SAP Intranet (called SAPNet) served as a central place with links to all updated information. This way, technologies allowed remote counterparts to keep updating their knowledge about what was going on, including plans and progress.

A variety of collaborative technologies were used in different situations. A phone was used for urgent matters, for regular updates between managers, and to resolve misunderstandings. For situations that required knowledge sharing between remote counterparts Application Sharing Tool (AST) or VC were used. For example, an AST was typically used remotely (i) for discussions that involved showing slides (usually remote counterparts use AST to give presentations, simultaneously using the phone to explain the slides and to discuss issues); and (ii) for discussing technical issues (e.g. code reviews, debugging), in this case the AST was used for taking control of a computer remotely.

Twice a month VC sessions that involved managers and developers from all three locations were organized to discuss progress and other issues. For example:

> Whenever a new colleague joins our team or any of the teams in the other locations, in the next VC we will have an introduction round like "these are new colleagues that have joined." So though you have not

met them physically, you get to know that this is the person, he exists there, things like that. (Akhilesh)

This way counterparts from dispersed locations got to know the composition of a remote team and could know whom to contact. This helped to streamline knowledge sharing between remote counterparts.

Finally, email was typically used for low priority tasks and issues, and tasks that could not be completed in real time because of time-zone differences.

Social coordination

Social coordination mechanisms aimed to create the social capital of the global team. A particular effort was put into building up shared experiences, and creating transactive memory among dispersed team members. Social mechanisms included team-building activities and mutual adjustment which aimed to reduce knowledge gaps, build relationships, and maintain team atmosphere between dispersed members. Furthermore, frequent interactions and systematic communications between remote counterparts were considered important to ensure effective coordination over distance.

The remote counterparts did not have a history of working together before they were merged into one group. Therefore transactive memory in this group had been developing since the project started. Having transactive memory was important as it influenced the amount of information that needed to be shared, and had an impact on the efficiency of communications, as illustrated by the following quote:

A simple one-line question can result in a ten-page answer. It can be a very lengthy answer, a one-line reply. The level of detail you get in the answer depends on how well you know that person. Because if the person knows me very well and knows in what areas I am working, then he can decide how much information I will need. Is one line good enough for him or should I explain to him over three pages so that he knows what is happening? (Sudhir)

To bridge the knowledge gap and facilitate knowledge sharing between the teams in the early stages of the project Sudhir (manager of the Bangalore team) organized a team-building exercise there in which key members of Walldorf and Palo Alto teams participated, together with the local team. The team-building exercise gave an opportunity for key members to meet in person, learn about areas of expertise of remote counterparts and their working experience, learn about cultural differences, and create space for social interactions. This exercise helped to reduce the possibility of conflicts and misunderstandings in the future:

> The team-building exercise improved relationships among the KM Collaboration group, because earlier communications were only in a formal way, and after the team-building activity we really knew people much better, it became easier to communicate and communications became more informal. (Jyothi)

This way, the team-building exercise was used to promote knowledge sharing processes. It was the first major step toward bridging knowledge gaps between dispersed team members and toward developing trust: "The end result of that exercise was that the entire team feels more comfortable to work together. Now they know each other and trust each other better" (Stefan).

Mutual adjustment included setting up rules of communications which helped people to adjust to communication styles and reduce misunderstandings and confusions that typically happen as a result of different cultural backgrounds. For example, agreement was reached that Indian team members would not take it personally when Germans are too direct. Compared to Indians, Germans usually are very direct and "brutally precise" in communicating what they have in mind and, typically, this is one of the biggest challenges in German–Indian teams.

Facilitating interactions between remote counterparts included face-to-face interactions and over distance. For example, regular teleconferences between software managers in Walldorf, Bangalore, and Palo Alto, and transatlantic VCs with all team members every couple of months, helped to keep knowledge of all parties up to date.

Baan case: Analysis

The E-Enterprise group was relatively young: the first products were released in 1999. Some people in Hyderabad had been working in a globally distributed environment before joining the group. However, because of a general Baan policy to reduce travel expenses, and because the E-Enterprise organization structure had changed several times since the group was established, team members did not have a history of working together: the majority of them did not know each other and did not know the composition of the dispersed team. Therefore, in Baan, transactive memory among dispersed team members was not developed.

Furthermore, team members in the Netherlands and India had different cultural backgrounds in terms of national culture and organizational culture (newcomers and people from Baan ERP group), and they did not have a common technical background. Therefore, there was a gap in common understanding of the technology and the processes team members were supposed to follow. Moreover, it was reported that often people in the Hyderabad office were not aware of what was happening in the Barneveld office: they were not updated about changes in requirements and dependencies between the products, and were not aware of product and technology roadmaps.

In this section, four types of coordination practices that were (or were not) in place in the E-Enterprise group are presented. The implications of (the lack of) coordination practices for knowledge processes between globally dispersed team members are discussed and illustrated using quotations made by interviewees.

Coordination by organization design

The organization design of the E-Enterprise group was continuously changing: people, their roles, products, product requirements, processes, ownership, and physical location of tasks – all these were changing very fast. Moreover, too many people in different roles were involved in the management of each product included in the E-Enterprise Suite, so that some responsibilities were overlapping. Combined with other circumstances (e.g. the sequentially changing ownership discussed below), a situation emerged where everybody was involved but nobody was responsible. Interviewees (in different roles) were asked to list the people involved in the management of different E-Enterprise products and to describe their roles and responsibilities. From the descriptions provided by the interviewees it followed that sometimes people had different views on what they or their colleagues were supposed to do.

Lack of stable organization design and clearly defined roles created flaws in knowledge flows between globally distributed teams: some information was lost because there were no clearly defined communication channels; team members had very limited knowledge about their remote counterparts; and often did not know whom to contact at remote sites if issues emerged.

Work-based coordination

Work-based coordination in the E-Enterprise group was very limited. First, there were no clear divisions of work between the Indian and Dutch teams. For example, between 1999 (when the first version of E-Enterprise Suite was developed) and 2002 (when the interviews were carried out) ownership of the common platform – E-Enterprise Server – was transferred from India to the Netherlands and then back to India.

Changing ownership had implications for knowledge processes: there was always a need to understand the product developed by another team (which is often more difficult than to develop a product from scratch), and there was never a complete knowledge of the product and the logic behind it. For example, as Sujai explained:

> It's difficult to visualize the idea when it is not yours. If we have the knowledge of the existing product then we're building on top of it, it's easy. But sometimes it happens that the understanding of the existing architecture is not very good because we are not there from the beginning: the initial product has been transferred from there [the Netherlands] to here [India]. (Sujai)

Furthermore, there was no feeling of "our" product because it was inherited from another team: "I expect one of the important things that should happen within E-Enterprise Baan or anywhere is that more ownership must be felt by everybody" (Vijaya). Everything seemed to be in transition and unstable. This situation reduced morale in the group and increased tensions between Indian and Dutch group members. This tense relationship, in turn, reduced motivation of remote team members to share knowledge.

There was a strong technical dependency between the E-Enterprise Server and the seven products comprising the E-Enterprise Suite. These dependencies existed because the combinations of products had to work together. Technical dependencies on the E-Enterprise Server caused problems relating to (i) specifications and (ii) schedules across products which needed to be synchronized. In addition, the technical dependencies also caused knowledge and information dependencies between the dispersed teams. Vijaya explained:

> The dependency on the Netherlands is causing problems. Dependency on information, dependency on knowledge (even in terms of simple design documents, for example, functional designs, or technical

designs, they are not complete), dependency on requirements, because everything is centralized in Holland and then that has to be shared with us so that we can proceed. (Vijaya)

Taking into account the numerous dependencies discussed above, there was no structured approach to identify and coordinate these dependencies:

> One thing that is missing right now in E-Enterprise is that at any time you can't look into any document to see what are the exact dependencies involved. Right now they're coming with something like a dependency matrix. But so far we didn't have that. So it's generally like if you want to know tomorrow whatever dependency with another product, you have to actually talk to the team members or the Architect or the Consultant. There is no central store or central repository. (Satish)

However, it is important to note that there were some attempts in the E-Enterprise group to establish work-based coordination. For example, Baan tried to standardize development methods and processes: "We want to have common processes across the locations. We try to achieve a uniform standard for all these. So that is a basic aim of this. Though we have not reached it in all the areas, but in certain areas we are making steps" (Jeevan).

As work-based coordination in the E-Enterprise group was very limited, the remote team members suffered from information flaws and lack of knowledge sharing. In particular, the lack of common knowledge about the evolving product was mentioned as critical:

> We have an existing architecture and we need to build future products based on this architecture, so understanding the existing architecture is most important to be able to build on top of it. We have completed realization from our side [E-Procurement and E-Sourcing] and E-Enterprise Server has also completed their realization. But now we need to integrate E-Enterprise Server into our applications. So for that we need a lot of knowledge about E-Enterprise Server. (Sujai)

Technology-based coordination

The E-Enterprise group was well equipped with the technologies required to enable working in a globally distributed environment. Technologies were considered very important: "this is actually one of the most important things: technology comes to our rescue in working in a distributed environment" (Venkat). Different technologies were used to save on travel costs between the Netherlands and India, as Venkat explained:

> Quite some time back, before all of these tools came into practice, we used to travel to the Netherlands and they used to travel here in order to meet us, especially at the start of a new release or to share some important needs that stretch over a long time. Even for small purposes people used to travel. That was becoming expensive and they [Baan] had to think of alternatives, then all of these media came in the picture. Then the VC was immediately applied. We started using VC, and we don't have to go to the Netherlands: we are saving a lot of dollars. (Venkat)

A variety of collaborative technologies was used in different situations. Typically email was used for quick queries and describing a problem prior to a phone call. The phone was used in situations when an urgent response was required and to resolve conflicting situations: "Telephone was usually involved when a lot of emails have been exchanged and certainly we feel that everyone is talking differently and it is taking too much time and no one is coming to any conclusions, then we start organizing a telephone call" (Srinnivas). Overall, there was also a tendency to minimize the use of the phone because of the costs involved.

ASTs – in particular NetMeeting and Webex – were often used for knowledge sharing activities during meetings between sites and with customers. VC was used occasionally for updates between managers from dispersed locations.

In the E-Enterprise group collaborative tools were mainly used for coordination and knowledge sharing purposes between individual team members. However, there was no configuration management tool in place to coordinate technical dependencies between products included in the E-Enterprise Suite (problems caused by lack of compatibility between versions of different products, discussed above).

Social coordination

In the E-Enterprise group social coordination between dispersed team members was very limited. Visiting the other country was difficult for people involved in the group because Baan was "trying to make cost-cutting measures, and they tried to shift everything to one location to reduce the communication costs" (Sridar). Therefore, the majority of team members have never been to the remote location and did not know who their remote counterparts were.

Lack of social coordination caused a number of problems. In particular, there was a lack of team atmosphere between teams in Hyderabad and Barneveld: from interviews of members of both teams, tensions between the teams became evident:

> The major issue is that people don't perceive that on the other side, they're not reciprocating our needs: what we want, during which time, what priority we have. They don't see the same priority as our people see, and vice versa. So there is always a gap. (Jeevan)

Interviewees were convinced that meeting their remote counterparts would give them a possibility to develop rapport, learn about cultural differences, and share views on different issues. This would help to bridge cultural and knowledge gaps:

> Personally I feel meeting the people would help you resolve the tasks more quickly, because you can really think and feel the person when you are actually talking. For example, assume two people, one has never come to India and the other has never gone to Holland. If they are interacting, there would be some gaps. But if they had an interaction at a personal level at some point in time, then the interaction would really be better, the response will be generally quicker. (Phani)

It was mentioned that understanding of cultural differences could help to bridge knowledge gaps and improve working relationships. For example, Ganesh (Process Manager for Baan Hyderabad) explained that understanding of cultural differences helps to define better processes that would be acceptable for Dutch and Indian cultures:

> When we write the process plan there are a lot of cultural issues that come into the picture. How to deal with this particular area? I can give you an example on quality assurance – a critical area. In the Indian culture, quality assurance is an important topic – people don't mind someone checking the work they do, but if you compare with our counterpart: in the Netherlands sometimes people don't like this. Because the counterpart, the Netherlands team, have a different

culture – individualistic. So there will be some resistance on that front sometimes. Once we understand this and appreciate the cultural factors, then we can define a better plan.

Discussion

In this section we compare results from the successful and unsuccessful cases. As an initial step, we compare the existence or absence of coordination mechanisms. Then we will assess how the role of coordination mechanisms in these organizations impacted on knowledge processes and ultimately on coordination outcomes.

Coordination mechanisms at SAP and Baan

In contrast to the E-Enterprise group of Baan, managers of the SAP KM Collaboration group implemented a number of coordination practices which aimed to facilitate knowledge processes between dispersed teams. Table 4.2 lists the coordination mechanisms identified in the SAP case, grouped according to the four categories of coordination mechanisms. The sign "+" is used to illustrate existence of a coordination mechanism, "–" indicates lack of a mechanism.

Coordination mechanisms and knowledge processes

Organization design. At SAP, a number of coordination mechanisms were employed to facilitate sharing and integration of knowledge between the dispersed teams. Various forms of organization design enabled handling knowledge processes differently. For example, direct contacts were used to promote unbiased and efficient knowledge transfer. This established and maintained transactive memory (who knows what and who is doing what) and enabled knowledge integration. By contrast, at Baan, organization design did not define clear communication channels to support knowledge and information flows between the teams in the Netherlands and India. This caused breakdowns in the coordination of work done at remote sites. Often, people in the Hyderabad office were not aware of plans and changes in products and technology originated by the Barneveld office. This limited the knowledge processes between dispersed teams which, in turn, did not help the teams to achieve a coordinated outcome.

Table 4.2 Coordination mechanisms: comparison of results across cases

Coordination mechanisms	SAP case (successful)	Baan case (unsuccessful)
Coordination by organization design		
Contact person/liaison	+	–
Mini-teams	+	–
Direct contact	+	–
Work-based coordination		
Enabling flexible project management techniques, planning by milestones	+	–
Making efficient division of work	+	–
Using specifications to guide the work	+	–
Using standard tools, SOP, and methodologies	+	+
Technology-based coordination		
Shared software development tools	+	+
Internet-enabled ICT infrastructure	+	+
Wide range of media and collaborative technology	+	+
Shared databases	+	–
Technology-enabled representation/visibility	+	–
Social coordination		
Team-building	+	–
Mutual adjustment	+	–
Facilitating interactions	+	–
Designing systematic communications	+	–

Work-based coordination. Both companies, SAP and Baan, used project plans and product specifications to coordinate work between locations. However, the companies used these coordination mechanisms differently. For example, in SAP (i) updated specifications were available on the intranet, and (ii) remote teams were informed about any modifications through their contact persons (technical architects). Through these mechanisms SAP ensured that the new knowledge is captured, and made explicit and accessible for all team members despite their geographical location. However, in Baan there was no central point of access to updated documents and, often, employees used outdated specifications to design their products. Both companies put efforts into standardization of tools and methods across locations to reduce knowledge gaps and create common knowledge about these tools and procedures. At the time of data collection Baan was implementing standard development methods and processes across locations. SAP standard tools and methods were implemented at the very early stages of the project, which helped to facilitate knowledge processes between remote teams through shared (similar) understanding of standards and made easier integration of deliverables of remote teams into the single (joint) outcome. Further various strategies for division of work in global projects is discussed in Chapter 7.

Technology-based coordination. Various technologies deployed at SAP helped to amplify knowledge processes across dispersed locations: Web access and synchronization of data ensured that all teams had access to the latest files. At Baan there was an attempt to have a central requirements database. However, requirements were changing so quickly that the database was not up to date. Code was synchronized via the databases at two locations. At SAP, various collaborative technologies were available for dispersed team members: for example internal phone lines (a five-digit number) between Bangalore and Walldorf made it easy to contact remote counterparts. These collaborative technologies were used in a *proactive* manner, for example for updates and knowledge sharing during various meetings between managers and developers, organized on a regular basis. In Baan, team members at both locations had a variety of collaborative technologies as well. However, different from SAP, at Baan these collaborative technologies were used largely in a *reactive* manner to fill in knowledge and information gaps; for instance for clarifications and to resolve problems. The roles that technology plays in global projects is discussed in Chapter 9.

Social coordination. At SAP, social coordination played an important role in building social capital at a global team level. As three dispersed teams were merged into one group in the beginning of the project, members of these teams had to build relationships such as trust and rapport from scratch. The team-building exercise and short visits were organized to give developers and key players an opportunity to meet in person in an informal environment and get to know each other. This helped to create transactive memory and build relationships among the team members. By contrast, Baan did not have coordination mechanisms in place aimed at building social capital between dispersed team members. Furthermore, many of the people interviewed did not know their remote counterparts in person. Baan tried to reduce project costs by avoiding traveling, thus reducing the opportunity of remote team members to meet in person. As a result, there were tensions between team members in Hyderabad and Barneveld. Tensions reduced the motivation of remote team members to communicate and share knowledge, unless this was considered absolutely necessary. Therefore, communications between the teams were often postponed to the integration stages and were initiated by emerging problems.

Knowledge processes and coordinated outcomes

In SAP, the managers of the KM Collaboration group realized the importance of the sharing and integration of knowledge across dispersed locations at the early stages of the project and put a lot of effort into setting up and facilitating knowledge processes across dispersed locations. It was particularly important to create transactive memory between dispersed team members, to share knowledge about the cultures of the remote counterparts, and to achieve a common understanding of the evolving product. Interviewees from SAP said that knowing who knows what at a remote location enabled them to reduce development life cycle because team members knew whom to contact for a specific problem and the response was quicker. As a result, they were able to achieve a successful coordinated outcome: "We just went through a merger, so setting up a global project was not an easy task. Despite all the difficulties we managed to have a successful second software release in eight months" (Stefan).

The success of the project outcome is also supported by external evidence. According to JupiterResearch, a leading research and consulting company in emerging technologies, SAP Enterprise Portal was recognized as the third largest software solution, with 17 per cent of the US market in 2002. The studied project developed SAP Collaboration tools as one of the main features of the SAP Enterprise Portal.

At Baan, managers of the E-Enterprise group had limited coordination mechanisms in place that would facilitate knowledge processes. Subsequently, there were numerous knowledge gaps between team members in India and the Netherlands. Moreover, the E-Enterprise global team did not develop transactive memory as team members did not know who their remote counterparts were. Often interdependencies between products developed at remote locations were discovered at the last moment and this resulted in integration problems (instead of careful advance planning). As a result, working in a globally distributed environment proved to be problematic for the E-Enterprise group, and in the summer of 2002 the development office in the Netherlands was shut down.

Conclusions

This chapter has developed a knowledge-based perspective on coordination and demonstrated its applicability in the context of globally distributed software projects. The increasing move toward globally dispersed work, and the resulting implications for knowledge creation, sharing, and integrating, we suggest, make our model both heuristically and as an explanatory device eminently applicable as a basis for research in many other contexts where coordination is a key concern.

In terms of practical implications, the chapter illustrates micro-coordination practices in relation to four types of knowledge processes. We compared a successful project (SAP) with an unsuccessful project (Baan). But an even more important finding emerges. Instead of focusing on coordination mechanisms *per se*, and (as found in many studies) over relying on the efficacy of tools and technologies as coordination mechanisms (Cheng *et al.*, 2003/4; Smith and Blanck, 2002; Ebert and De Neve, 2001; Mockus and Weiss, 2001; Majchrzak *et al.*, 2000) to ensure successful outcomes, managers should consider their organization in terms of knowledge processes and not just as information flows. They must then focus on how coordination mechanisms facilitate knowledge processes in all four areas. Here our research suggests that technologies are most useful for *amplifying knowledge management processes*, that is, for allowing knowledge sharing. Organization design *facilitates knowledge flows* across organizations and teams. Work-based mechanisms *make knowledge explicit and accessible*, while social mechanisms are needed to *build social capital* and exchange knowledge and ideas. (This is further explored in Chapter 8.) While these mechanisms can and do have multiple uses, it is clear that unless management practices take on board their various knowledge pay-offs, coordination in increasingly knowledge-intensive work environments will become much more problematic.

The framework developed in this chapter proposes a one-directional, singular relationship between coordination mechanisms and knowledge processes. However it is possible that one coordination mechanism (or combination of them) affects more than one knowledge process. While it is possible that each mechanism affects mainly one knowledge process, the effect on other knowledge processes cannot be totally ignored. Therefore in our further research we will investigate the interrelationships between coordination mechanisms and knowledge processes.

Finally, it is important to note that our findings are based on two case studies and therefore, by definition, meet to only a limited extent the criteria of generalizability. In this research we generalize (i) from data to description (i.e. empirical statements presented above) and (ii) from description to the theory (the proposed research model) that is generalizable within the case setting (Lee and Baskerville, 2003). However, in order to generalize from the theory to descriptions of other settings, further research needs to be conducted in these other settings.

References

Adler, P. S. (1995) "Interdepartmental Interdependence and Coordination: The Case of the Design/Manufacturing Interface," *Organization Science*, 6(2), 147–67.

Akgun, A. E., Byrne, J., Keskin, H., Lynn, G. S., and Imamoglu, S. Z. (2005) "Knowledge Networks in New Product Development Projects: A Transactive Memory Perspective," *Information & Management*, 42(8), 1105–20.

Barkhi, R., Amiri, A., and James, T. L. (2006) "A Study of Communication and Coordination in Collaborative Software Development," *Journal of Global Information Technology Management*, 9(1), 44–61.

Battin, R. D., Crocker, R., and Kreidler, J. (2001) "Leveraging Resources in Global Software Development," *IEEE Software* (March/April), 70–7.

Bechky, B. A. (2003) "Sharing Meaning Across Occupational Communities: The Transformation of Understanding on a Production Floor," *Organization Science*, 14(3), 312–30.

Bigley, G. A. and Roberts, K. H. (2001) "The Incident Command System: High Reliability Organizing for Complex and Volatile Task Environments," *Academy of Management Journal*, 44(6), 1281–99.

Boland, R. J. (1991) "Information Systems Use as a Hermeneutic Process," in *Information Systems Research: Contemporary Approaches & Emergent Traditions* (Eds, Nisen, H. E., Klein, H. H., and Hirschheim, R.) North-Holland, New York, NY, pp. 439–58.

Boland, R. J. and Tenkasi, R. V. (1995) "Perspective Making and Perspective Taking in Communities of Knowing," *Organization Science*, 6(4), 350–72.

Bowker, G. and Starr, S. (1999) *Sorting Things Out: Classification and Its Consequences*, MIT Press, Cambridge, MA.

Brown, J. S. and Duguid, P. (2001) "Knowledge and Organization," *Organization Science*, 12(2), 198–213.

Carlson, J. R. and Zmud, R. W. (1999) "Channel Expansion Theory and the Experiential Nature of Media Richness Perceptions," *Academy of Management Journal*, 42(2), 153–70.

Carmel, E. (1999) *Global Software Teams: Collaborating across Borders and Time Zones*, Prentice-Hall, Upper Saddle River, NJ.

Cheng, L., DeSouza, C. R. B., Hupfer, S., Patterson, J., and Ross, S. (2003/4) "Building Collaboration into IDEs," *Queue*, 1(9), 40–50.

Ciborra, C. U., Orlikowski, W. K., Failla, A., Patriotta, G., Bikson, T. K., Suetens, N. T., and Wynn, E. (1996) *Groupware & Teamwork: Invisible Aid or Technical Hindrance?*, John Wiley, Chichester.

Cramton, C. D. (2001) "The Mutual Knowledge Problem and Its Consequences for Dispersed Collaboration," *Organization Science*, 12(3), 346–71.

Crowston, K. (1997) "A Coordination Theory Approach to Organizational Process Design," *Organization Science*, 8(2), 157–75.

Crowston, K. and Kammerer, E. E. (1998) "Coordination and Collective Mind in Software Requirements Development," *IBM Systems Journal*, 37(2), 227–45.

Davenport, T. H., De Long, D. W., and Beers, M. C. (1998) "Successful Knowledge Management Projects," *Sloan Management Review*, 39(2), 43–57.

Davenport, T. H. and Prusak, L. (2000) *Working Knowledge: How Organizations Manage What They Know*, Boston, MA, Harvard Business School Press.

Donnellon, A., Gray, B., and Bougon, M. G. (1986) "Communication, Meaning, and Organized Action," *Administrative Science Quarterly*, 31(1), 43–55.

Dougherty, D. (1992) "Interpretive Barriers to Successful Product Innovation in Large Firms," *Organization Science*, 3(2), 179–202.

Ebert, C. and De Neve, P. (2001) "Surviving Global Software Development," *IEEE Software* (March/April), 62–9.

Faraj, S. and Sproull, L. (2000) "Coordinating Expertise in Software Development Teams," *Management Science*, 46(12), 1554–68.

Gabarro, J. J. (1990) "The Development of Working Relationships," in *Intellectual Teamwork: Social and Technological Foundations of Cooperative Work* (Eds, Galegher, J., Kraut, R. E., and Egido, C.) Lawrence Erlbaum, Hillsdale, NJ, pp. 70–110.

Galbraith, J. R. (1973) *Designing Complex Organizations*, Lawrence Erlbaum, Reading, MA.

Giddens, A. (1991) *The Consequences of Modernity*, Polity Press, Cambridge.

Gittell, J. H. and Weiss, L. (2004) "Coordinating Networks within and across Organizations: A Multi-level Framework," *Journal of Management Studies*, 41(1), 127–53.

Goodhue, D. L. and Thompson, R. L. (1995) "Task-Technology Fit and Individual Performance," *MIS Quarterly*, 19(4), 213–35.

Grant, R. M. (1996) "Toward a Knowledge-Based Theory of the Firm," *Strategic Management Journal*, 17 (Winter), 109–22.

Hendriks, P. (1999) "Why Share Knowledge? The Influence of ICT on the Motivation for Knowledge Sharing," *Knowledge and Process Management*, 6(2), 91–100.

Herbsleb, J. D. and Mockus, A. (2003) "An Empirical Study of Speed and Communication in Globally-Distributed Software Development," *IEEE Transactions on Software Engineering*, 29(6), 1–14.

Jarvenpaa, S. L., Knoll, K., and Leidner, D. E. (1998) "Is Anybody out there? Antecedents of Trust in Global Virtual Teams," *Journal of MIS*, 14(4), 29–64.

Kogut, B. and Zander, U. (1996) "What Firms Do? Coordination, Identity, and Learning," *Organization Science*, 7(5), 502–18.

Kotlarsky, J. and Oshri, I. (2005) "Social Ties, Knowledge Sharing and Successful Collaboration in Globally Distributed System Development Projects," *European Journal of Information Systems*, 14(1), 37–48.

Krauss, R. M. and Fussell, S. R. (1990) "Mutual Knowledge and Communicative Effectiveness," in *Intellectual Teamwork: Social and Technological Foundations of Cooperative Work* (Eds, Galegher, J., Kraut, R. E., and Egido, C.) Lawrence Erlbaum, Hillsdale, NJ.

Kumar, K., van Fenema, P. C., and Von Glinow, M. A. (2005) "Intense Collaboration in Globally Distributed Work Teams: Evolving Patterns of Dependencies and Coordination," in *Managing Multinational Teams: Global Perspectives* (Eds, Shapiro, D. L., von Glinow, M. A., and Cheng, J. L. C.) Elsevier, Oxford, pp. 127–54.

Lee, A. S. and Baskerville, R. L. (2003) "Generalizing Generalizability in Information Systems Research," *Information Systems Research*, 14(3), 221–43.

Levesque, L. L., Wilson, J. M., and Wholey, D. R. (2001) "Cognitive Divergence and Shared Mental Models in Software Development Project Teams," *Journal of Organizational Behavior*, 22, 135–44.

Liew, A. (2007) "Understanding Data, Information, Knowledge and their Inter-Relationships", *Journal of Knowledge Management Practice*, 8(2).

Lorand, R. (2000) *Aesthetic Order*, Routledge, London.

Majchrzak, A. and Malhotra, A. (2004) "Virtual Workspace Technology Use and Knowledge-Sharing Effectiveness in Distributed Teams: The Influence of a Team's Transactive Memory," *Knowledge Management Knowledge Base. http://knowledgemanagement.ittoolbox.com/documents/document.asp?i=3164.*

Majchrzak, A., Rice, R. E., King, N., Malhotra, A., and Ba, S. (2000) "Computer-Mediated Inter-Organizational Knowledge-Sharing: Insights from a Virtual Team Innovating Using a Collaborative Tool," *Information Resources Management Journal*, 13(1), 44–54.

McCann, J. E. and Galbraith, J. R. (1981) "Interdepartmental Relations," in *Handbook of Organizational Design* (Eds, Nystrom, P C. and Starbuck, W. H.) Oxford University Press, New York, 2, pp. 60–84.

Miles, M. B. and Huberman, A. M. (1994) *Qualitative Data Analysis: An Expanded Sourcebook*, Sage, Thousand Oaks, CA.

Mintzberg, H. (1979) *The Structuring of Organizations*, Prentice Hall, Englewood Cliffs, NJ.

Mockus, A. and Weiss, D. M. (2001) "Globalization by Chunking: A Quantitative Approach," *IEEE Software* (March/April), 30–7.

Moreland, R. L. (1999) "Transactive Memory: Learning Who Knows What in Work Groups and Organizations," in *Shared Cognition in Organizations: The Management of Knowledge* (Eds, Thompson, L., Messick, D., and Levine, J.) Lawrence Erlbaum, Mahwah, NJ.

Ngwenyama, O. K. and Lee, A. (1997) "Communication Richness in Electronic Mail: A Critical Social Theory and the Contextuality of Meaning," *MIS Quarterly*, 21(2), 145–67.

Nidumolu, S. R. (1995) "The Effect of Coordination and Uncertainty on Software Project Performance," *Information Systems Research*, 6(3), 191–219.

Nidumolu, S. R. (1996) "A Comparison of the Structural Contingency and Risk-based Perspectives on Coordination in Software-Development Projects," *Journal of Management Information Systems*, 13(2), 77–113.

Nonaka, I. (1994) "A Dynamic Theory of Organizational Knowledge Creation," *Organization Science*, 5(1), 14–37.

Oettinger, A. G. (1999) "Introduction," in B. M. Compaine and W. H. Read (eds), *The Information Resources Policy Handbook: Research for the Information Age*, MIT Press, Cambridge, MA.

Olson, J. S. and Olson, G. M. (2004) "Culture Surprises in Remote Software Development Teams," *Queue*, 1(9), 52–9.

Orlikowski, W. J. (1992) "The Duality of Technology: Rethinking the Concept of Technology in Organizations," *Organization Science*, 3(3), 398–427.

Orlikowski, W. J. (2002) "Knowing in Practice: Enacting a Collective Capability in Distributed Organizing," *Organization Science*, 13(3), 249–73.

Quinn, R. W. and Dutton, J. E. (2005) "Coordination as Energy-in-Conversation," *Academy of Management Review*, 30(1), 36–57.

Sarker, S. and Sahay, S. (2004) "Implications of Space and Time for Distributed Work: An Interpretive Study of US–Norwegian System Development Teams," *European Journal of Information Systems*, 13(1), 3–20.

Smith, P. G. and Blanck, E. L. (2002) "From Experience: Leading Dispersed Teams," *Journal of Product Innovation Management*, 19, 294–304.

Spender, J.-C. and Grant, R. M. (1996) "Knowledge and the Firm: Overview," *Strategic Management Journal*, 17 (Winter), 77–91.

Strauss, A. L. and Corbin, J. M. (1998) *Basics of Qualitative Research* Sage, Thousand Oaks, CA.

Szulanski, G. (1996) "Exploring Internal Stickiness: Impediments to the Transfer of Best Practice within the Firm," *Strategic Management Journal*, 17 (Winter), 77–91.

van de Ven, A. H., Delbecq, A. L., and Koenig, R. Jr (1976) "Determinants of Coordination Modes within Organizations," *American Sociological Review*, 41 (April), 322–38.

van Fenema, P. C. (2002) "Coordination and Control of Globally Distributed Software Projects," Department of Decision and Information Sciences, Erasmus University, Rotterdam School of Management, Rotterdam, 572.

von Hippel, E. (1994) "Sticky Information" and the Locus of Problem Solving: Implications for Innovation," *Management Science*, 40(4), 429–39.

Walsham, G. (2002) "Cross-Cultural Software Production and Use: A Structurational Analysis," *MIS Quarterly*, 26(4), 359–80.

Wegner, D. M. (1987) "Transactive Memory: A Contemporary Analysis of the Group Mind," in *Theories of Group Behavior* (Eds, Mullen, G. and Goethals, G.) Springer Verlag, New York.

Zuboff, S. (1988) *In the Age of the Smart Machine: The Future of Work and Power*, Basic Books, New York.

CHAPTER 5

Expertise management in a distributed context: The case of offshore information technology outsourcing

Ilan Oshri, Julia Kotlarsky, Leslie P. Willcocks, and Paul C. van Fenema

Introduction

The offshore outsourcing of information technologies (IT) started in the 1990s, following the outsourcing trend in manufacturing industries. In particular, the recent trend has been characterized by offshoring of various IT processes and services to external contractors at offshore locations. Indeed, low labour costs combined with the search for skilled workforces have promoted a shift in strategic IS development toward considering outsourcing to offshore locations. In doing so, firms have set up development centers in India and Israel and have more recently considered the Philippines, China, and other countries. In recent years, the scale of outsourcing projects has increased significantly as the considerations involved in outsourcing to offshore locations have been extended from simple and repetitive tasks and processes to those that involve strategic and knowledge-intensive activities (Quinn, 2000), such as the development and implementation of strategic IT systems.

As outsourcing projects become more complex and may involve multiple stakeholders, the parties involved require well developed and accessible distributed expertise such as specialized skills and knowledge. Such capability, i.e. the management of distributed expertise, is considered a key resource for software development (Faraj and Sproull, 2000).

Research has previously reported that experts from different companies and remote sites, specializing in multiple areas, have jointly engaged in sharing expertise in order to innovate and design new products (Malhotra *et al.*, 2001). While such evidence is valuable in understanding knowledge processes in distributed contexts, past studies have, so far, paid little attention to the processes involved in managing expertise in distributed contexts in general, and in offshore outsourcing settings in particular. Clearly, a successful software development effort depends on a timely and accurate coordination of expertise (Faraj and Sproull, 2000). And yet such expertise is often developed based on local training and learning routines (DeSouza and Evaristo, 2004). Furthermore, while solving problems, remote counterparts in offshore outsourcing projects are expected to integrate their knowledge and expertise and offer clients innovative ideas to transform their business (Willcocks and Lacity, 2006). Such arguments have been outlined in Chapter 1, and it was suggested in Chapter 2 that developing a transactive memory system may assist in managing distributed expertise. In this chapter we seek to develop further ideas of how distributed expertise can be managed.

In fact, the study of the management of expertise is wide and diverse. Nonetheless, the vast majority of the studies on expertise management have tended to separate three key components essential for leveraging local expertise globally, namely: the development, coordination, and integration of expertise. Furthermore, past studies on expertise development have mainly emphasized the role that knowledge creation plays in the development of expertise in co-located contexts (e.g. Oshri *et al.*, 2006; Lave and Wenger, 1991), while studies on expertise coordination have tended to emphasize the role that information plays in bringing together expertise, in the form of directories that map out the pool of expertise available within the organization (Nevo and Wand, 2005). Considering expertise development processes separately from expertise coordination activities may result in an incomplete theoretical construct that does not explain how knowledge creation activities relate to the cataloging of the location of expert knowledge. To address this gap, this chapter seeks to link expertise development, coordination, and integration activities by exploring how the knowledge created during expertise development activities is catalogued and is made available in the form of a cataloguing system that offers access to "where knowledge lies." Furthermore, in developing, coordinating, and integrating expertise, globally distributed teams seek, on the one hand, to develop a distributed mode of expertise management to allow the emergence of expertise in remote locations so that work can be divided based on local expertise, and, on the other hand, such teams may consider a joint mode of expertise development in which the entire global team may benefit from the collective experience embedded within the team. We explore the development of expertise and the coordination of knowledge through a cataloguing system, by considering either a joint or a distributed approach to expertise management.

Following this introduction, the chapter explores the concept of expertise and the theoretical foundation of its development, coordination, and integration. This conceptual contribution is followed by an in-depth case study of an offshore outsourcing project in which expertise was managed onsite and offshore. The chapter concludes by providing theoretical and practical implications.

Understanding the concept of expertise management

From a knowledge perspective, there are two views of expertise. One view perceives expertise as the possession of specialized knowledge and skills (Faraj and Sproull, 2000), such as technical and domain knowledge that is abstract and tacit to a great extent (Hinds and Bailey, 2000). According to this view, teams, either dispersed or co-located, are simply a means to bring together people from various domains of expertise. The second view considers expertise to be context-dependent, embedded in practice (e.g. Fitzpatrick, 2003; Orlikowski, 2002) and developed through participation in organizational activities (e.g. Oshri *et al.*, 2006; Lave and Wenger, 1991). According to this view, teams provide the platform and context in which these interactions and practices are exercised and through which expertise jointly emerges. According to this view, largely adopted by this chapter, *expertise* is defined as the ability to act *knowledgeably* within a specific domain of application (Gasson, 2005). Expertise is also often referred to in the literature as *know-how* or *competence*, which is the ability to apply knowledge to develop and improve products and processes (McEvily *et al.*, 2004), or the ability to achieve skillful performance (Orlikowski, 2002). In a way, the concept of expertise is closely related to the notion of *knowing in practice* (*ibid.*).

The concepts of expertise and knowledge indeed relate to each other; however, we maintain that they are not synonymous (Willem and Scarbrough, 2002). For one, we argue that expertise refers to a specific type of knowledge that is dynamic and evolving in nature. In this regard, *embodied knowledge* and skills possessed by individuals (Fitzpatrick, 2003) represent the notion of expertise discussed in this chapter. Such knowledge is accumulated over years of experience in a specific area. Furthermore, embodied knowledge is *context-dependent* (*ibid.*), situated in a particular setting (Orlikowski, 2002). Lastly, such knowledge is inseparable from the practice of doing, and is constantly evolving and changing through a recurrent practice that involves varying activities and contexts.

In line with past discussions about the dispersed nature of knowledge (Petsch *et al.*, 1997; Tsoukas, 1996), expertise at the team and organizational level can indeed be perceived as distributed. In this regard, recent years have witnessed a further dispersal of expertise (Petsch *et al.*, 1997: 1039). For example, teams involved in outsourcing projects are often located onsite, offshore, and nearshore. This presents new challenges to the management of expertise, as remote counterparts engage in creating and sharing context-dependent knowledge. At the same time, remote counterparts are expected to share and exploit knowledge in a fashion that brings expertise to bear in a timely manner (Faraj and Sproull, 2000), regardless of its origin or physical location.

A review of the expertise and knowledge management[1] literature suggests that the management of expertise consists of three major processes, namely expertise *development* (e.g. Lave and Wenger, 1991), *coordination* (e.g. Faraj and Sproul, 2000) and *integration* (e.g. Alavi, 1994). While each expertise management process has its distinct characteristics, the three processes depend on each other (see Table 5.1).

Expertise development involves the acquisition of know-how through learning. By this we mean that expertise is developed when members of a team engage in learning and problem-solving activities to come up with new products and services. Such expertise can be developed through training sessions and formal education programs. At the same time, by being involved in a particular project, skills and expertise may potentially be enhanced as members of a team interact with their counterparts, and confront and solve new problems. In this sense, expertise development is the learning process through which individuals and groups develop skills, know-how, identity, and meaning to facilitate their participation in organizational activities.

Expertise coordination refers to team-situated interactions aimed at managing expertise dependencies (Faraj and Sproull, 2000: 1555). In this regard, expertise coordination as a process ensures that individuals at each site have the requisite know-how, and that they know who knows and does what. The notion of expertise coordination has been associated with the concept of Transactive Memory (TM). A Transactive Memory System (TMS) has been defined as the combination of individual memory systems

Table 5.1 Expertise development, coordination, and integration in distributed contexts

	Expertise development	Expertise coordination	Expertise integration
Emphasis in terms of unit of analysis	• Individual and intraproject level	• Project and inter-project level	• Interproject and organizational level
Processes	• Participation in projects • Acquisition of know-how through learning and sharing • Transferring and enhancing expertise base	• Search processes for existing solutions	• The diffusion (and adoption) of global best practices
Outcome of processes	• Upgrade know-how and skills-base	• Problem solving through the transfer of expertise in a timely manner	• Innovation and "avoiding reinventing the wheel"
Challenges	• Do individuals have the expertise needed to perform their tasks?	• Are individuals aware of who knows what and how such an expertise can be brought to bear?	• Would individuals get involved in global innovation and adopt global best practices?

and communications (also referred to as "transactions") between individuals. The group-level TMS is constituted by individuals using each other as a memory source. Transactions between individuals link their memory systems; through a series of processes (i.e. encoding, storing, and retrieving) know-how is exchanged. Individuals encode information for storing and retrieval, similar to a librarian entering details of a new book in the particular library system before putting it on the shelves. Through encoding, knowledge is categorized (i.e. assigned labels that reflect the subjects of the knowledge) in order to systematically store the location of the know-how, but not the know-how itself. Then, individuals store this information internally (building their own memory), or externally (storing it in artifacts or indirectly in other people's memories). And lastly, information about the location of the expertise is retrieved when someone else asks for it (Nevo and Wand, 2005). Retrieval thus consists of two interconnected subprocesses: person A asks person B for information; person B retrieves the information. As Nevo and Wand (2005: 551) put it: "Knowledge is encoded, stored and retrieved through various transactions between individuals." Expertise coordination, therefore, attempts to achieve awareness of the existence of expertise and the alignment of expertise across various experts and tasks, in the sense that task dependencies (Goodhue and Thompson, 1995; van de Ven *et al.*, 1976) and expertise dependencies are addressed effectively. In this regard, coordination results in a concerted awareness of dispersed expertise availability and could potentially enable the employment of expertise in a timely and accurate manner (Faraj and Sproull, 2000).

Expertise integration is the process that brings together know-how in an effective and efficient way to develop new concepts and innovations. As opposed to expertise coordination, which aims at creating awareness of the existence of expertise, expertise integration assumes value creation through cross-fertilization and interactions between experts (McEvily *et al.*, 2004; Grant, 1996; Alavi, 1994). Consequently, experts bring their know-how together, often expertise that is drawn from various disciplines and that is based on years of experience, to innovate with new concepts, products, and processes. In doing so, the integration of expertise attempts to address future needs (e.g. business transformation and innovation) rather than to solve present problems (e.g. maintenance issues). In line with the literature on knowledge integration (Grant, 1996), the integration of expertise facilitates the organization's ability to sense, interpret, and respond to new opportunities and threats in a dynamic business environment (Alavi, 1994).

There are several aspects relating to the characteristics of expertise and knowledge that affect a firm's ability to develop, coordinate, and integrate expertise. The following section will discuss these aspects in depth, aiming to identify the challenges associated with the management of distributed expertise.

The management of distributed expertise: The dilemma and its implications

The management of expertise may face challenges that can be behavioural, for example the lack of motivation (Hinds and Bailey, 2000), be it managerial or technological (von Hippel, 1998, 1994; Tyre and von Hippel, 1997; Szulanski, 1996) in nature. In the context of a distributed environment, one dilemma could be imperative for the management of expertise; namely, whether to jointly or locally develop expertise. By this we mean that distributed teams can jointly develop expertise by incorporating the entire team in learning activities. On the other hand, distributed teams may pursue an approach in which the development of expertise will be distributed, resulting in the specialization of individuals and teams in a particular area. The first approach can be seen as a joint approach, whereas the latter would be a distributed approach to developing expertise.

Taking either a distributed or joint approach to expertise development may have implications for the coordination and integration of expertise. Coordinating expertise may require the development of an organizational memory system, known as the transactive memory system (TMS). Through this memory system individuals can encode, store, and retrieve information about "who knows what" and "who does what" from codified and personalized directories. Updating the directories of a TMS is critical for the coordination of expertise, as experts may develop new skills and acquire recent information about markets and products. While the joint development of expertise may offer more opportunities to update directories about "who knows what" and "who does what" through interactions between remote counterparts, the investment in creating "common grounds" (Cramton, 2001) for knowledge exchanges can be rather costly and problematic to achieve. Furthermore, a joint development of expertise may create duplications of expertise across locations beyond what is necessary, and may impose information overload on individual team members (Petsch *et al.*, 1997).

The distribution of expertise, on the other hand, offers advantages in terms of the division of work, which could offer fewer dependencies between remote counterparts, and could prevent miscommunications between them (Carmel and Tjia, 2005). Indeed, the diversity of perspectives and knowledge asymmetries may increase the global team capability to create new knowledge (Malhotra and Majchrzak, 2004; Petsch *et al.*, 1997) and enhance the quality of their decision-making processes (Huang *et al.*, 2003). At the same time, such a distributed approach may result in fewer opportunities to share learning and may create difficulties to integrate expertise due to insufficient mutual understanding induced by team members having different interpretive frameworks and sets of expertise (Malhotra and Majchrzak, 2004; Petsch *et al.*, 1997; Alavi, 1994). Based on the literature cited above, Table 5.2 summarizes the dilemma and the implications involved in a joint or a distributed approach to developing expertise.

In line with these observations, this chapter seeks to explore the approach taken by distributed teams at a case study company, TCS,

Table 5.2 Expertise management: The dilemma and its implications

	Expertise development	Expertise coordination	Expertise integration
	Joint expertise development		
Benefits associated with jointly developing expertise	• Creating common grounds for knowledge sharing • Facilitating the development of a TMS (that extends beyond the boundaries of co-located teams)	• Ability to bring expertise to bear beyond a single co-located team by accessing information about "who knows what" and "who does what"	• Knowledge integration of learning generated in past and present projects through intensive formal and informal interactions
Challenges of jointly developing expertise	• High investment in creating "common ground" between remote counterparts • Higher task dependency may result in miscommunications and in design problems • Duplications of existing assets that may result in "reinventing the wheel" • May create high cognitive load on individual team members		
	Distributed expertise development		
Benefits associated with separately developing expertise	• High degree of specialization of teams in a particular area • May avoid the duplication of expertise bases and "reinventing the wheel" • May allow fewer dependencies between tasks	• Because of fewer dependencies between tasks, there is less need to bring expertise to bear beyond the boundaries of a dispersed team • A powerful TMS within co-located teams that supports problem solving within a team	• Knowledge integration produces information that is relevant and contributes directly to the line of products and markets within this specific domain and market
Implications of separately developing expertise	• Difficulties of exploiting learning generated in remote locations or other knowledge domains • An overview perspective of "who knows what" and "who does what" is mainly developed at middle management level • Little knowledge integration between domains: to integrate knowledge between domains, dispersed teams need to rely on well-defined interfaces agreed in advance		

concerning their expertise management, the challenges faced and solutions introduced to cope with the implications presented above.

About this research

To explore the management of expertise in offshore settings our primary case selection criterion was to find an outsourcing project that was globally distributed and required the development, coordination, and integration of expertise. A key project of TATA Consultancy Services (TCS) was selected and studied in depth in the context of expertise management. This project involves the outsourcing of ABN AMRO IT-infrastructure support and the development of new systems by TCS. The project necessitated complex and challenging expertise development, and the coordination and integration of activities between onsite and offshore locations, as remote counterparts needed to transfer knowledge while learning about the client systems as well as engaging in codevelopment and implementation activities. Evidence was collected from interviews, project documentation, and observations (Yin, 1994; Eisenhardt, 1989). Interviews were conducted at two remote sites: at the onsite location in Amsterdam with TCS and ABN AMRO personnel, and in Mumbai (India) at the offshore location with TCS personnel. Interviewees were chosen to include (i) counterparts working closely at remote locations, and (ii) diverse roles such as executives, managers, and developers. In total, 52 interviews were conducted. They lasted on average 1.5 hours; they were recorded and transcribed in full. A semi-structured interview protocol was applied, to allow the researchers to clarify specific issues and follow up with questions. Data analysis followed several steps. It relied on iterative reading of the data using open-coding techniques (Strauss and Corbin, 1998), to sort and refine themes emerging from the data (Miles and Huberman, 1994). In particular, three themes that represent the concept of *expertise management* were carefully studied: development, coordination, and integration of expertise. Each process was examined in relation to joint and distributed approaches to expertise management. Statements that were found to correspond with these three themes were selected, coded, and analyzed using Atlas.ti – Qualitative Data Analysis software (Weitzman, 2000; Miles and Huberman, 1994). The first step in our data analysis aimed to examine expertise development, coordination, and integration processes. It involved reading through the interview transcripts and collected documents, then (i) coding statements that illustrated various elements of expertise development, coordination, and integration, and (ii) marking evidence of the approach regarding the way expertise was developed and shared, i.e. either joint or distributed. During this stage, chunks of text (paragraphs or sentences) describing expertise management processes were coded. Then, to understand how expertise had been managed in this particular outsourcing project, we analyzed statements in each of these three categories to identify the specific processes that contribute to the development, coordination, and integration of expertise.

The ABN AMRO bank – TCS outsourcing project: Expertise management processes

To understand the complexity involved in managing expertise across dispersed locations, we first describe the challenges faced in this project. Following this, the results of the case study will be presented. Some background information about TCS and the outsourcing deal with ABN AMRO can be found in the Appendix.

Expertise development processes at TCS

There are several domains within which expertise can be developed, such as technology-, business-, and managerial-oriented expertise. We have observed that when it comes to technology- and business- (market-) oriented expertise, TCS followed an approach that promoted a joint development of expertise at the project and the organizational levels. There were several processes and organizational mechanisms that TCS put in place to ensure that expertise was developed in a joint manner, such as a tightly managed learning process between onsite and offshore teams, a global expertise management system, and a joint expertise development program.

The learning process between onsite and offshore teams contributes to the development of technological expertise relating to client systems as well to a better understanding of ABN AMRO business processes and

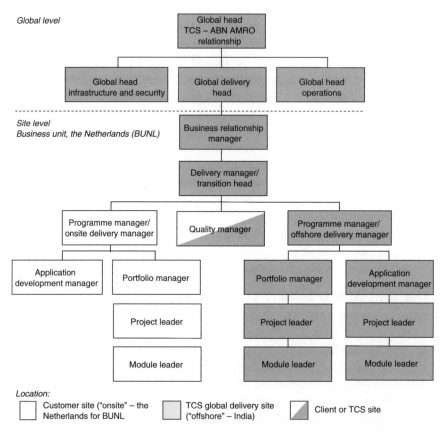

Figure 5.1   The organizational structure of ABN AMRO – TCS project team

environment. Members of the onsite and offshore teams jointly learned about client systems and acquired new knowledge regarding maintenance and problem-solving concerning the IT infrastructure at the client site. This learning activity took place mainly during the transition phase. While the teams were distant from each other, the processes and structures implemented by TCS ensured that the expertise developed onsite would be shared with the offshore team. For example, the offshore team was organized as a mirror image of the onsite team to ensure that each offshore expert corresponded with and learned from a particular individual, who held the same role title, from the onsite team (see Figure 5.1). Furthermore, the learning between onsite and offshore teams took place through the application of standardized templates that captured the know-how held by the client and shared it with the offshore team. One Project leader from Mumbai offshore team described this as follows:

We share the documents that were prepared at the onsite and the minutes of the meeting prepared at the onsite. So the discussion that has been carried on at onsite, the onsite person passes [to offshore] through email and we [offshore] receive it.

The codification of knowledge through the use of these standardized templates enabled the offshore team to examine and learn the technological aspects involved in supporting the client systems as well as to identify know-how gaps that had not been properly addressed by the onsite team. To ensure that expertise had been properly learned and absorbed by the offshore team and that the know-how acquired could be appropriately (re)applied in problem-solving scenarios, the offshore team "played back" the know-how acquired to the onsite team, as well as solved problems generated by the client. The Relationship Manager of the Amsterdam offshore team explained the concept of "playback":

While we are doing the knowledge transition, we have multiple checkpoints where we have what we call this "play back" session, where we play back the knowledge that we have actually learned or gathered from the Bank. Then we also involve our offshore teams and onsite teams, play it back to the Bank saying, "This is what I understand." And we also make sure that we start the sessions from the business side because it is not just a burden for our people to understand a particular application of a particular technology. But it's also important for them to understand the end customer.

Through such "playback" exercises, the onsite and offshore teams ensured that know-how gaps, which are in fact expertise deficiencies of either team, would be detected and eliminated. In other words, the teams identified the areas in which expertise had been jointly developed as well as those areas that required additional joint expertise development.

In addition to the organizational structure and the joint learning process, TCS have also developed a process that ensures that the pool of expertise at the project and organizational level will be monitored and, where needed, expertise levels will be upgraded. For example, Centres of Excellences (CoEs) at TCS played a role in monitoring and indicating which expertise should be upgraded when there was a gap between existing and needed expertise within a project. CoEs are known to be networks of experts who have advanced know-how and experience in a particular market or technological domain. However, at TCS these CoEs played a far more significant role, by monitoring the level of expertise and conducting a gap analysis to ensure that expertise was updated with industry standards. Indeed, TCS introduced CoEs in several domains, related to technologies (e.g. Windows-based technologies, Java-based technologies) and specific industries (Financial CoE) and services (e.g. Service Practice CoE). A member of the Oracle CoE described how he monitored expertise:

> Every month, I do a technical health-check review of those projects. Now these reviews are different from all the quality reviews. Our quality reviews are done against the quality check lists and quality guidelines. These reviews [CoE Reviews] are done from a technology perspective: for example if I am doing a project review, I try to find out whether the project is using the most advanced solutions.

Another member of CoE described the involvement of his CoE in expertise development processes:

> We have internally a learning and development group who are conducting various training programs depending on the need associated with the project's requirements, and to support that we have our individual learning plan . . . we assess the people on the basis of the knowledge that particular resource has and the knowledge that is required for the project and we do a gap analysis about the areas that require further development. Once we do the gap analysis the system tells us, "Okay he needs to do this, this, and this to reach the appropriate level." At this stage the person has to undergo this training. We give him a particular timeframe in which he can do all these knowledge acquisition activities so he builds up his knowledge.

The involvement of CoEs in expertise development is of particular importance, as these networks are bodies of knowledge and best practices in certain fields, but are also a repository of information of "who knows what" across the organization. This aspect will be discussed in more detail in the section about expertise integration.

While such expertise development activities were mainly conducted within an outsourcing project, other processes within TCS ensured that expertise would be developed across the organization. For example, training activities concerning specific technologies were offered to employees regardless of their geographical locations or association with a particular project or industry. Courses were mainly offered by the Global Learning and Development Group and could be taken online or by physically attending a module. In parallel, project leaders could identify an expertise deficiency in a particular area and could request an upgrade of the team's expertise base to correspond with the level needed by the industry. Consequently, a tailored module would be offered to the team, which ensured the joint development of expertise in that particular area.

To summarize, expertise development at TCS mainly took place within offshore outsourcing projects during which the onsite and the offshore teams jointly developed expertise that was required for future maintenance and development of client systems. Additional activities ensured that expertise was developed also in a distributed manner through training schemes.

Expertise coordination processes at TCS

The coordination of expertise is required to find solutions and answers to either technological or business challenges that are not in the possession of the team. In such situations, team members will start looking for the required expertise within their local or global project team or in the other projects. A successful expertise coordination activity often results in locating an expert who can share his or her know-how with the information seeker(s). Finding the most appropriate expert in a timely manner has always been a key challenge for dispersed teams. To achieve this, the coordination of expertise at TCS mainly relied on two memory systems. One was a transactive memory system (TMS) that was created within a particular offshore outsourcing project (between onsite, offshore, and nearshore teams) in which most individuals developed an awareness of "who knows what" and "who does what". The second memory system was a much broader memory system consisting of a corporate-wide Expertise Management System that was put in place and that was updated regularly by TCS to ensure that expertise could be brought to bear in a timely manner beyond the boundaries of an outsourcing project.

The organization of the outsourcing project team, in onsite and offshore locations, as a mirror image, i.e. using almost identical roles and titles for the offshore and onsite teams, created an expertise directory with regard to the information about "who knows what" and "who does what". These pointers to expertise holders were created and constantly updated during the transition and steady state phases, as remote counterparts continuously interacted with each other to ensure the joint development of expertise. For example, during a specific learning activity, an onsite expert would create a document that captured the know-how involved in maintaining a specific system, and would make this know-how available to his or her remote counterparts based offshore. In doing so, the onsite expert first created a pointer in the expertise directory to a particular area of expertise of which he or she possesses the required know-how to maintain this system. Following the sharing of know-how with counterparts from the offshore team, an update of the expertise directory with regard to where such expertise lies would take place within the entire global team. In other words, through intensive knowledge exchanges between onsite and offshore teams, the types of expertise and their location within the teams were made transparent to the entire global team. The directory of expertise emerged as a set of documentations and entries in databases (i.e. a codified directory) as well as information stored in people's memory about "who knows what" (i.e. a personalized directory). The codified part of this directory was implemented through a project portal accessible through the TCS intranet for members of the project team only. In collaboration with ABM AMRO, a dedicated TCS team created Project Portal (internally called Knowledge Base), which contains links to all project and system documents created during the knowledge transfer phase. Furthermore, this Knowledge Base contains information about the experts involved in the project, their contact details and other relevant information. At the time of data collection in Mumbai (June 2006), two TCS associates worked full-time on the development and maintenance of this system.

In addition, other processes were put in place at TCS to ensure that expertise could be brought to bear in a timely manner from outside the boundaries of an outsourcing project. TCS introduced a system that coordinated expertise across the entire firm, called Integrated Competency and Learning Management (ICLM). TCS designed and implemented this system to manage employees' competencies, monitor skills adjustments, and offer learning modules and individual development programs according to future needs. The Head of Human Resources of TCS Europe explained:

> This system is actually a differentiator from the employee and the organization point of view... The ICLM provides an overall end-to-end view of the learning and competence... Every employee in the world would have access to this system. So if you have any requirement, say that you need a person with a background in banking, experience in acquisitions, and also one who accomplished a project involving international customers, then you put the data in the system, and you will exactly see who is the right person for the job at TCS.

In addition to staffing individuals according to their skills, the ICLM system offered search capabilities for expertise available globally that could not be located through the project-based TMS. In this regard, at the organizational level, the coordination of expertise, in the sense of bringing specific expertise to a particular location in a timely manner, was carried out through the ICLM system. To ensure that the directories of the system were up-to-date, a dedicated team was put in place in India that monitored data entry, handled requests from TCS employees, and issued information to them about learning modules.

Another vehicle through which expertise was coordinated at TCS was a technical database of reusable components (code) from various projects, stripped of confidential client data. A dedicated team checked entries of individual team members submitted to this database, filtered these entries and made sure that the most appropriate keywords were assigned to each entry. Individual team members, regardless of their geographical location and project association, who sought solutions to a particular technological problem, could access this database through the TCS intranet and search for reusable components. While a reusable solution was the main outcome of this activity, information about who would be the expert of that particular technology was also provided. Through this tool, remote counterparts could contact the expert for consultation prior to employing the reusable component. Similarly, TCS developed a database that contained business history, i.e. a brief overview, and lessons learned from past projects, accessible through the TCS intranet. Through this system team members could find information about projects and contact individuals involved in these projects for advice.

In conclusion, at TCS the coordination of expertise within a specific outsourcing project relied heavily on the TMS developed during knowledge exchanges between onsite and offshore teams. The joint approach to expertise development in an outsourcing project supported the build-up of an expertise directory through which remote counterparts could locate experts regardless of their geographical location. When it came to expertise coordination between and across outsourcing projects, TCS introduced organizational mechanisms in the form of the ICLM system, a technical and business database, to offer information seekers search mechanisms and insure that expertise would be made available in a timely manner.

Expertise integration processes at TCS

The joint development of expertise within the ABN AMRO – TCS outsourcing project helped TCS to deal with typical expertise integration challenges such as different mindsets and lack of understanding between experts. Interviewees claimed that TCS employees involved in a distributed outsourcing project developed common understanding of specific systems, concepts, and terminology because of the structures, work practices, and learning processes described above.

However, the sharing of learning beyond the boundaries of an outsourcing project and the integration of expertise across projects and domains still posed a challenge to TCS. Indeed, leveraging knowledge and expertise to develop new products and services required the facilitation of learning across functional areas, market knowledge, and various technologies that were globally distributed and sometimes remotely related. To tackle this challenge, TCS introduced various mechanisms to ensure that know-how and learning generated in one project would be shared in other projects. One vehicle through which expertise was integrated at TCS was the Centres of Excellence (CoEs), described above. One manager from Mumbai described the role of one technological CoE in bringing together expertise:

> These are the people who can solve the problems in certain areas so we have a team of certain virtual members, anywhere between 30 and 50... These are the people who try to address [the problem] if the technical support team cannot address those things.

A key role for the CoE was to ensure that expertise and knowledge developed in one place would be reapplied in other projects. In this regard, the CoE facilitated the reapplication and integration of expertise from almost the beginning of the project, by offering expertise and solutions developed in other projects and by connecting experts in a particular field with the project team, to advise them on best practices and approaches to carry out their outsourcing project. One member of CoE explained:

> That is [the start of the project] where the CoE helps the project, mainly in whatever can be leveraged from CoE in the benefit of the project. And then we get in all the various stages of the project till it gets wound up, and once it gets wound up we again get involved and analyze what are the things which we can take back to the CoE so that it can be (re)utilized somewhere else.

Indeed, when projects do not apply best practices, members of CoEs make sure that the know-how required for the proper execution of an outsourcing project, according to TCS best practices, will be shared with the project team. In this regard, CoEs were responsible for acquiring know-how from internal or external sources and sharing it with project teams. The member of the Oracle CoE added:

> All those aspects which might lead to a risk from a technical perspective ... [we are] also looking at the skill sets which are required for the project and the right set of skills and if there are any gaps there, how we can bridge those gaps, either through training or maybe through consultation or maybe inviting over an alliance partner.

Another mechanism for expertise integration across technological and market knowledge domains that TCS employed was knowledge-exchange events and seminars that were organized on a regular basis in different geographical locations. For example, technological fairs were organized a few times a year at major TCS development sites (e.g. May 2006 in Mumbai). In this case, experts from different technological domains offered information about different aspects relating to the use and implementation of their technologies. This knowledge exchange event was organized in the form of a traditional trade fair in which TCS employees walked from stand to stand to learn about and assess the applicability of existing solutions to their project.

To summarize, the integration of expertise at TCS took place at two levels, namely project and organizational. The integration of expertise at the project level relied on TMS that had been developed and updated through intense interactions between remote counterparts. Indeed, the approach taken by TCS, to jointly develop expertise as described above, supported the development of a TMS and offered more opportunities for members of the global outsourcing project to integrate their expertise. At the same time, new ideas and innovations were sought outside the boundaries of an outsourcing project through other vehicles such as CoEs, trade fairs, and training. While the use of external sources of knowledge in the form of CoEs is a distributed approach to expertise management, the TMS-based approach can be seen as a joint approach to expertise integration.

Summary of findings and discussion

The objective of this chapter was to explore expertise management processes in distributed contexts. The case of the ABN AMRO – TCS outsourcing project illustrates the complexity involved in managing distributed expertise. For one, the management of expertise in such projects involves the coordination and integration of expertise that is both locally and globally developed. In addition, the case illustrates aspects relating to project and organization expertise that need to be coordinated and integrated. Similarly, expertise development at TCS involved knowledge codification processes as well as processes that encourage the sharing of tacit knowledge. The following sections address these aspects, starting with the summary of the findings presented above.

The evidence presented above suggests that TCS followed an approach in which expertise was developed both within and across projects. The company pursued a joint approach to expertise development, in particular between onsite and offshore teams, but also a distributed approach across the organization through training activities that upgraded the skills base of TCS employees regardless of their geographical location. Both joint and distributed approaches to expertise development and division of work will be discussed in Chapter 7.

In terms of expertise coordination, TCS invested in activities that created a TMS between onsite and offshore teams through which dispersed team members developed awareness about "who knows what" and "who does what". To support the coordination of expertise beyond the boundaries of an outsourcing project, TCS implemented an ICLM system and various mechanisms that offered search mechanisms for knowledge seekers and provided them with access to existing expertise and in-house solutions.

The integration of expertise was mainly evident at the organization level. One key vehicle through which lessons learnt and insights gained were shared was through the CoEs. These networks of experts ensured that members of project teams were aware of the latest know-how and best practices possessed by TCS. They also made certain that the project's skill-level was adequate to meet the outsourcing challenge. Expertise integration also took place within an outsourcing project; however, intraproject expertise integration was perceived by interviewees as limited in its scope. In this regard, CoEs were the forces behind incorporating cutting-edge innovative ideas from the industry into project teams. Table 5.3 summarizes the findings of this study.

Evidence from this case also suggests that expertise development, coordination, and integration are interconnected. In particular, we propose that the joint approach to developing expertise between onsite and the offshore teams resulted in the development and the updating of a TMS (Yoo and Kanawattanachai, 2001) that stretched beyond the boundaries of a single team. Indeed, recent studies have suggested that a TMS can be expanded within an organization through the application of information

Table 5.3 Expertise management at project and organization levels

	Expertise development	Expertise coordination	Expertise integration
Project	Joint developed expertise through tightly managed knowledge transfer processes between onsite and offshore teams and development of knowledge base	A TMS that supports the development of a collective awareness of "who knows what"	Expertise integration within an outsourcing project mainly meant reusing existing ideas. Limited in exposure to external innovations
Organization	Distributed mode of expertise development through on-line training and courses	Information technologies in the form of technological and past projects databases and ICLM system that offered search mechanisms of existing expertise and experts	Knowledge-exchange events and CoEs that brought in new ideas and innovations from other projects and the industry

systems (Nevo and Wand, 2005). This study suggests that a joint development of expertise could, as well, result in expanding the boundaries of a TMS, as members of a global team encode, store, and retrieve information regarding their expertise through the use of databases, documents, and person-to-person interactions. Similarly, we have observed that while the boundaries of such a TMS may have expanded beyond the onsite and the offshore team, the ability to coordinate expertise beyond the boundaries of a single outsourcing project were rather limited, unless team members had used information systems in the form of the ICLM system (Majchrzak *et al.*, 2005) or other search mechanisms to locate needed expertise. In this respect, the joint development of expertise is limited in its impact on the development of an organization-wide TMS, and therefore may not provide the support needed to coordinate expertise across the organization. Lastly, evidence suggests that the integration of expertise is strongly connected with the development of expertise. Indeed, past studies have expressed concerns that the development of local expertise might, in fact, limit possibilities for expertise integration, as project teams would rather prefer to implement practices developed locally (DeSouza and Evaristo, 2004) than adopt new practices and innovations proposed by experts who were not part of the local team. Our analysis suggests that because CoEs at TCS were involved in both expertise development and expertise integration, these experts were able to negotiate the nature of the local practices implemented by the team, assess these practices in relation to the global practices, and offer avenues to local teams so that global practices could be followed while local needs were considered. Indeed, we have learned that while TCS has built a repository of templates for software development processes, these templates, in some cases, have been adjusted to accommodate local needs. Such changes in the global practices were reported to the appropriate CoE, which evaluated the reusability of these changes and, following this assessment process, the revised template was made available to the entire organization.

Implications for researchers

To summarize, the evidence suggests that TCS pursued a hybrid approach to expertise development, in which both joint and distributed approaches to expertise development were carried out, and through which the coordination and integration of expertise were supported through intra- and interproject knowledge integration mechanisms. Our findings confirm observations made by past studies that both joint and distributed approaches to expertise development have been applied by distributed teams. Yet this study contributes to the relevant literature by considering the project and organizational level as two planes within which expertise development can be carried out in a different manner. Indeed, as the evidence suggests, TCS pursued a joint approach to expertise development at the project level while developing expertise in a distributed manner at the organizational level.

There are other aspects related to the management of expertise arising from the TCS outsourcing case. For example, the joint development of expertise appears to rely on the codification of know-how captured by the onsite team. Indeed, the evidence suggests that the codification and documentation of knowledge acquired during these exchanges between onsite and offshore teams were imperative for creating a knowledge-base of expertise needed to maintain clients' systems. Furthermore, the process of codifying knowledge created a terminology accepted by both onsite and offshore teams concerning the processes and the technologies involved in maintaining clients' systems (Argyres, 1999). Lave and Wenger (1991) described at length the practice-based approach to developing expertise. In particular, they emphasized in their study how expertise is transferred from an expert to a novice, for example in the case of midwives. Such practice-based processes required the participation of a newcomer in activities, and in problem-solving and organizational activities, through which a newcomer gains the know-how required to perform his or her duties, assumes more responsibilities, and gradually shifts from the periphery to the centre of activity within a team or an organization.

However, our case illustrates a rather different approach to developing expertise, in which project members codified the know-how required for carrying out their duties, minimized face-to-face interactions and relied on standardized procedures when learning about clients' processes and technologies. This observation raises the following question: Why does expertise development at TCS present a rather different approach from that observed in the relevant literature (i.e. Lave and Wenger, 1991)?

We suggest that distributed teams such as the TCS outsourcing project team, as opposed to co-located teams, invest in creating pointers to the know-how necessary to carry out specific activities rather than in learning and absorbing the know-how necessary for successfully executing these activities. While past studies mainly focused on the process through which knowledge is created during expertise development processes (Sole and Edmondson, 2002), we offer an explanation in which the expertise development process, such as that described above, can also be seen as a process through which individuals create information about the location of the know-how and expertise necessary to execute a particular activity. Indeed, interpersonal exchanges as a source of expertise development in dispersed teams has been consistently proven to be difficult; therefore such teams build an information repository that ensures that expertise can be coordinated when needed and that the pointers to the knowledge are known and can easily be accessed and updated by the entire team. Through the use of standardized templates, documents, and a tight learning process, this TCS outsourcing team built a cataloguing system in which pointers to where knowledge and expertise reside was made available to the entire team. In this regard, our findings contribute to the literature on expertise development by considering information processes as part of the process of developing expertise.

Implications for practitioners

For practitioners, the evidence presented above raises a question about the preferred approach to managing expertise in the sense of a distributed versus a joint approach to its development. We propose that, on the one hand, a distributed approach to expertise development may encourage the exploration of new ideas and the acquisition of cutting-edge knowledge within a globally distributed project; however, such an explorative approach could produce a distributed expertise base that is troublesome to map out and manage, resulting in inabilities to coordinate expertise in a timely manner. On the other hand, pursuing an approach that relies on a joint approach to expertise development may result in the development of an expertise system that is exploitative in nature. As observed in the above case, members of an outsourcing project could easily access each other's expertise and bring it to bear in a timely manner. However, such an approach can be overly exploitative, lacking innovative ideas to transform the client's and the vendor's business. We propose a hybrid approach, in which the management of expertise encourages the exploitation of expertise within globally distributed outsourcing projects and yet explores the development and integration of expertise from external sources of knowledge which could overcome the dilemma presented above. Depending on project characteristics, a shift in emphasis from a joint to a distributed expertise development approach might be appropriate. Such project characteristics may include (i) similarity of clients' businesses, thus justifying investments in cross-project mechanisms, and also (ii) the level of turnover in the vendor teams.

Note

1. In reviewing the knowledge management literature we focused on the literature that addresses embodied specialized knowledge and skills embedded in practice (that fits our definition of expertise).

References

Alavi, M. (1994) "Computer-Mediated Collaborative Learning: An Empirical Investigation," *MIS Quarterly*, 18(2), 159–74.

Argyres, N. S. (1999) "The Impact of Information Technology on Coordination: Evidence from the B-2 'Stealth' Bomber," *Organization Science*, 10(2), 162–80.

Carmel, E. and Tjia, P. (2005) *Offshoring Information Technology: Sourcing and Outsourcing to a Global Workforce*, Cambridge University Press, Cambridge.

Cramton, C. D. (2001) "The Mutual Knowledge Problem and Its Consequences for Dispersed Collaboration," *Organization Science*, 12(3), 346–71.

DeSouza, K. C. and Evaristo, J. R. (2004) "Managing Knowledge in Distributed Projects," *Communications of the ACM*, 47(4), 87–91.

Eisenhardt, K. M. (1989) "Building Theories from Case Study Research," *Academy of Management Review*, 14(4), 532–50.

Faraj, S. and Sproull, L. (2000) "Coordinating Expertise in Software Development Teams," *Management Science*, 46(12), 1554–68.

Fitzpatrick, G. (2003) "Emergent Expertise Sharing in a New Community," in *Sharing Expertise: Beyond Knowledge Management* (Eds, Ackerman, M. S., Pipek, V., and Wulf, V.) The MIT Press, Cambridge, MA, pp. 81–110.

Gasson, S. (2005) "The Dynamics of Sensemaking, Knowledge, and Expertise in Collaborative, Boundary-Spanning Design," *Journal of Computer-Mediated Communication*, 10(4), http://jcmc.indiana.edu/

Goodhue, D. L. and Thompson, R. L. (1995) "Task-Technology Fit and Individual Performance," *MIS Quarterly*, 19(4), 213–35.

Grant, R. M. (1996) "Prospering in Dynamically-Competitive Environments: Organizational Capability as Knowledge Integration," *Organization Science*, 7(4), 375–87.

Hinds, P. J. and Bailey, D. E. (2000) *Virtual Teams: Anticipating the Impact of Virtuality on Team Process and Performance*, Annual Meeting of the Academy of Management, Best Papers Proceedings, Toronto.

Huang, J. C., Newell, S., Galliers, R. D., and Pan, S.-L. (2003) "Dangerous Liaisons? Component-Based Development and Organizational Subcultures," *IEEE Transactions on Engineering Management*, 50(1), 89–99.

Lave, J. and Wenger, E. (1991) *Situated Learning Legitimate Peripheral Participation*, Cambridge University Press, Cambridge.

Majchrzak, A., Malhotra, A., and Richard, J. (2005) "Perceived Individual Collaboration Know-How development through Information Technology-Enabled Contextualization: Evidence from Distributed Teams," *Information Systems Research*, 16(1), 9–27.

Malhotra, A. and Majchrzak, A. (2004) "Enabling Knowledge Creation in Far-Flung Teams: Best Practices for IT Support and Knowledge Sharing," *Journal of Knowledge Management*, 8(4), 75–88.

Malhotra, A., Majchrzak, A., Carman, R., and Lott, V. (2001) "Radical Innovation Without Collocation: A Case Study at Boeing-Rocketdyne," *MIS Quarterly*, 25(2), 229–49.

McEvily, S. K., Eisenhardt, K. M., and Prescott, J. E. (2004) "The Global Acquisition, Leverage, and Protection on Technological Competencies," *Strategic Management Journal*, 25(8–9), 713–22.

Miles, M. B. and Huberman, A. M. (1994) *Qualitative Data Analysis: An Expanded Sourcebook*, Sage Publications, Thousand Oaks, CA.

Nevo, D. and Wand, Y. (2005) "Organizational Memory Information Systems: A Transactive Memory Approach," *Decision Support Systems*, 39(4), 549–62.

Orlikowski, W. J. (2002) "Knowing in Practice: Enacting a Collective Capability in Distributed Organizing," *Organization Science*, 13(3), 249–73.

Oshri, I., Pan, S. L., and Newell, S. (2006) "Managing Trade-offs and Tensions between Knowledge Management Initiatives and Expertise Development Practices," *Management Learning*, 37(1), 63–82.

Petsch, W., Becker, S., and Glynn, S. (1997) *Managing Teamwork in a Highly Distributed Project*, Americas Conference on Information Systems, Association for Information Systems, Indianapolis.

Quinn, J. B. (2000) "Outsourcing Innovation: The New Engine of Growth," *Sloan Management Review*, 41(4), 13–28.

Sole, D. and Edmondson, A. (2002) "Situated Knowledge and Learning in Dispersed Teams," *British Journal of Management*, 13: S17–S34.

Strauss, A. L. and Corbin, J. M. (1998) *Basics of Qualitative Research*, Sage, Thousand Oaks, CA.

Szulanski, G. (1996) "Exploring Internal Stickiness: Impediments to the Transfer of Best Practice within the Firm," *Strategic Management Journal*, 17 (Winter), 77–91.

Tsoukas, H. (1996) "The Firm as a Distributed Knowledge System: A Constructionist Approach," *Strategic Management Journal*, 17(Winter), 77–91.

Tyre, M. J. and von Hippel, E. (1997) "The Situated Nature of Adaptive Learning in Organizations," *Organization Science*, 8(1), 71–83.

van de Ven, A. H., Delbecq, A. L., and Koenig, R. Jr (1976) "Determinants of Coordination Modes Within Organizations," *American Sociological Review*, 41 (April), 322–38.

von Hippel, E. (1994) "'Sticky Information' and the Locus of Problem Solving: Implications for Innovation," *Management Science*, 40(4), 429–39.

von Hippel, E. (1998) "Economics of Product Development by Users: The impact of 'Sticky' Local Information," *Management Science*, 44(5), 629–44.

Weitzman, E. A. (2000) "Software and Qualitative Research," in *Handbook of Qualitative Research* (Eds, Denzin, N. K. and Lincoln, Y. S.) Sage, Thousand Oaks, CA, pp. 803–20.

Willcocks, L. P. and Lacity, M. (2006) *Global Sourcing of Business and IT Services*, Palgrave, Basingstoke.

Willem, A. and Scarbrough, H. (2002) *Structural Effects on Inter-Unit Knowledge Sharing: The Role of Coordination Under Different Knowledge Sharing Needs*, Third European Conference on Organizational Knowledge, Learning and Capabilities, Athens.

Yin, R. K. (1994) *Case Study Research: Design and Methods*, Sage, Newbury Park, CA.

Yoo, Y. and Kanawattanachai, P. (2001) "Developments of Transactive Memory Systems and Collective Mind in Virtual Teams," *The International Journal of Organizational Analysis*, 9, 187–208.

CHAPTER 6

Offshore outsourcing: Operating in emerging market economies

Katy Mason and Ilan Oshri

Introduction

Given a progressively more competitive global environment, it is increasingly being contended that the central factor in the success and survival of organizations is the effective management of buyer–supplier networks (Gummesson, 2002; Thorelli, 1986). We define a "buyer–supplier network" as a web of interdependent firms working together to supply services and products to one focal buyer (Möller *et al.*, 2005; Möller and Törrönen, 2003). One example of a buyer – supplier network is an outsourcing relationship in which the buyer is based in a developed market and the supplier is located in an emerging market. In this regard, such firms are increasingly less likely to behave in isolation when developing customer and competitor oriented strategies. In doing so, these firms are required to develop unique learning capabilities in order to improve their responsiveness to customers (Day, 2002; Schultze and Boland, 1997; Slater and Narver, 1995). Such issues have been explored within the marketing literature (Baker and Sinkula, 2002; Schultze and Boland, 1997; Slater and Narver, 1995), management learning literature (Loasby, 1999; Senge, 1990) and international business literature (Zander, 2003; Minbaeva *et al.*, 2003). For example, Nobeoka *et al.* (2002) found that suppliers were able to lever their organizational learning through the development of strong interfirm relationships with multiple customers. Such learning resulted in both new product development and process innovation. Similarly, Zahay and Handfield (2004) suggest that the organizations most likely to innovate are those which posses the ability to learn and share information within interfirm relationships. In this regard, the literature suggests that clear benefits emerge from an organization's ability to learn from its supply network (van den Bosch *et al.*, 1999).

Indeed, past research has illustrated the point that firms develop abilities to learn by acquiring and utilizing external and internal knowledge (Minbaeva *et al.*, 2003). For example, the study of learning capacity provides substantial evidence that absorptive capacity significantly affects a firm's ability to learn (Lane *et al.*, 2001). The generic processes through which learning processes can be established in distributed contexts have been discussed in Chapter 5. In this chapter we seek to explore the specific areas of learning imperative for setting up distributed development, in the context of offshoring. In this regard, while the vast majority of these studies focus on understanding the key determinants affecting the firm's ability to learn, this study seeks to explore the specific challenges faced, and capabilities learnt and developed, when a firm forms a buyer–supplier network.

Following a brief review of the learning literature, four propositions are offered. These propositions examine the links between network success and (i) relationships within the network; (ii) changes in value perceived by the customer; (iii) firm (company) boundaries; and (iv) network structure and type. Network success is defined as the member's motivation to engage in future transactions between members of the network (Gallivan, 2001). Evidence from a leading supplier of aerospace systems that engaged in developing an international buyer–supplier network illustrates our assumptions about the impact of these factors on network success and the need to develop learning capabilities in these areas. The chapter concludes by offering practical and theoretical implications.

Learning in a network context

The ability of a firm to learn has been widely studied in the literature. In developing learning capabilities, it has been argued, firms should consider the level of prior knowledge, the organizational form, and the motivational, coordination, and socialization capabilities that affect a firm's ability to learn, absorb, and reapply knowledge (Jansen *et al.*, forthcoming).

Nonetheless, an organization's capacity to learn is not absolute but rather varies with the learning context (Lane *et al.*, 2001). In this regard, international buyer–supplier networks present a challenging case for both suppliers and buyers for the following reasons. First, the learning generated within a network is highly contextual, thus posing challenges to the parties involved to reapply learnt lessons in other contexts without engaging in significant knowledge reconfiguration activities (Verona and

Ravasi, 2003). Second, the quality of the learning generated within a network depends on the value perceived by its members. In this regard, a buyer could benefit more from a larger network; however, a larger network may reduce control over the quality of learning, as the value perceived and investment in learning by members of the network will be reduced. Lastly, a buyer–supplier network that involves geographically dispersed suppliers offers fewer if any opportunities to create socialization capabilities that are imperative for generating learning between members of the network.

Recent years have witnessed unparalleled growth in firms seeking to develop and manage interfirm relationships, and specifically buyer–supplier networks, through the exploration and expansion of different forms of collaborative and partnering agreements (Murray et al., 2005; Webster, 1992). Two distinct streams of literature concerning the development of the supply network concepts have emerged (Lamming, 2000). The first stream is the largely descriptive research on industrial networks and their conduct emerging from industrial marketing and purchasing (see, for example, Möller et al., 2005; Möller and Törrönen, 2003). The second stream of literature on supply chain management is more prescriptive in nature and is grounded in the fields of strategic management, operations management, and logistics (see, for example, Nishiguchi, 1994; Womack and Jones, 1994). More recently, researchers have attempted to foster a more holistic approach. For example, the integration of the concepts of relationship management and value, traditionally associated with the industrial marketing and purchasing perspective, have increasingly been integrated with concepts of firm boundaries and network typologies and structures, more typically allied with the logistics and strategic management fields (Jüttner et al., 2006; Langabeer and Rose, 2001).

In this way, the quality of relationships is thought to differentiate "network organisations" from "networks of organisations" (Möller et al., 2005; Alexsson and Easton, 1992). Research in this field has increasingly emphasized the importance of both effectiveness (emerging from the industrial marketing and purchasing tradition) and efficiency (more typically associated with the operations and logistics tradition) to networks of organizations. As Achrol (1997: 59) explains, "a network organisation is distinguished from a simple network . . . by the density, multiplicity and reciprocity of ties and a shared value-system defining membership roles and responsibilities". While it is recognized that these networks come in many forms, such as supply, distribution, or R&D, this chapter focuses on buyer–supplier networks. That is, the network organization formed by a buyer and its stable interorganizational ties with strategically important suppliers. The following section explores four emergent themes associated with buyer–supplier network success.

Learning in supply networks: Propositions

The literature highlights four areas that may affect the network success: (i) relationship, (ii) value, (iii) firm boundaries, and (iv) network structure and type. We examine these themes in the context of a buyer–supplier network and offer a set of propositions that explores the relationships between these four areas and learning.

Relationships and supply networks

The industrial and purchasing literature has focused considerable attention on the importance of relationships between individuals and firms both on a local (Paniccia, 1998) and a corporate level (Welsh and Wilkinson, 2005). Indeed, much of this literature acknowledges and examines issues relating to relationship-building, such as trust, commitment, and cooperation, which arise within interfirm and network relationship development (Kwon and Suh, 2004; Farrelly and Quester, 2003; Lanfield-Smith and Smith, 2003; Sánchez and Pérez, 2003). In this way, the development of supply networks requires managers to select appropriately and invest valuable resources in supply network members. Gadde and Snehota (2000) recognize the substantial participation and cost involved in building relationships within networks, but they argue that such costs must be more than offset by relationship benefits. However, developing and maintaining good relationships can be challenging. Vaaland and Håkansson (2003), for example, recognize the potential for conflict but suggest the use of governance mechanisms as a method of using conflict to strengthen business relationships. Similarly, Håkansson and Ford (2002) explore three paradoxes associated with networks: opportunities and restrictions of networks; influencing and being influenced within networks; and controlling (and being controlled) within networks. In their view, networks should interact by using tools to help decision-makers understand their context. Specifically, they argue that no one relationship can be understood without reference to the wider network. Håkansson and Ford (2002) explain:

> The development of any one relationship between two companies will depend on a number of factors: on what has happened in the past in the relationship; on what each of the two parties has previously learned in its other relationships; on what currently happens between the companies in the relationship and in others in which they are involved; on the expectations of both companies of their future interactions; on what happens in the wider network of relationships in which they are not directly involved.

In this regard, the recognition that firms and networks learn from their own and others' experiences, related to the specific context within which they operate, suggests that the assimilation and reapplication of this knowledge is likely to be of importance to the continuation of the network (Gallivan, 2001). Therefore, learning from the specific context within which the network relationships reside may result in a higher perceived success of the network by its members. We propose that:

P_1: Perceived network success is increased when firms have high learning capabilities for developing context-specific relationships knowledge.

Value and supply networks

Maintaining strategic importance through a value proposition which is attractive to the network is a key issue for suppliers. As customers seek to make key decisions on whether to invest in new supplier relationships, to maintain and develop important relationships or to divest from low-value relationships, suppliers may seek to focus on strengthening their customer value strategies. These involve anticipating and responding to changes in customers' desired values. That is, suppliers continuously seek to identify and understand the changes in value that customers wish to see being offered (Flint and Mentzer, 2000).

While some progress has been made in understanding how value is perceived by customers, much of this work has been carried out in a consumer context (for example, Lai, 1995; Holbrook, 1994) rather than in a business-to-business environment (notable exceptions being Fredriksson and Araujo, 2003; Ulaga, 2003; Gassenheimer *et al.*, 1998). Further, such research has largely focused on current perceived value by customers rather than customers' desired value change. However, as

Flint *et al.* (2002) observe, although the literature makes little direct reference to customers' desired value changes, several papers comment on the dynamic nature of value (for example, Richins, 1994).

According to Flint and Mentzer (2000) there are five aspects that represent the dynamic nature of value. These aspects concern the customer-desired value changes. They can be labelled as (i) the value hierarchy levels (where customers may change the attributes they desire from suppliers), (ii) the form the desired value change takes, (iii) the rate of the desired value change, (iv) the magnitude of the change, and (v) the volatility of customer value change. While these observations are key to understanding the dynamic nature of value, they are limited to dyadic relationships and do not explore the supply network perspective (also see Ulaga, 2003; Flint *et al.*, 2002). Although Fredriksson and Araujo (2003) explore value through a different lens, namely the performance measurement of suppliers, their findings provide additional support to the above observation that value can be seen as dynamic, complex, multidimensional, and cross-functional.

The network perspective on value also considers the notion of value as a dynamic concept; however, the network literature differs in its interpretation of value in that it conceives value in terms of systems (Parolini, 1999) rather than purely from the customer perspective. For example, Möller *et al.* (2005) argue that the different value platforms that firms perceive and share within a network affect the type of network that develops. They suggest that core value production drives an efficient production and delivery system, that relational value production drives a product innovation supply network focused on creating new solutions supporting the customers' businesses, and that future-oriented value production drives a radical innovation for new business opportunities. Furthermore, Möller *et al.* (2005) hold that these value platforms are, broadly speaking, hierarchical, and that firms must achieve one as a foundation for the next. This progression requires firms to build capabilities to enable them to achieve the goals set for each value platform. In this way, the dynamic nature of desired customer value is likely to be affected by the way in which the buyer–supplier network evolves, and vice versa. In this regard, the development of a sensing mechanism for changes in value perception is more likely to lead to continued success of the network. Thus developing learning capabilities with regard to the changes in value perceptions of network members is likely to leverage perceived network success. We propose that:

P_2: Perceived network success is increased when firms have a developed learning capability for sensing changes in value perception.

Firm boundaries and capabilities

Traditionally, the marketing and strategy literatures have sought to identify firm boundaries from an ownership perspective (Holmstrom and Roberts, 1998; Williamson, 1975; Coase, 1937). However, recent research has argued that the boundaries of the firm are determined by the capabilities necessary to undertake productive activities. The capabilities approach to the firm sets out to find integration mechanisms that sustain the division of labour among agents with incomplete, dispersed, and disparate knowledge, as well as to help the process of creating and testing knowledge (Kogut and Meitu, 2000; Loasby, 1998; Piore, 1992). Furthermore, a second category of activities is increasingly becoming accepted as central to the identi-fication and management of firm boundaries (Araujo et al., 2003). This second group of activities, often referred to as indirect or ancillary capabilities (Loasby, 1998; Langlois and Robertson, 1995) is concerned with the capabilities of firms to interact with customers, suppliers, and other external agents. The ancillary capabilities perspective marks an important shift in the way firms define their operations and presents them with a greater degree of fluidity and flexibility. Mahoney (1992) examined the isomorphic nature of ownership and long-term relationships within supply chains. In this sense, it is not the ownership of physical assets that deter-mines the way firms create and offer added value for customers, but, rather, it is what capabilities reside within the network and how they are utilized.

Thus, value creation capabilities cross firm boundaries and create bridges for the development of supply networks (Araujo et al., 2003; Möller and Törrönen, 2003). This observation calls for further under-standing of firm boundaries in the context of networks. Dyer and Singh (1998), for example, discuss the phenomenon of critical resources span-ning firm boundaries. Pettigrew et al. (2002) identify the rising interest of strategy scholars in networks as repositories of resources. In line with these studies, the resource pool is seen as the network and is not restricted to the traditional ownership boundaries associated with a single firm. We argue that the most effective and efficient utilization of network resources can be achieved only if firms learn how to capture resource and capability information and utilize it to their best advantage. Further, when firms are able to do this, their perception of the network's success is positively affected. Therefore, we propose that:

P3: Perceived network success is increased when firms have developed learning capabilities for acquiring knowledge regarding network resources and capabilities.

Network structure and type

Many researchers in the field of supply networks have commented on the need for them to develop and operate in accordance with their specific context (Holmen *et al.*, 2003; Gadde and Håkansson, 2001; Harland *et al.*, 2001). As Holmen *et al.* (2003) observe, both macro and micro contexts are likely to impact on the type of network structure adopted. Holmen *et al.*'s (2003) network structure taxonomy suggests how managers might benefit from adopting a mix of different supply structures dependent on context and need. In this regard, it is suggested that executives need to manage and develop relationships with suppliers, as well as conceptualize and foster appropriate relationships between groups of suppliers. This has implications for the way firms select their partners (Gadde and Håkansson, 2001) and for the level of involvement network members have in shaping and managing micronets within the greater network structure. As Dubois and Gadde (2000) explain, the experience (and learning) that network members develop from prior network involvement is likely to influence the way they behave and contribute to the development of new supply networks. In line with this argument, we claim that if firms are able to develop mechanisms and procedures to capture learning about network types and contexts, they may be in a stronger position to apply this knowledge correctly in future network development. Therefore, we propose that:

P_4: Perceived network success is increased when firms have a developed learning capability for acquiring knowledge about network structure and type.

The communications and coordination technologies available today have changed the way firms organize, structure, and manage their business networks. As Mills *et al.* (2004) observe, while existing firms develop supply networks slowly or rapidly, dependent on the competitive and environmental conditions in their markets, contemporary entrepreneurs starting businesses today can rapidly create a supply network that less than ten years ago could not have been attempted. If firms develop their learning capabilities to apply the lessons learned through relationship management within networks, and identify, communicate, and develop solutions for changing perceived customer value, resources, and network structures, then we argue that it is likely that such networks will have an increased probability of success. We explore these propositions in the following sections, in which the research design, empirical data, and analysis are presented and discussed.

About this research

The research is based on a single case study, semi-structured inter-views and on-site observations. Data collection methods included 37 in-depth interviews with eight senior executives and front-line managers. All interviews were recorded and transcribed. Data were coded and analyzed to examine the relationships between perceived network success and (i) context-specific relationship knowledge, (ii) changes in the value perceptions of network members, (iii) network resources and capabilities, and (iv) network structure and type (Figure 6.1). Other data sources used in the study included minutes of meetings, tender documents, quarterly reviews, and diaries kept by participants.

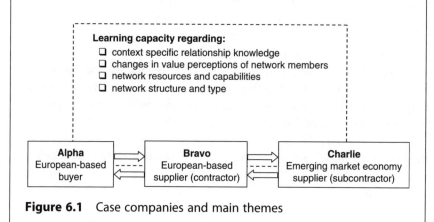

Figure 6.1   Case companies and main themes

Case analysis and findings

We now describe the areas of learning developed by the network. Some background information about Alpha can be found in the Appendix.

Learning for relationship context

While we subscribe to the suggestion that the success of a particular network is, in some way, determined by the degree of learning developed by members of this network, we seek to explore further this proposition from a relationship management perspective, attempting to identify the relationship factors that are likely to influence perceived network success. The mechanisms and processes through which the assimilation of context-specific relationship knowledge is captured are also examined. Our findings identify three factors that appear to frame the context of a relationship: (i) the perceived corporate identity each firm held of the other, (ii) the experience they had of trading with each other (including the tendering and supplier selection process), and (iii) the basis of the supply agreement that had been reached. This context appeared to provide the platform from which levels of trust, openness, commitment, and cooperation evolved. The case analysis also suggests that context-specific relationship knowledge evolved as a direct result of network interactions between the network members. These interactions appeared to have affected changes in the relationship context over the 18-month period of the case study. The dynamic nature of the relationship context was illustrated by our case.

Pre-contract, none of the studied teams had worked together. Nonetheless, other teams from Alpha, Bravo, and Charlie had previously worked together. A separate division of Alpha works directly with Charlie; however, the division of Alpha involved in this study had no direct experience of working with Charlie. Similarly, on an individual level, none of the individuals involved in our case study had previously worked with each other. Further, Alpha and Bravo had only previously worked with each other on a purely subcontracting basis, referred to by the parties as a "bums on seats" approach. This form of contracting required that design engineers were sourced and supplied by Bravo to sit and work in-house at Alpha, alongside Alpha employees. They were contracted on an hourly rate to do a specific job that was detailed and managed by Alpha. A sudden upturn in the economic environment had resulted in the identification of new business opportunities for Alpha. This created significant demand for contract design engineers within the marketplace, and had levered hourly rates considerably. This situation was highlighted by a detailed make/buy analysis, which resulted in Alpha deciding to try and create more stability, and, thus, in a move away from this kind of subcontracting. The key challenge was identified as: How might Alpha create or find a valuable resource of design engineering skills that fitted their specialist requirements, and that provided low variable cost without compromising quality?

In an effort to move toward their desired scenario, Alpha sought bids from suppliers. The criteria they developed required that a future supplier should offer: (i) the potential for developing a supply network; (ii) direct experience of sourcing routine engineering from emerging market economies; (iii) previous local experience and expertise in more sophisticated design engineering; and (iv) expertise to manage these outsourced work streams as a single package. This not only represented a shift from the use of subcontractors on an hourly rate, but also the potential for the supplier to develop specialized added value through the management of resources and expertise across the multiple work streams. As an Alpha representative explained: "I want to be able to package it [the work] and let them manage it."

The size of the contract was estimated to be a turnover of £1m within the first year and £4m by the end of the second. To facilitate the desired business model Alpha held a suppliers conference, which began with Alpha's presentation of what they were looking for. An interviewee recalled: "What we did was we overlaid the final slide ... with something like, "our reputation is in your hands" ... I wanted to make it clear to everybody in the room, that this was not just another supply arrangement". Indeed, the consequences of failure were described by Alpha as "dire". An interviewee explained that the message was, "not just about cost, [but] also about management of risk".

After the Alpha presentation, the six suppliers were invited to present their bids. One of the requirements detailed by Alpha in the invitation to tender had been that the supplier should seek to reduce their cost base by seeking to source some routine engineering offshore. Indeed, the contract would eventually be structured to incentivize this behaviour.

While Alpha recognized offshore sourcing as a significant area where costs might be minimized, they remained concerned about their lack of experience in this area. Bravo was awarded the contract because they were viewed as the only company that understood what Alpha was trying to achieve. The Alpha representatives felt that the majority of the suppliers at the conference did not fundamentally understand the concept of the supply network as Alpha conceptualized it. One interviewee commented: "I couldn't close the gap ... I couldn't get them [the other suppliers] to grasp the issue of the business model being new and not business as usual." These dealings created the context for the beginning of the relationship between Alpha and Bravo, with Charlie as an approved supplier.

Shortly after the contract was awarded to Bravo, interviewees from the network organizations spoke of the importance of honesty and openness in their dealings with one another. They spoke about fostering an atmosphere of trust. Communications appeared to be frequent, with multiple face-to-face meetings, telephone conversations and emails between Alpha and Bravo, and Bravo and Charlie senior managers and directors. However, as the relationship evolved, differences from the forecast work streams (upon which the contract was based) emerged, and forced the parties into renegotiating the flat rate of pay for contracted hours. At this time, interviews revealed that, despite the understandable tensions associated with the need to renegotiate rates, significant trust had developed between certain individuals at Alpha and Bravo. Further, these personal relationships had facilitated a high degree of openness and the parties appeared to have developed a deeper understanding of each other's difficulties, and, in this way, of the network context within which they operated.

During the first year of the contract, the Alpha team, involved in developing the Bravo/Charlie network, learnt much about the relationship context. They learnt how to foster and build trust, whom to share commercially sensitive information with, how and when to share it, and how to reach new agreements that satisfied the needs of all parties. This learning was illustrated by one employee commenting:

> We'll keep ploughing a furrow ... because we said that this was something that was a foundation for organic growth, we're looking to find things to add into it and that is starting to happen ... we are trying to grow it and it's not easy. There're tensions between ourselves and Bravo and there's tension between various parts of Alpha but I think we'll work it through and we'll work it through better than we would have done because there's a relationship to maintain.

Other interviewees also commented on the knowledge gained during the set-up of the network, as well as on their motivation to engage in additional activities within the network. For example, interviewees six months into the contract noted that "we've achieved ... a better understanding of the customer community [within the network]". Another participant observed how, as their relationships had developed and they had learnt how to overcome difficulties, the process had become "self-smoothing". They explained "it just takes a lot of the hurly-burly out of it and it has worked well from my perception and so we're trying to grow it". A further interviewee described the learning process, explaining, "it takes a bit of sort of sinking in, and that's in essence what we're doing ... and on the whole I think it's working ... we'll get better as we do more".

The evidence suggests that such experiences generate a sense of positive learning within the network, contributing to members' motivation to continue the development of the relationship within the network. Furthermore, this knowledge was absorbed and shared by members of the network and in this way demonstrates the learning capacity of the network.

The mechanisms put in place to capture and manage these evolving relationship factors were largely team-based and dependent on the day-to-day communications of individuals. One interviewee explained that the need to develop an open culture between the two firms had resulted in an agreement with Bravo being offered space on-site at Alpha. This principle was taken further as the relationship developed. Within a few days of the start of the contract, the senior line managers from Alpha and Bravo were physically sitting next to each other in an open-plan office so that they could continuously communicate with each other, face-to-face, and address issues as they arose. One interviewee observed: "George [Alpha] and Bert [Bravo] are sitting next to each other and talking each day and there's this self-levelling mechanism going on day-by-day."

Additionally, each organization developed an escalation procedure so that if managers felt they needed advice they could easily and instantaneously escalate the problem up the organization to their seniors. Gradually, procedures were developed to collect and disseminate information at the right time, in the right format, to front-line managers and workers in the supply network. One interviewee explained: "There was one incident where we got the delivery dates wrong. We've now developed a standard procedure and supporting documentation to provide everyone working on that job with the transparency they need."

There were understandable teething problems with directing and completing work streams, with interviewees observing that the process of establishing such procedures often facilitated frank exchanges of views. However, there was also a consensus amongst participants that such procedures had come to represent the openness and trust that the parties had endeavoured to create.

To summarize, we suggest that a capacity to assimilate context-specific relationship knowledge, particularly where such knowledge relates to positive experiences, has been developed within the studied network (Cohen and Levinthal, 1990). We also argue that this capacity has led to network success in terms of members' motivation to continue the development of the network (Gallivan, 2001). Such capacity can be developed when individuals understand the situation and difficulties of the different parties and have a basic understanding of the procedures required as to how to go about solving arising difficulties: then, they are better positioned to consider ways to develop the network further.

Learning for value

When customers' values change or evolve, suppliers are given the task of identifying and reacting to these changing customer needs and wants.

In this regard, we set out to explore (i) how these changes in values might be identified and captured, (ii) how firms are able to learn about such changes in value perceptions, and (iii) how this impacts on perceived network success.

At the beginning of the contract, interviewees were asked to describe the value they thought the contract would deliver, and specifically on the value they thought they required presently, compared with that which they might require in future. Responses regarding current value largely concurred with Möller *et al.*'s (2005) core value platform, whereby Alpha's focus appeared to be on efficient productivity and delivery systems. This perspective was reflected in the responses of interviewees throughout the network. The observation is also consistent with Möller *et al.*'s (2005) argument of value as a hierarchical system: *core value* to *relational value* to *future-oriented value*. Hence, at the beginning of the relationship, according to Möller *et al.* (2005), it would be expected that core values would prevail.

When asked about value three months, six months and then 12 months into the contract, interviewees throughout the network still found it difficult to identify possible changes in value. Table 6.1 presents statements from interviewees reflecting on changes in perceived value over time. Despite the strong tendency for respondents to claim that value had not changed in any significant way, we argue that such changes are observable. In particular, as time moved on interviewees tended to associate, more frequently, perceived value with the development of the network and with their motivation to further invest in the network.

Furthermore, we argue that the respondents' reaction to changes in value over time appears to concur with Möller *et al.*'s (2005) recognition of a shift toward the relational platform whereby firms begin to value innovation and the supply network begins to focus on creating new solutions to support the customer business.

Our explanation is that the difficulties interviewees had in identifying this fundamental change in value could be due to the perspective and discussions that developed during the bidding period, and it could be argued that, right from the outset, *relational value* was envisaged. Our analysis suggests that this appears to have always been part of the *"long game"*. The initial focus, as the network emerged, was to establish a successful core value platform, from which a relational platform could be more clearly conceived and developed. This observation has important implications for learning capacity on two levels. First, it seems to suggest that as a result of previous experiences and their knowledge of one another, the supply network members had already absorbed and learnt

Table 6.1 Interviewees' observations reflecting changes in perceived value over the first 12 months of the contract

Interviewee	Contract signing	Three months later	Six months later	Twelve months later
A	"it's the low value stuff … routine engineering"	"it's just the routine work really"	"we're growing faster than expected"	"we've far exceeded the forecast head count and they're asking us to do much more added value work than we'd anticipated"
B	"the added value comes from us managing work streams"	"we'll provide value by handling packages of work"	"there's a learning curve … but we're actually now doing jobs that were never in the initial contract"	"now there are one or two other types of engineering support that we're providing them, that they're rolling into the model"
C	"the scope review suggests 50% will go offshore"		"they've dealt with more of the higher skilled stuff than we'd imagined"	"that will be part of the organic growth we're aiming for"
D	"this is new, we are pioneers … we're trying to understand what they want and show them what we can offer"	"the head count here is growing … we're recruiting hard to deliver"	"and that is completely off spec … it's new"	"I'm working on the basis that it will just run and run, that way we'll have to not perform for us to lose"

something about how to progress with the type of innovation-led network they ultimately aimed to achieve, and were implementing this learning by taking a step-by-step approach to the evaluation of their new supply network: documentary evidence of procedures support this view.

Second, this observation suggests that the network was aware of the need for capturing ongoing information regarding how the second platform of relational value might be achieved. In this regard, the mechanisms created to capture this information, framed as dimensions of value by Flint and Mentzer (2000), appeared strongly associated with procedures developed to track perceived network success. Specifically, fortnightly meetings with front-line network managers on different work streams, and quarterly reviews involving senior managers from network members, incorporated network success measures, including work stream allocation and completion rates, satisfaction with work in progress and work completed, delivery time scales and job transparency.

This phenomenon was illustrated by the attention that centred on Bravo when their merger was agreed with a significant player in their industry. Within days of the merger, Bravo was presenting to senior managers within Alpha (incorporating the Alpha team and their seniors), their increased capabilities and resources that had materialized as a result of the merger. As the network members attempted to anticipate future changes in value and future needs for services, the repositioning of both parties' value propositions were clear, conscious, and visible. The presentation developed into round-table discussions as the conference progressed. In this way, attempts by the supply network to absorb changing value perceptions appear closely associated with the perceptions of network success; thus suggesting that perceived network success is increased when the learning capacity of the supply network regarding changing perceived value is high.

Learning for resources and capabilities

The decision by Alpha to enter into a long-term relationship and to create a supply network within this area marks a shift in the way the firm thinks about and manages capabilities. It impacts on decisions regarding where the capabilities reside. In some cases, capabilities reside in parallel within the various supply network members. These parallel capabilities offer greater flexibility and fluidity of task allocation. For example, some capabilities need to be developed by all firms and, in addition, need to evolve over time. These might include specialist capabilities such as the use of CAD technology or ancillary capabilities associated with firms interacting with each other (see Loasby, 1998; Langlois and Robertson, 1995). Ancillary capabilities can then be developed later as a broader network capability. The mechanisms created by organizations to monitor and assess supply network success create procedures that drive the development of increasingly effective mechanisms, developing, locating, and utilizing resources and capabilities that exist within the network to maximum effect.

Specialist capabilities, such as low-skilled design engineering tasks in the form of remodelling designs for new CAD technologies, exist as latent capabilities within Alpha while being developed and exercised in Charlie. The management of these resources requires each network member to have a current and dynamic understanding of where these capabilities reside and how they might be best utilized and managed.

In this way, some capabilities are developed externally but reside within the network rather than within the traditional boundaries of the core firm (Alpha). Learning associated with resource utilization and the management of capabilities that has moved beyond the traditional boundaries of the firm presented some challenges for the supply network. As Bravo had agreed a flat hourly rate of pay for all jobs given to them regardless of complexity, the objective was to assign more highly skilled jobs to Bravo employees situated onsite at Alpha, where they could be managed by Bravo as part of an on-site team. With these tasks, Bravo would make a loss, as the hourly rate they paid the more highly skilled engineers was greater than that covered by the flat rate being paid by Alpha to Bravo. The losses were to be compensated for by the difference in the significantly lower offshore rate Bravo paid Charlie, thus offering Alpha the benefit of increased stability in cost management and Bravo the ability to leverage profitability by good resource utilization and management and the potential to develop capabilities offshore through their relationship with Charlie. Thus, less highly skilled design engineering work (considered to be low risk) would then be completed offshore using the capabilities developed by Charlie.

Despite the detailed procedures and requirements communicated to Charlie personnel, and the training paid for and executed by Alpha and Bravo, instances of front-line workers from Charlie being unable to complete basic re-engineering tasks presented initial difficulties for the network. Understanding and managing the offshore resources created, "a headache" for the Bravo team. This, to a large extent, was not visible to the Alpha team but represented a steep learning curve for both Bravo and Charlie. As one interviewee pointed out, while these offshore tasks were relatively low-skilled, they still represented a critical resource (see Dyer and Singh, 1998) and, in this regard, the ability of the network to deliver on these capabilities (both from a technical and commercial perspective) was central to the success of the network. In this way, it can be seen that the effective and efficient exploitation of network resources can only be realized when firms capture and utilize resource and capability information. Talking at the beginning of the contractual agreement period, one Bravo interviewee observed:

> As we do more of this, we'll get better at it. The way I see it is, that we'll add value by managing the resources. As we are able to do this the network will grow and the added value that comes from managing the process increases and increases as the network does.

In this regard, perceived network success increased when firms had a high learning capacity for knowledge relating to the network's resources and capabilities. As the capacity of the network to manage the different work streams developed, so too did the perceived success of the network. When questioned on this topic, interviewees' responses included, "[I]t's working well", "I'm pretty satisfied with it on the whole", and "I think there's great potential."

Learning for network structure and type

When Alpha originally envisaged a supplier solution that incorporated offshore sourcing they explored the viability of two different network structures. The first would require Alpha to source and manage the offshore relationship themselves, while the second would be to draw up a contract with an intermediary who would manage the offshore sourcing and offer a stable, single flat rate for routine re-engineering work. Influenced by their lack of experience of the offshore market, together with the quality and nature of the bids presented to them, Alpha selected the latter. One interviewee explained:

> We had seven [companies] selected for this last [supplier selection] stage. We gave the suppliers half a day each to come and tell us how they were going to do this, how they were going to execute the task, what's the transition plan, what risks did they perceive, how they were going to make it happen. I think there were seven left on the deck ... we sat and listened and we asked questions ... it became clear that Bravo and [one other] were the only two that would meet the commercial criteria as well as the technical ones and then we sat down and we worked through structured negotiation with each. We couldn't get the others to understand the difference between risk and price.

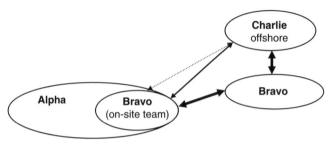

Key:
Heavier lines indicate a greater frequency of communication flows.
Arrows indicate the direction of communication flows.

Figure 6.2   The Alpha–Bravo supply network

It was at this stage that the structure of the network, the responsibilities, and the likely communication and work flows were explored. The resulting network is represented in Figure 6.2. In accordance with the traditional supply chain perspective (see Figure 6.1), the majority of the communication flows are between Alpha and Bravo and Bravo and Charlie. This horizontal, linear approach is consistent with the traditional tiered supply system employed by Alpha. However, the structure differs from this more traditional approach as it incorporates an embedded supplier. That is, Bravo has been integrated into the mechanisms and procedures of Alpha. This draws Charlie into a web-like structure of communication flows. Hence communication links exist, directly between the embedded Alpha/Bravo teams and Charlie (represented by a solid, two-way arrow in Figure 6.2), and occasional, infrequent contact directly between Charlie and Alpha (represented by a lighter, dotted line). The boldness of the arrows indicates the direction, strength, and frequency of communications within the network. These network communications have developed as the network evolved through its various problem-solving activities. An Alpha interviewee explained: "If we're putting this work out, we can't just expect them to pick it up. There has to be a learning curve. And we can help them in that ... it's in our interest." A Bravo interviewee echoed this point: "We've discussed the learning curve [with Alpha], and in principle they understand this ... they're directly involved with the training and getting our people and where we've needed it, the Charlie people, up to speed ... and that's great."

The establishment of authority and hierarchy within the network seems to set important boundaries for participants. While the communications web that exists appears to increase the learning capacity of the network, the responsibility for the management of work flows and revenues is clear. As one participant indicated: "[W]e each have a commercial interest to protect ... it's only when we are successful in creating shared objectives that this can work ... so we can't just throw all caution to the wind."

This said, the overwhelming consensus among interviewees was one of sharing learning to facilitate the achievement of the shared objectives, and this in turn increases perceived supply network success. This was particularly evident where interviewees had benefited directly from the successful training of network members, through increased satisfaction with the work carried out for them by their supplier. As one interviewee observed:

> You can't just take anybody and sit them at a terminal and say right, go away and use it. You've got to train them in what the system is ... we've done the training in a couple of ways. We've actually taken Bravo people and put them on our training courses, we've had people help, actual Alpha people in the working environment help, so on the job type training... Bravo ... then trained their own people, so essentially we've got some key people trained by Alpha and then Bravo are then training up their own people.

Therefore, understanding and learning about the characteristics of the network and the way it is structured helps network members to create shared understandings of the processes and mechanisms through which communications and work must flow. Based on the above evidence, we conclude that perceived network success is increased when firms have a high capacity for acquiring knowledge regarding network structure and type.

Conclusions and implications

The key objective of this chapter was to explore how learning of particular areas has evolved within a supply network and how it has affected the perception of network success. Based on the evidence presented above, we argue that a firm's ability to assimilate knowledge from a supplier network will significantly and positively affect: (i) the degree of *trust* developed between members of the network, (ii) the *value* perceived from being part of the network, (iii) the firm's ability to effectively utilize *capabilities* within the network, and (iv) its ability to shape the *structure* of the network and to use this structure to create a shared understanding of how the network works. It was also evident from the case study that as relationships, value, capabilities, and network structure developed, and members of the network became more aware of these factors as central to the development and continuation of the network, the potential for network success increased. This has several implications for both theorists and practitioners.

From a research viewpoint, this chapter has three main contributions to make. Firstly, it is a direct response to the calls of earlier commentators for further research into how supplier networks learn and absorb knowledge (Storck, 2000). Furthermore, the chapter contributes to our understanding of dynamic supply networks through the identification of specific learning requirements, in the form of trust, changing value, capabilities, and structures, through which learning capacity can be focused and developed. In particular, this study makes an attempt to move away from understanding dyadic relationships in a supplier network by focusing on the complex, multifaceted nature of relationships in a multiplayer supply network.

Secondly, this study offers a unique opportunity to observe how the relationships between members of a supply network take shape and co-evolve over time. Past studies on co-evolution have focused, by and large, on the interactions between firms and industries as the key context that shapes their behaviours. Against this approach, this study has considered the multiple tiers of an industry as the context within which the learning takes place.

Thirdly, this chapter advances the understanding of learning in general, and in network settings, in particular. As earlier claims suggest, developing learning capabilities within a supply network is challenging because of the limited control that the players have over the learning and learning-generating mechanisms within the network. This study suggests that in addition to the prior knowledge needed to improve the firm's ability to assimilate new and related knowledge (Cohen and Levinthal, 1990), experiences involved in the generation of the learning, which are contextual to the knowledge creation process and are also socially embedded in the cultures and norms of the players involved, serve as enablers of the transfer of learning within a network. We also observe that learning, as a capability, is a dependent of the value perceived by members of the network. In this regard, our findings suggest that a shift in the desired value created within the network may take place, thus raising a possibility that learning is in itself a dynamic phenomenon that may change as the network grows and generates value to its members.

From a practical viewpoint, this study highlights two areas that may contribute to the management of a supply network. Firstly, the mechanisms through which learning can be developed within a supply network are critical for supporting the development of the network. In order to ensure members' willingness to keep developing the network, managers should invest in activities that not only generate value but also support the dynamic nature of value in supply networks: in particular, in procedures that facilitate routine observation and that record changing customer needs and customer difficulties as they arise. Such procedures might take the form of fortnightly meetings and scope reviews. In this way, the concept of value, what is needed and what can be developed, can evolve in line with the building of capabilities and experience.

Secondly, a supply network may significantly benefit from the development of shared identity. In line with Sethi's (2000) concept of superordinate identity, we argue that a supply network may enjoy a higher success rate should members of the network identify with the network's goals rather than with their origin organizations. Members of the network, thus, have to invest in creating shared goals and cultivating social ties between the partners involved. Creating a superordinate identity may assist in shifting management's traditional conception of supplier networks as transaction-based entities that generate financial value to the parties involved, to entities that are value-based, generating various types of values (e.g. learning) to members of the network. In creating a superordinate identity, members of the network should consider physically co-locating partners, co-deciding on procedures, and clearly communicating the goals of the network. Furthermore, members of the network should ensure that the changing value desired and generated from the network is captured and communicated to the parties to avoid conflict generation within the network.

References

Achrol, R. S. (1997) "Changes in the Theory of Interorganizational Relations in Marketing: Toward a Network Paradigm," *Journal of the Academy of Marketing Science*, 25(1), 56–71.

Alexsson, B. and Easton, G. (1992) *Industrial Networks: A New View of Reality*, Routledge, London.

Araujo, L., Dubois, A., and Gadde, L. (2003) "The Multiple Boundaries of the Firm," *The Journal of Management Studies*, 40(5), 1255.

Baker, W. E. and Sinkula, J. M. (2002) "Market Orientation, Learning Orientation and Product Innovation: Delving into the Organization's Black Box," *Journal of Market-Focused Management*, 5(1), 5.

Coase, R. H. (1937) "The Nature of the Firm," *Economica*, 4, 386–405.

Cohen, W. and Levinthal, D. (1990) "Absorptive Capacity: A New Perspective on Learning and Innovation," *Administrative Science Quarterly*, 35, 128–52.

Day, George S. (2002) "Managing the Market Learning Process," *The Journal of Business & Industrial Marketing*, 17(4), 240.

Dubois, A. and Gadde, L. E. (2000) "Supply Strategy and Network Effects – Purchasing Behaviour in the Construction Industry," *European Journal of Purchasing and Supply Management*, 6(3–4), 207–15.

Dyer, J. H. and Singh, H. (1998) "The Relational View: Cooperative Strategy and Sources of Interorganizational Competitive Advantage," *The Academy of Management Review*, 23(4), 660.

Farrelly, Francis and Quester, Pascale (2003) "The Effects of Market Orientation on Trust and Commitment: The Case of the Sponsorship Business-to-Business Relationship," *European Journal of Marketing*, 37(3/4), 530.

Flint, D. J. and Mentzer, J. T. (2000) "Logisticians as Marketers: Their Role When Customers' Desired Value Changes," *Journal of Business Logistics*, 21(2), 19–45.

Flint, D. J., Woodruff, R. B., and Fisher Gardial, S. (2002) "Exploring the Phenomenon of Customers' Desired Value Change in a Business-to-Business Context," *Journal of Marketing*, 66(4), 102–17.

Fredriksson, Peter and Araujo, Luis (2003) "The Evaluation of Supplier Performance: A Case Study of Volvo Cars and Its Module Suppliers," *Journal of Customer Behaviour*, (2), 365–84.

Gadde, L. and Håkansson, H. (2001) *Supply Network Strategies*, John Wiley, Chichester.

Gadde, L. and Snehota, I. (2000) "Making the Most of Supplier Relationships," *Industrial Marketing Management*, 29, 305–16.

Gallivan, M. J. (2001) "Striking a Balance between Trust and Control in a Virtual Organization: A Content Analysis of Open Source Software Case Studies," *Information Systems Journal*, 11(4), 227–304.

Gassenheimer, J. B., Houston, F. S., and Davis, J. C. (1998) "The Role of Economic Value, Social Value and Perceptions of Fairness in Interorganizational Relationships Retention Decisions," *Journal of the Academy of Marketing Science*, 26, 322–37.

Gummesson, E. (2002) "Relationship Marketing in the New Economy," *Journal of Relationship Marketing*, 1(1), 37.

Håkansson, H. and Ford, D. (2002) "How Should Companies Interact in Business Network?," *Journal of Business Research*, 55, 133–9.

Harland, C. M., Lamming, R. C., Zheng, J., and Johnsen, T. E. (2001) "A Taxonomy of Supply Networks," *Journal of Supply Chain Management*, (Fall), 37–40.

Holbrook, M. B. (1994) "The Nature of Consumer Value," in *Service Quality: New Directions in Theory and Practice* (Eds, Rust, R. T. and Oliver, R. L.) Sage, Newbury Park, CA, pp. 21–7.

Holmen, E., Håkansson, H., and Pedersen, A.-C. (2003) "Framing as a Means To Manage a Supply Network," *Journal of Customer Behaviour*, 2, 385–407.

Holmstrom, B. and Roberts, J. (1998) "The Boundaries of the Firm Revisited," *Journal of Economic Perspectives*, 12(4), 73.

Jansen, J. J. P., van den Bosch, F. A. J., and Volberda, H. W. (forthcoming) "Managing Potential and Realized Absorptive Capacity: How Do Organizational Antecedents Matter?," *Academy of Management Journal*.

Jüttner, U., Christopher, M., and Baker, S. (2006) "Demand Chain Management-Integrating Marketing and Supply Chain Management," *Industrial Marketing Management*, 36(3), 377–92.

Kogut, B. and Meitu, A. (2000) "The Emergence of E-Innovation: Insights from Open Source Software Development," The Wharton School, University of Pennsylvania.

Kwon, I. G. and Suh, T. (2004) "Factors Affecting the Level of Trust and Commitment in Supply Chain Relationships," *Journal of Supply Chain Management*, 40(2), 4.

Lai, A. W. (1995) "Consumer Values, Product Benefits and Customer Value: A Consumption Behavior Approach," *Advances in Consumer Research*, 381–8.

Lamming, R. (2000) "Japanese Supply Chain Relationships in Recession," *Long Range Planning*, 33(6), 757.

Lane, P. J., Salk, J. E., and Lyles, M. A. (2001) "Absorptive Capacity, Learning, and Performance in International Joint Ventures," *Strategic Management Journal*, 22(12), 1139–61.

Lanfield-Smith, K. and Smith, D. (2003) "Management Control Systems and Trust in Outsourcing Relationships," *Management Accounting Research*, 14(3), 281.

Langabeer, J. and Rose, J. (2001) *Creating Demand Driven Supply Chains: How to Profit from Demand Chain Management*, Chandos, Oxford.

Langlois, R. N. and Robertson, P. L. (1995) *Firms, Markets and Economic Change: A Dynamic Theory of Business Intuitions*, Routledge, London.

Loasby, B. J. (1998) "The Organization of Capabilities," *Journal of Economic Behavior and Organization*, 35(2), 130–60.

Loasby, B. J. (1999) *Knowledge, Institutions and Evolution in Economics*, Routledge, London.

Mahoney, J. T. (1992) "The Choice of Organizational Form: Vertical Financial Ownership Versus Other Methods of Vertical Integration," *Strategic Management Journal*, 13(8), 559.

Mills, J., Schmitz, J., and Frizelle, G. (2004) "A Strategic Review of Supply Networks," *International Journal of Operations and Production Management*, 24(10), 1012–36.

Minbaeva, D., Pedersen, T., Björkman, I., Fey, C., and Park, H. J. (2003) "MNC Knowledge Transfer, Subsidiary Absorptive Capacity and HRM," *Journal of International Business Studies*, 34(6), 586–99.

Möller, K. and Törrönen, P. (2003) "Business Suppliers' Value Creation Potential: A Capability-Based Analysis," *Industrial Marketing Management*, 32, 109–18.

Möller, K., Rajala, A., and Svahn, S. (2005) "Strategic Business Nets – Their Type and Management," *Journal of Business Research*, 58, 1274–84.

Murray, J. Y., Kotabe, M., and Zhou, J. N. (2005) "Strategic Alliance-Based Sourcing and Market Performance: Evidence from Foreign Firms Operating in China," *Journal of International Business Studies*, 36(2), 187.

Nishiguchi, T. (1994) *Strategic Industrial Sourcing*, Oxford University Press, New York.

Nobeoka, K., Dyer, J. H., and Madhok, A. (2002) "The Influence of Customer Scope on Supplier Learning and Performance in the Japanese Automobile Industry," *Journal of International Business Studies*, 33(4), 717–36.

Paniccia, I. (1998) "Network Perspectives on Interfirm Conflict: Reassessing a Critical Case in International Business," *Organization Studies*, 19(4), 667.

Parolini, C. (1999) *The Value Net: A Tool For Competitive Strategy*, Wiley, Chichester.

Pettigrew, A., Thomas, H., and Whittington, R. (2002) *Strategic Management: The Strengths and Limitations of a Field*, Sage, London.

Piore, M. J. (1992) *Fragments of a Cognitive Theory of Technological Change and Organisational Structure*, Harvard Business School Press, Boston, MA.

Richins, M. L. (1994) "Special Possessions and the Expression of Material Values," *Journal of Consumer Research*, 21(3), 522.

Sánchez, A. M. and Pérez Pérez, M. (2003) "Cooperation and the Ability to Minimize the Time and Cost of New Product Development within the Spanish Automotive Supplier Industry," *Journal of Product Innovation Management*, 20(1), 57.

Schultze, U. and Boland, R. J. (1997), "Hard and soft information genres: an analysis of two Notesdatabases," *Proceedings of the Thirtieth Hawaii International Conference on System Sciences*, 6, Wailea, HI, US, 40–9.

Senge, P. M. (1990) "Building Learning Organizations," *Sloan Management Review* (Fall).

Sethi, R. (2000), "Superordinate Identity in Cross-Functional Product Development Teams: Its Antecedents and Effect on New Product Performance," *Journal of the Academy of Marketing Science*, 28(3), 330–44.

Slater, S. and Narver, J. (1995) "Market Orientation and Learning Organisation," *Journal of Marketing*, 59(3), 63–74.

Storck, J. (2000) "Knowledge Diffusion through 'Strategic Communities'," *Sloan Management Review*, 41(2), 63–74.

Thorelli, H. B. (1986) "Networks: Between Markets and Hierarchies," *Strategic Management Journal*, 7(1), 37.

Ulaga, W. (2003) "Capturing Value Creation in Business Relationships: A Customer Perspective," *Industrial Marketing Management*, 32, 677–93.

Vaaland, T. I. and Håkansson, H. (2003) "Exploring Interorganizational Conflict in Complex Projects," *Industrial Marketing Management*, 32, 127–38.

van den Bosch, F. A. J., Volberda, H. W., and de Boer, M. (1999) "Coevolution of Firm Absorptive Capacity and Knowledge Environment: Organizational Forms and Combinative Capabilities," *Organization Science*, 10(5), 551.

Verona, G. and Ravasi, D. (2003) "Unbundling Dynamic Capabilities: An Exploratory Study of Continuous Product Innovation," *Industrial and Corporate Change*, 12(3), 577.

Webster (1992) *Webster's Dictionary*, Oxford University Press, Oxford.

Welch, C. and Wilkinson, I. (2005), "Network Perspectives on Interfirm Conflict: Reassessing a Critical Case in International Business," *Journal of Business Research*, 58(2), 205.

Williamson, O. E. (1975) *Markets and Hierarchies: Analysis and Antitrust Implications*, Free Press, New York.

Womack, J. P. and Jones, D. T. (1994) "From Lean Production to the Lean Enterprise," *Harvard Business Review*, 72(2), 93.

Zahay, D. L. and Handfield, R. B. (2004) "The Role of Learning and Technical Capabilities in Predicting Adoption of B2B Technologies," *Industrial Marketing Management*, 33, 627–41.

Zander, U. Kogut, B. (2003) "Knowledge of the Firm and the Evolutionary Theory of the Multinational Corporation," *Journal of International Business Studies*, 34(6), 516.

CHAPTER 7

Globally distributed component-based software development: An exploratory study of knowledge management and work division

Julia Kotlarsky, Ilan Oshri, Jos van Hillegersberg, and Kuldeep Kumar

Introduction

Global distribution of software development has become widespread over the last 15 years (Herbsleb and Moitra, 2001). Moreover, there are a number of economic and technical drivers that are likely to accelerate further the growth of distributed software development. For one, to access a larger pool of expertise, often in low-cost geographical locations, many companies are switching to globally distributed software development or offshore outsourcing of software products and services. On the technological side, continuing innovations in Information and Communication Technology (ICT) improve the possibilities to cooperate in a distributed mode.

Indeed, geographical distance, and the time-zone and cultural differences associated with global distribution, have caused problems for globally distributed software teams in achieving successful collaboration. A growing number of studies have reported problems regarding collaboration in distributed work, such as coordination breakdowns (Cheng *et al.*, 2004; Carmel, 1999), lack of understanding of a counterpart's context (Cramton, 2001), and different language competencies across remote sites (Sarker and Sahay, 2004). Other studies have argued that globally distributed work may exacerbate the chance of misunderstandings (Olson and Olson, 2004; Battin *et al.*, 2001), lack of trust (Cramton, 2001; Jarvenpaa *et al.*, 1998), asymmetry in distribution of information among sites (Carmel, 1999), difficulty in collaborating due to different skills and training, and mismatches in Information Technology (IT) infrastructure (Sarker and Sahay, 2004).

The practices recommended to overcome these difficulties have mainly focused on a division of work that minimizes the need for intersite coordination and, therefore, communication and synchronization (Herbsleb and Mockus, 2003; Ebert and De Neve, 2001; Mockus and Weiss, 2001; Repenning *et al.*, 2001). To achieve this, it was recommended that "tightly coupled work items that require frequent coordination and synchronization should be performed within one site" (Mockus and Weiss, 2001).

In this regard, past research (e.g. Carmel, 1999) has indicated that the adoption of Component Based Development (CBD), which aims to reduce the costs involved in developing new products and to improve time to market of new products through the reuse of components across multiple products (Huang *et al.*, 2003), may also facilitate globally distributed software development. According to this view, components can be developed independently from remote locations (Repenning *et al.*, 2001) and, therefore, mitigate some coordination breakdowns associated with the traditional, non-CB globally distributed software development (Carmel, 1999). Put simply, each site should take responsibility to develop a particular component with minimum intersite communication and coordination activities (Repenning *et al.*, 2001). Such a development approach has indeed been discussed in Chapter 5. In this chapter we claim that such an approach may in fact result in fewer opportunities to reuse components because remote sites may have limited exposure to the knowledge of components developed by other remote teams and because of the limited knowledge sharing between remote counterparts (Kotlarsky and Oshri, 2005).

In this chapter we report on two companies that followed an approach in which the development of a component was jointly carried out across several sites. We explore the capabilities that were imperative to achieve component reuse in globally distributed CBD projects. We provide a historical background of CBD, followed by a review of the literature on it in globally distributed software development projects. The research method section then poses the key questions that the studied companies were facing and explain the research approach, exploratory in nature, adopted for this study. The following section, based on the empirical evidence, provides the rationale that guided the companies in pursuing a division of work based on the expertise available within the dispersed teams regardless of their geographical location (as opposed to the approach in which one site takes ownership of the development of a particular component). The empirical section outlines the capabilities developed by these companies in order to support component reuse in globally distributed CBD projects. Lastly, practical implications are offered to managers and engineers.

Component-based development: Background

CBD has its roots in manufacturing. Since the mid 1960s, when the concept of modular production was introduced (Starr, 1965), *modular* (later referred to as *component-based*) product architectures became dominant in manufacturing industries. Indeed, the trend to develop products that have a *component-based* (CB) architecture is well established in automotive, electronics, aircraft, and other industries, and it has been successfully used for setting up globally distributed design and production activities. For example, in the computer industry, Dell products include components produced by different vendors in various locations. In the automotive industry, the design of a car and the manufacture of car components both involve designers and component suppliers at various dispersed locations (Olin *et al.*, 1999). Even a very large and complex product such as an aircraft could be developed from remote locations, as in the case of Boeing-Rocketdyne (Malhotra *et al.*, 2001), Boeing 777 (Yenne, 2002), and Airbus.

In the software development industry, *Component-Based Development* involves (i) the development of software components and (ii) the building of software systems through the integration of pre-existing software components (Bass *et al.*, 2000). *Components* are units of independent production, acquisition, and deployment that interact with each other to form a functioning system (Szyperski, 1998). Being self-contained and replaceable units, components can be reused across a number of products, and be replaced by more recent and advanced versions of components in a "plug-and-play" manner, as long as the interfaces across the components comprising the products are compatible.

Indeed, the idea to develop software components goes back to the early days of computer systems in the form of subroutines and subroutine libraries. In this regard, the transition in software development took place as "programmers observed that they could insert subroutines extracted from their previous programmes, or even written by other programmers, and take advantage of the functionality without having to concern themselves with the details of coding. Generally useful subroutines were collected into libraries, and soon very few people would ever again have to worry about how to implement, for example, a numerically well-behaved double-precision cosine routine" (Clements, 1995). Nevertheless, until the mid 1990s reusability was limited because module interfaces were programming-language specific and even platform specific. Also, specification techniques to document module interfaces were insufficiently developed. Finally, the Internet, as an effective means to facilitate the development and distribution of software modules, was not as widespread as it is today. These limitations have hindered the development of global software component reuse (Traas and Hillegersberg, 2000).

With the introduction of software component technologies in the mid 1990s, such as Enterprise JavaBeans, Microsoft COM, and CORBA (Peters and Pedrycz, 2000), there have been expectations that CBD will offer additional avenues to software development and reuse opportunities. As opposed to a monolithic system, a CB system has a number of advantages for production and competitiveness. In particular, a CB system allows changes to be made to isolated functional elements of the product without affecting the design of other components (Ulrich and Eppinger, 2000). Furthermore, a CB system supports the rapid customization of products through the reuse of existing standardized components, resulting in an improved product variation, higher utilization of existing assets, better reliability of products (Vitharana, 2003), shorter time to market (Huang et al., 2003; Vitharana, 2003; Crnkovic and Larsson, 2002; Kim, 2002; Bass et al., 2000), and lower costs associated with product development (Ravichandran and Rothenberger, 2003; Kunda and Brooks, 2000).

Along with this positive outlook, some possible challenges associated with CBD that co-located software development teams have faced have been reported in the literature. For example, it has been argued that "it often took longer to develop a reusable component than to develop a system for a one-off purpose" (Huang et al., 2003). Other studies have reported difficulties associated with the management of CBD in co-located projects, such as a lack of stable standards, lack of reusable components, and problems related to the granularity and generality of components (Vitharana, 2003; Crnkovic and Larsson, 2002).

Component-based development in globally distributed software development contexts

As discussed above, globally distributed teams represent a new organizational form that has emerged in conjunction with the globalization of socio-economic processes. Such teams have replaced the traditional single-site hierarchy and the functional department structure for various reasons. For one, companies in developed nations have outsourced parts of their IT services and business processes to developing nations (Carmel and Agarwal, 2002). Short-cycle development and the launch of new products and software for global markets has required expertise from a range of geographical areas (DeSouza and Evaristo, 2004). Indeed, an increasing number of companies are setting up software development in a globally distributed mode and at the same time are adopting a CBD methodology. At the basis of this approach is the assumption that in globally distributed software development particular parts of large software systems reappear with sufficient reliability such that common parts can be written once, rather than many times, and that common systems can be built through reuse rather than being rewritten over and over.

Alongside such advances in software development, recent years have witnessed the emergence of open source software (OSS) development. OSS projects develop "software whose source code is distributed without charge or limitations on possible modifications and distributions by third parties" (Crowston and Scozzi, 2002: 3). In most cases, the development of OSS is entirely global and is voluntarily carried out by individuals sometimes through the application of component-based development principles such as the use of JavaBeans. While there are some similarities between OSS and commercially driven globally distributed CBD projects in terms of the application of specific methodologies and development tools, being a commercially driven effort as opposed to the voluntary process associated with OSS (Murugesan, 1999), project managers of globally distributed CBD can consider aspects relating to the way a component will be developed that ensure that the challenges reported above relating to coordination breakdowns across remote sites will be minimized.

In this regard, the adoption of CBD by globally distributed software development teams has indeed created expectations that some coordination breakdowns associated with the traditional, non-CB globally distributed software development would be mitigated (Carmel, 1999) through the organization of distributed work. For example, it has been argued that each site could take ownership of a particular component to develop it independently, with a reduced degree of intersite communication and coordination (Repenning *et al.*, 2001). Indeed, this process would facilitate the globalization of the software industry, as components could be developed remotely with minimum intersite coordination (Turnlund, 2004; Repenning *et al.*, 2001).

From a knowledge processes viewpoint, such an approach, in which each site takes responsibility for the development of a particular component, may result in fewer opportunities for the entire project team to share knowledge about existing components available for reuse. Research has indeed shown that the knowledge embedded in a design can be contextual and specific to a particular business context to the extent that the transfer of any solution, be it a component or a programme, from one project team to another often requires intensive communications between members of these teams (Oshri and Newell, 2005). This is because in most cases a component will need to be modified before being reapplied in another product. Against past expectations that CBD would result in fewer communication and coordination activities, we claim that in pursuing CBD principles, remote teams are more likely to intensify their communication and coordination activities in an attempt to increase the reuse rate of existing components.

Table 7.1 summarizes the issues revolving around coordination, communication, and knowledge processes in global traditional (non-CB) software development and in global CBD projects.

To illustrate our claim, evidence from two globally distributed CB software development projects is presented below. First, evidence relating to the way components were developed within these projects is outlined; then the capabilities developed by these companies are analyzed and discussed.

About this research

An in-depth case study of three globally distributed CBD projects – two at TATA Consultancy Services (TCS) and one at LeCroy – was carried out. We adopted a qualitative, interpretive approach. The main goal of the empirical research was to explore:

1. Which division of work approach (e.g. one site owns a particular component, or a joint development utilizing expertise regardless of its geographical location) was implemented by TCS and

LeCroy, and how this division of work affected intersite coordination efforts between remote sites
2. What capabilities were critical in supporting component reuse in the globally distributed CBD environment.

Evidence was gathered through a variety of sources, such as interviews, documentation, and archival records (Yin, 1994; Eisenhardt, 1989). Interviews were conducted at two remote sites per company: in Switzerland, India, and the US for TCS, and in Switzerland and the US for LeCroy. Background information about TCS and LeCroy can be found in the Appendix. Interviewees were chosen to include (i) counterparts working closely from remote locations, and (ii) diverse roles such as managers and developers. In total, 20 individuals were interviewed (14 at TCS and 6 at LeCroy: see additional information about the interviewees in the Appendix). Interviews lasted 1 hour and 30 minutes on average; they were recorded and fully transcribed. A semi-structured interview protocol was applied to allow the researchers to clarify specific issues and follow up with questions. Data were triangulated through interviews with team counterparts in different locations and through the use of project documents. Data analysis followed several steps. It relied on iterative reading of the data using the open-coding technique (Strauss and Corbin, 1998), and sorting and refining themes emerging from the data with some degree of diversity (Miles and Huberman, 1994).

Component-based development: Expertise-based or location-based division of work

Despite the expectation that CBD would enable a division of work based on *geographical location*, in which one site takes responsibility for the development of a particular component, thus reducing the need for intersite coordination required to complete a particular development (Repenning *et al.*, 2001), evidence from both TCS and LeCroy suggests that dividing the work based on *technical or functional expertise* enabled these companies to achieve a high rate of component reuse and product variation. In addition, a division of work based on expertise enabled them to utilize the knowledge and expertise of their employees regardless of their geographical location,

Table 7.1 Challenges in global software development projects

	Global non-CB software development	Global CB software development	
	Challenges	Expectations	New challenges
Coordination	Breakdown of traditional coordination mechanisms (Rafii, 1995; Espinosa and Carmel, 2003; Cheng et al., 2004) Lack of complete picture about what is going on at remote locations (Carmel, 1999) Difficulties to work in different time zones (Karolak, 1999; Kobitzsch et al., 2001) Delays in distributed collaborative work processes (Jarvenpaa and Leidner, 1999; Herbsleb et al., 2000) Different tools, technologies, ICT infrastructure (Sarker and Sahay, 2004)	Each site could take ownership of particular components and work on them independently without much need for inter site coordination (Carmel, 1999; Colbert et al., 2001; Repenning et al., 2001)	Even when remote sites had ownership of particular components, extensive inter site coordination was required (IBM case in Carmel, 1999) Difficulties to manage a complex integration process across sites if components are fine grained (Turnlund, 2004) A concern raised in recent studies that there is a need to coordinate onsite–offshore activities related to component development, modification, and integration (Alexandersen et al., 2003)
Communication	Loss of communication richness (Carmel, 1999) Language barriers (Sarker and Sahay, 2003)	Opportunity to reduce communication needs between sites as each site is working on different components (Colbert et al., 2001; Repenning et al., 2001)	Remote sites know less about specific and contextual knowledge embedded in solutions Remote sites know less about the area of specialization of their remote counterparts

	Misunderstandings caused by cultural differences (Battin et al., 2001; Olson and Olson, 2004) Lack of informal, inter-personal communications (Herbsleb and Mockus, 2003)	Remote sites possess limited knowledge of the "big picture", i.e. new developments in other sites are less visible
Knowledge processes	Lack of understanding of counterpart's context (Orlikowski, 2002) Asymmetry in distributing information among sites (Carmel, 1999) Lack of trust and motivat on to collaborate (Jarvenpaa and Leidner, 1999)	Intensive knowledge processes within remote sites and fewer across remote sites	Risk of "reinventing the wheel" if intersite coordination and communication activities are reduced Differences in the specialization domains developed in each site, e.g. site A specializes in the banking sector while site B specializes in the insurance sector. This could hinder the development of complementary solutions and the implementation of agility in design that offers future integration of existing solutions Differences in the level of technical expertise developed within sites that could hamper the quality of knowledge transfer processes from team A to B when a particular component is reused

thus allowing these companies to access the pool of expertise available in offshore locations. Lastly, an expertise-based division of work approach required remote engineers and managers to interact and consult with remote counterparts in order to solve design issues.

In dividing the work between the sites, some ground rules were followed. For example, at TCS the first activities that required direct customer contact and access to the customer's site, such as user requirements and release management, were done *onsite*. Self-contained activities, such as coding and unit testing, were, on the other hand, sent *offshore*, to take advantage of the cost, quality, and availability of offshore personnel. As one interviewee explained, the onsite team was sending requirements offshore: "Because the expertise and major source code are here [offshore, in Gurgaon], and mainly because of the expertise, it is quicker and easier to work here" (Pankaj, TCS).

The composition of the onsite team included experts who provided expertise in those areas required at the customer location. One manager described the areas of expertise developed onsite:

> Technical people look at technical and architectural issues, functional people look at the functionality and the development of the functionality. Support people handle the configuration management, the Groupware, the other various tools which are being used by the team. (Sanjay, TCS)

On the other hand, activities that required involvement of the client and close interactions among the TCS developers were conducted in a mixed onsite–offshore manner. Overall, the majority of the activities required extensive communications, and onsite and offshore teams conducted them jointly through frequent communications using ICTs and visits to remote sites. The only activities that were done independently at the offshore location were coding and unit testing.

At LeCroy the division of work was also based on the technical domains (areas of expertise) of the engineers. Anthony, LeCroy's Chief Software Architect, describes the division of work in the following way: "What happened was, part of it was based on who was free at that time, and part of it was where the expertise was."

The software team in Geneva was responsible for most of the original core code in the oscilloscope: these were the developers who had written the original code for oscilloscopes since the mid 1980s. Anthony continued: "So they were also the natural guys to work on the next generation, or defining the next generation."

Maine was another location where the architect of the product was based and who collaborated with the team. This person had worked in New York for many years and had spent a year working in Geneva. In 1999 his family decided to move back to Maine and telecommute from there. Jon, a system architect, moved to Maine, and from there he simply carried on the work that he had been doing in Geneva.

Originally five people, Jon in Maine and four people in Geneva, developed the basics of the Maui. Later on in the development process, additional people in New York and Geneva started to work on the new platform, jointly developing new features. This approach to development required a high utilization of the Integrated Development Environment and the employment of collaborative technologies. As the manager of Geneva team pointed out:

> We use MSN Messenger – every member of the software development group appears on the list. So, for having a chat with someone, wherever they may be in the world in the given time, you just need to double-click on their name and start typing a line. (Anthony, LeCroy)

To summarize, both companies, TCS and LeCroy, have chosen to utilize the expertise available within their globally distributed CBD projects regardless of their geographical locations. In doing so, the companies recognize the need to develop capabilities that will allow these teams to jointly develop software components based on CBD principles.

Capabilities supporting globally distributed component-based software development

The division of work approach pursued by TCS and LeCroy posed these companies new challenges. In particular, as these companies attempted to reuse components across different projects (for TCS) and products (for LeCroy), and improve product flexibility through the application of CBD principles, three areas had become critical in achieving success: (i) intersite coordination, (ii) knowledge management, and (iii) communication channels.

Intersite coordination capabilities

Two areas of capabilities were developed by TCS and LeCroy that supported intersite coordination activities. The first area, which is generic in nature, involved a high-speed, wide-band ICT infrastructure that ensured connectivity between remote sites. The ICT infrastructure supported rapid access to the network, shared resources (e.g. server and project repository, databases), and Web access to common resources. For example, as Corey LeCroy (Vice-President of Information Systems) outlined:

> The role of the WAN, server and applications pool, how file shares are set up, conferencing tools, and just plain network speed are of very high importance . . . and no firm trying to execute globally distributed CBD successfully can do so without the right infrastructure.

The second area of capabilities was developed mainly in-house to support joint development activities carried out across remote sites, without increasing the intersite coordination overhead. These included the following capabilities:

- *Automated management of interdependencies between components and related files.* This capability allows for managing dependencies between components. Managing these interdependencies is not a problem as long as the number of components is small, because in such a case the dependencies can be modelled and understood visually. However, when the number of components becomes high, visual understanding is no longer an option. To manage interdependencies between a high number of components, LeCroy developed an in-house tool that supported rapid update of changes, four times a day, by automatically building components that had changed since the last "build", thus utilizing time-zone differences. One manager from LeCroy explained:

> We have a server that builds four times a day all the components, and produces "release binaries". So I don't have to build every component locally. If someone changes the hardcopy component and they put it back, it will be rebuilt on the server and then in the morning I can import that component and just use it. (Larry, LeCroy)

This capability allowed developers from NY and Geneva to access the latest versions of the development files when they started their working day.

- *Bug tracking capability.* The complexity involved in developing components from several remote locations created new challenges in terms of tracking bugs and managing versions of components and products. This is because each single bug being reported required its source to be tracked and traced (i.e. whether it had originated from one of the customers or from an internal development team), and required the location of all the components in which this particular code was reused. In CBD there is a need to trace bugs on three different levels: first, on the system level, where customers report problems with their specific product; second, on the product level, where errors are detected in a specific product version; and finally, on the component level, where the fault is located. The need to trace bugs is closely related to version and configuration management, because any modification in the component could lead to an upsurge of new versions of different products which already exist in several versions (see a similar claim by Crnkovic and Larsson, 2002). Therefore, it is imperative to carefully record links between components, products, and systems so that tracing errors on all levels is possible. This requirement may not be unique to CBD; however, what is specific to the component-based approach is the mapping between products and components and the management of error reports on product and component level, which is the most difficult part of the management involved in CBD (*ibid.*). Indeed, for bug tracking TCS used a combination of tools: MS-Access for issues registration and resolution, and PVCS Tracker for defect logging, tracking, and analysis. At LeCroy, for instance, the use of automated tools for bug tracking helped to speed up the development by utilizing time-zone differences. As the manager of the Geneva team explained: "I would not say that time differences are a disadvantage, and close to a release or big milestone they can be a big advantage. Because problems, bug fixing, can be passed on from time zone to time zone" (Anthony, LeCroy).

- *Standardization and centralization of the tools and methods* across locations was perceived as imperative by TCS and LeCroy for the effectiveness of component reuse, mainly because software development activities such as building and testing a code could be carried out on the central server. Some of the technologies implemented to facilitate this capability are: Web access, replicated databases, and a single (integrated) development environment. To facilitate the standardization of processes and learning among newcomers, TCS and LeCroy created a Guide that explains how to use tools and methods.

Knowledge management capabilities

Ensuring a high degree of component reuse requires knowledge management capabilities. One key challenge that TCS faced, for example, was that several Quartz implementation projects for different clients were running in parallel, and the people involved in different Quartz implementations did not have a direct exposure to the work that other project teams were engaged in. Therefore, several knowledge management mechanisms were introduced by TCS that facilitated the transfer and reuse of components across product teams. For example, TCS created a new role in the form of a *programme manager*, who coordinated all Quartz implementations and was aware of new components being developed for a specific customer, and who facilitated the reuse of components across different Quartz implementations at different geographical locations. This way, TCS exploited customer-specific components by adding them to the Quartz package, so that, with each new Quartz implementation, TCS increased the variety of components/functionalities that this product offered to potential clients. For example, after implementing Quartz at Royal Skandia UK, an insurance company, where Quartz was implemented as an investment engine, insurance products were added to the next version of Quartz:

> A lot of changes were made to the basic Quartz system just to be able to integrate it with the insurance business. We had to build in a lot of things that deal with policy administration and policy distribution, which are not particularly bank products. This way typical insurance products were added to Quartz: they were released as the next version of Quartz. (Sanjay, TCS)

To facilitate the reuse of knowledge and components in a globally distributed environment, engineers were encouraged to rotate between onsite and offshore locations to bridge knowledge gaps between the two sites.

LeCroy, on the other hand, developed a "component toolbox," a *repository of components* that implemented functionalities common to the oscilloscopes and oscilloscope-like instruments. These components included (i) hundreds of mathematical functions, one component per functionality; (ii) Graphical User Interface components that provide the user interface; (iii) core components that allow the systems to work together and provide the basic instrument capabilities; and (iv) acquisition board driver components responsible for controlling the acquisition hardware of an oscilloscope.

Based on this knowledge management system, a specific oscilloscope could be built by selecting and integrating these components with oscilloscope-specific acquisition and application systems. Furthermore,

LeCroy introduced an integrated development environment on the central server, accessible for all members of the dispersed team. Centralization of tools in one location ensures one single environment for all remote locations. For the LeCroy software team, there are no "local" tools as such: all are located at one central place. For example:

> Version Control System (VCS) – Perforce – exists in Geneva and guys access it here [in New York] the same way over WAN, so the only difference there is: from here it takes a little longer to access it, speed is slower. It doesn't matter where you are in the world, you still can access the same single VCS. (Anthony, LeCroy)

Indeed, managing knowledge across sites required both companies to invest in unique repositories but also to identify individuals from the globally distributed teams who could share the knowledge created in one team with the others. By doing so, TCS, for example, was able to develop quickly its Quartz platform and offer solutions in new or related markets. Enabling knowledge flow between remote sites to increase the possibilities of reuse was also largely supported by the communication capabilities developed by TCS and LeCroy.

Communication channels

In light of the division of work applied by both TCS and LeCroy, the development of communication channels and capabilities that ensure the flow of information with minimum breakdowns and misunderstandings between remote sites was considered critical in their globally distributed CBD environments. To cope with this challenge, both TCS and LeCroy encouraged *frequent communications* between remote members and introduced design rules aiming to make communications more effective. For example, these companies encouraged systematic and frequent communications in the form of regular teleconferences between software managers in dispersed locations, and transatlantic videoconferences with the entire team, every one or two months. Such communications helped to coordinate expertise across locations and utilize better the dispersed knowledge. For example, as the onsite manager of the Dresdner project explained: "Between us [offshore] and our onsite team we say 'we'll do this portion of the job because we have more competent people here who can look at this part, and you can look at that portion of the job.' It's mutual communication" (Sunil, TCS).

This helped to streamline information flows between dispersed teams. In addition, attention was given to *improving the style and content of communications*, which helped to reduce misunderstandings and confusion induced by different cultural backgrounds. This was particularly important for the LeCroy global team, where people from different cultures collaborated over distance. For example, as one interviewee explained:

> I have a lot of experience working with a lot of foreign cultures. In some cultures if you are on the phone explaining something to somebody and they don't understand it – they still say "I understand." So the way I try to ensure that the information was received correctly is through a very detailed process of describing the issue. For example I say, "open this Web link. What do you see?" So it is very specific, very detailed. (Adrian, LeCroy)

Both companies encouraged *working flexibility*, in terms of working conditions, e.g. working from home, and working hours, which helped increase the overlap of working hours between dispersed locations so that teams could collaborate in real time.

Reuse at LeCroy and TCS: Some evidence

Both companies utilized the benefits offered by CBD, such as the ability to reuse components and to build product families rapidly by developing capabilities in the areas of intersite coordination, knowledge management, and communication. LeCroy's Maui CB architecture (platform) served as a basis for a number of future products, helped to reduce considerably time-to-market (an increased number of products offered to a market per year), and made possible the easy integration of LeCroy products with additional functionalities developed by third parties. After the first product (i.e. WaveMaster) based on the Maui architecture was launched in January, 2002, a large number of WaveMaster models and Disk Drive Analyzers, which are based on the Maui platform, were released, all as a result of a rapid recombination and reuse of existing components. In January, 2003, LeCroy launched the WavePro Oscilloscope series (7000, 7100, and 7300), which is also based on the Maui platform.

TCS Quartz CB architecture also supported the reuse of components across different implementations by adding customer-specific components to the Quartz package. Since the first Quartz implementation project started in 1998, Quartz has now been implemented in over 40 clients, and the platform has grown to include three different product families: Quartz Securities, Quartz Payments, and Quartz Financial. Furthermore, in the last three years, Quartz has been ranked among top 25 best-selling banking systems by the *International Banking Systems Journal.*

Discussion and implications

Before discussing the cases, it is important to note that our findings are based on two case studies and therefore, by definition, meet to only a limited extent the criteria of transferability (the extent to which the findings can be replicated across cases). Additional research across multiple case studies is needed in order to verify the insights reported in this chapter. With this in mind we can explore the approach to coordinating work and the capabilities developed by the studied companies, recognizing that not all the practices implemented by TCS and LeCroy would be appropriate in the context of other globally distributed CBD projects.

In developing these capabilities, TCS and LeCroy mainly focused on how to improve the rate of reuse when implementing CBD in globally distributed software development projects. To improve the rate of reuse of components, TCS and LeCroy followed an approach in which the development of components is jointly carried out by several remote sites instead of the more commonly found approach in which each site takes responsibility for a particular component. Managers from LeCroy and TCS indicated that while the approach in which dispersed sites jointly develop components requires a higher degree of coordination between dispersed project teams and intensified communication between remote counterparts, it also offers advantages in the form of knowledge integration (Walz *et al.*, 1993) and knowledge sharing (Kotlarsky and Oshri, 2005) across the various sites, processes that are imperative for component reuse. Against past expectations that CBD would mainly focus on developing component knowledge within particular teams (Colbert *et al.*, 2001; Repenning *et al.*, 2001), this study has illustrated how TCS and LeCroy have invested in developing component knowledge within and *across dispersed teams* to ensure that critical knowledge of components is available at more than one site. Through coordination mechanisms such as the automated management of interdependencies between components and standardized tools, remote counterparts were able to easily access work done in a different location and to continue the development or debugging of a particular component. This across-site participation in development and debugging activities assisted in expanding the knowledge relating to a particular component beyond the boundaries of the site involved. Furthermore, for remote teams who often work on several projects in parallel, this deeper familiarity with a particular component meant that they could assess the possibilities of reusing this component in other products or markets. For this reason, putting in place mechanisms that supported the sharing of component knowledge across various sites was critical to promoting component reuse at TCS and LeCroy.

The communication mechanisms implemented by both TCS and LeCroy further supported knowledge sharing and integration needed for component reuse. In line with the approach that component knowledge should be jointly developed across sites, TCS and LeCroy promoted the use of various communication methods (e.g. videoconferencing, chats, short- and long-term relocations). Communication styles were designed to ensure that remote sites would be able to understand each other and share component knowledge, despite language barriers and cultural diversity. As stated above, past studies anticipated that CBD principles would indeed reduce the need to communicate between sites. Our study suggests that in order to achieve a high rate of reuse, remote sites actually need to maintain a high degree of communication and utilize various means of communication in order to ensure that component knowledge is shared and the possibilities of reuse are improved.

Lastly, the implementation of certain knowledge management practices also contributed to the reuse achieved by these companies. In seeking to reuse components and by utilizing expertise residing in a project team regardless of its geographical location, these companies pursued an approach that promoted the capturing and distribution of explicit component knowledge as well as the sharing of tacit knowledge acquired through participation and involvement (Lave and Wenger, 1991). Indeed, TCS and LeCroy invested in mechanisms that captured both the explicit knowledge (e.g. via component repository) and tacit knowledge (e.g. via program managers) of a particular component, acknowledging the complexity involved in transferring knowledge between remote sites. In this regard, explicit knowledge about various components was captured and shared between remote sites through the codification and storage of design documents and components in a central repository. These documents and components could be retrieved by the entire global team in their search for reusable components. Tacit knowledge was acquired by the programme manager through his or her involvement in the design of various components, a process that allowed this person to develop understanding and reuse knowledge about markets, existing in-house solutions, and their suitability for emerging business opportunities, something that can hardly be codified and captured.

The capabilities developed by TCS and LeCroy are summarized in Table 7.2. Furthermore, we outline the benefits expected from a component reuse viewpoint when implementing these capabilities in globally distributed CB teams. While the evidence presented here is unique in the context of CBD in globally distributed teams, these capabilities are still firm-specific and therefore may vary from one company to another.

What implications does this study have for research and practice? From a research viewpoint, against the expectations of past studies, this study illustrates how globally distributed CBD project teams may make the most of component reuse opportunities by pursuing an approach in which remote sites jointly develop components. Indeed, in this study the costs associated with intersite coordination and communication activities are likely to be higher; however, the possibilities to reuse components can also be improved should companies invest in capabilities that promote knowledge sharing and knowledge integration activities. We further claim that intensive communication activities between globally distributed CBD remote teams may lead to the development of a "virtual shared memory" of the entire team, contributing to component reuse processes. In this regard, we align our findings with the emerging body of studies on Transactive Memory in the context of globally distributed teams. Transactive Memory as a concept highlights the need to build a shared memory in which person A knows what person B knows. Through such knowledge activities, often promoted through the utilization of various communication means, team and product performance could be improved (Akgun et al., 2005; Moreland and Myaskovsky, 2000), including the sharing and reuse of knowledge (Majchrzak and Malhotra, 2004; Faraj and Sproull, 2000).

In addition, in line with past research (Galliers and Swan, 1997; Land and Kennedy-McGregor, 1987) we have learned that globally distributed teams at TCS and LeCroy have often discovered opportunities to reuse existing components through involvement in development and via informal communication channels, and not always through formal knowledge management systems. Furthermore, the joint development of a particular component by several remote sites may impel a higher degree of standardization in terms of development tools, project methodologies, procedures, and documents, which is imperative in itself for CB software development. Indeed, some interviewees indicated that the

Table 7.2 Capabilities developed by TCS and LeCroy supporting globally distributed CBD

Capabilities implemented by TCS and LeCroy	Characteristics	Benefits
Inter site coordination capabilities		
Automated management of interdependencies between components and related files	Automatically building components that have changed since the last "build", four times a day, on the central server	Rapid update of changes: Members of dispersed teams have access to work done at remote site; they are aware of reusable components being developed elsewhere. Time-zone differences are utilized by programming "builds" of components to run during night time
Bug tracking across products and projects on system, product and component levels	Setting up bug tracking tool on the central server, enabling Web access	All components and products that are affected by the bug can be identified
Standardization of tools and methods across locations	Using similar tools and methods across dispersed locations, creating a Guide that explains how to use methods and tools	Ensuring compatibility and "integratibility" of files, components, and applications developed and used at remote locations speeds up the learning among newcomers
Centralization of tools	Centralizing tools used by dispersed team members on a central server, Web-access, Integrated Development Environment	Members of dispersed teams always work with updated files and have access to updated project and product documents
Knowledge management capabilities		
Component repository accessible from all dispersed locations	Creating repository of reusable components that implement functions common to majority of products	Enabling knowledge reuse across products Reducing time-to-market through reuse of existing components Increasing product variety Avoiding "not invented here" syndrome

(Continued)

Table 7.2 (Continued)

Capabilities implemented by TCS and LeCroy	Characteristics	Benefits
Program manager	Appointing program manager to have overview of all components being developed for different clients	Enabling knowledge reuse across projects Increasing product variety through reuse of customer–specific components in future products
Communication channels and capabilities		
Frequent communications	Organizing systematic and frequent communications between managers and developers of dispersed teams using online chat, email, teleconferencing, and videoconferencing	Streamlining information flows and coordinate activities between dispersed teams Time-zone differences are utilized by handing over bugs and some small tasks between the teams
Improving the style and content of communications	Adjusting style and content of communication (e.g. wording and selection of media) to personal and cultural characteristics of remote counterparts	Improving understanding between remote counterparts Reducing possibility of misunderstandings and conflicts
Working flexibility	Supporting flexible working conditions, e.g. equipment to enable working from home and flexible working hours	Enabling remote counterparts to collaborate in real time by increasing overlap in working hours

dispersed and yet highly integrated development process of components resulted in a set of standardized tools, procedures, and documents. In turn, a well-developed set of standardized tools, templates, and procedures may further improve the possibilities to reuse component knowledge.

Considering the exploratory nature of this study, we submit that our main contribution revolves around a number of pragmatic guidelines to companies that consider the application of CBD principles in their globally distributed environments. A theory related to CBD in globally distributed environments may emerge should future research confirm the findings reported in this study by conducting cross-industry surveys and

testing the relationship between the capabilities reported above and the success criteria of globally distributed CB software development projects.

While this case highlights the benefits associated with the joint development of a particular component regardless of the geographical location of the expertise, in practice we suggest that project managers should first assess whether such an approach is in their interest. Indeed, both TCS and LeCroy sought to improve the rate of reuse of their components and therefore pursued an approach that advanced knowledge sharing and knowledge integration across remote sites. In this regard, project managers should evaluate the objectives of their project to determine whether achieving cost efficiencies, often gained by outsourcing development activities to low-cost locations such as India, is more important than the investment in a long-term development of shared knowledge and reuse capabilities. A hybrid approach, in which some development activities will be jointly carried out across the remote sites and other activities will be centralized and accomplished in one location, is another possibility. In terms of the capabilities needed to support a joint development effort of a particular component across several sites, based on the evidence from TCS and LeCroy, Table 7.2 offers project managers some capabilities in the areas of the intersite coordination, communications, and knowledge management required for the sharing of knowledge and the reuse of components in CBD environments. Last but not least, we suggest that managers attempt to appoint project members based on their shared histories of collaboration in their area of expertise. In this way, members of a dispersed team will know each other, and their respective and shared communication and coordination routines, from past projects. Through such staffing strategies, the costs associated with intersite communication and coordination activities can be reduced, and the challenges associated with intersite coordination and communication activities can be overcome, while knowledge sharing and component reuse can be improved.

References

Akgun, A. E., Byrne, J., Keskin, H., Lynn, G. S., and Imamoglu, S. Z. (2005) "Knowledge Networks in New Product Development Projects: A Transactive Memory Perspective," *Information & Management*, 42(8), 1105–20.

Alexandersen, C., Kumar, K., and van Hillegersberg, J. (2003) *Bank-in-a-Box: Skandia's Agile and Customizable Financial Services Platform*, Society for Information Management (SIM), Chicago.

Bass, L., Buhman, C., Comella-Dorda, S., Long, F., Robert, J., Seacord, R., and Wallnau, K. (2000) *Market Assessment of Component-Based Software Engineering*, vol. I, Carnegie Mellon Software Engineering Institute (SEI), Chicago.

Battin, R. D., Crocker, R., and Kreidler, J. (2001) "Leveraging Resources in Global Software Development," *IEEE Software*, 18(2), 70–7.

Carmel, E. (1999) *Global Software Teams: Collaborating across Borders and Time Zones*, Prentice-Hall, Upper Saddle River, NJ.

Carmel, E. and Agarwal, R. (2002) "The Maturation of Offshore Sourcing of Information Technology Work," *MIS Quarterly Executive*, 1(2), 65–77.

Cheng, L., De Souza, C. R. B., Hupfer, S., Patterson, J., and Ross, S. (2004) "Building Collaboration into IDEs," *Queue*, 1(9), 40–50.

Clements, P. C. (1995) "From Subroutines to Subsystems: Component-Based Software Development," *From the American Programmer*, 8(11), 1–8.

Colbert, R. O., Compton, D. S., Hackbarth, R. L., Herbsleb, J. D., Hoadley, L. A., and Wills, G. J. (2001) "Advanced Services: Changing How We Communicate," *Bell Labs Technical Journal*, 6(1), 211–28.

Cramton, C. D. (2001) "The Mutual Knowledge Problem and Its Consequences for Dispersed Collaboration," *Organization Science*, 12(3), 346–71.

Crnkovic, I. and Larsson, M. (2002) "Challenges of Component-Based Development," *The Journal of Systems and Software*, (61), 201–12.

Crowston, K. and Scozzi, B. (2002) "Open Source Software Projects as Virtual Organizations: Competency Rallying for Software Development," *IEE Proceedings – Software*, 149(1), 3–17.

DeSouza, K. C. and Evaristo, J. R. (2004) "Managing Knowledge in Distributed Projects," *Communications of the ACM*, 47(4), 87–91.

Ebert, C. and De Neve, P. (2001) "Surviving Global Software Development," *IEEE Software*, 18(2), 62–9.

Eisenhardt, K. M. (1989) "Building Theories from Case Study Research," *Academy of Management Review*, 14(4), 532–50.

Espinosa, A. and Carmel, E. (2003) "Modeling Coordination Costs Due to Time Separation in Global Software Teams," Workshop on Global Software Development, International Conference on Software Engineering (ICSE), Portland, Oregon, US.

Faraj, S. and Sproull, L. (2000) "Coordinating Expertise in Software Development Teams," *Management Science*, 46(12), 1554–68.

Galliers, R. D. and Swan, J. A. (1997) "Against Structured Approaches: Information Requirements Analysis as a Socially Mediated Process,"

The Thirtieth Annual Hawaii International Conference on System Sciences, Hawaii.

Herbsleb, J. D. and Mockus, A. (2003) "An Empirical Study of Speed and Communication in Globally-Distributed Software Development," *IEEE Transactions on Software Engineering*, 29(6), 1–14.

Herbsleb, J. D., Mockus, A., Finholt, T. A., and Grinter, R. E. (2000) "Distance, Dependencies, and Delay in Global Collaboration," Conference on Computer Supported Cooperative Work, Philadelphia, PA.

Herbsleb, J. D. and Moitra, D. (2001) "Global Software Development," *IEEE Software*, 18(2), 16–20.

Huang, J. C., Newell, S., Galliers, R. D., and Pan, S. L. (2003) "Dangerous Liaisons? Component-Based Development and Organizational Subcultures," *IEEE Transactions on Engineering Management*, 50(1), 89–99.

Jarvenpaa, S. L., Knoll, K., and Leidner, D. E. (1998) "Is Anybody out There? Antecedents of Trust in Global Virtual Teams," *Journal of MIS*, 14(4), 29–64.

Jarvenpaa, S. L. and Leidner, D. E. (1999) "Communication and Trust in Global Virtual Teams," *Organization Science*, 10(5), 791–815.

Karolak, D. W. (1999) *Global Software Development: Managing Virtual Teams and Environments, IEEE Computer Society Press, Los Angeles, CA.*

Kim, S. D. (2002) "Lessons Learned from a Nationwide CBD Promotion Project," *Communications of the ACM*, 45(10), 83–7.

Kobitzsch, W., Rombach, D., and Feldmann, R. L. (2001) "Outsourcing in India," *IEEE Software*, 18(2), 78–86.

Kotlarsky, J. and Oshri, I. (2005) "Social Ties, Knowledge Sharing and Successful Collaboration in Globally Distributed System Development Projects," *European Journal of Information Systems*, 14(1), 37–48.

Kunda, D. and Brooks, L. (2000) "Assessing Organisational Obstacles to Component-Based Development: A Case Study Approach," *Information and Software Technology*, 42: 715–25.

Land, F. F. and Kennedy-McGregor, M. (1987) "Information and Information Systems: Concepts and Perspectives," in *Information Analysis: Selected Readings* (Ed., Galliers, R. D.) Addison-Wesley, Reading, MA.

Lave, J. and Wenger, E. (1991) *Situated Learning Legitimate Peripheral Participation*, Cambridge University Press, Cambridge.

Majchrzak, A. and Malhotra, A. (2004) "Virtual Workspace Technology Use and Knowledge-Sharing Effectiveness in Distributed Teams: The Influence of a Team's Transactive Memory". Knowledge Management

Knowledge Base DOI: *www.knowledgemanagement.ittoolbox.com*, accessed 26 September 2007.

Malhotra, A., Majchrzak, A., Carman, R., and Lott, V. (2001) "Radical Innovation Without Collocation: A Case Study at Boeing-Rocketdyne," *MIS Quarterly*, 25(2), 229–49.

Miles, M. B. and Huberman, A. M. (1994) *Qualitative Data Analysis: An Expanded Sourcebook*, Sage Publications, Thousand Oaks, CA.

Mockus, A. and Weiss, D. M. (2001) "Globalization by Chunking: A Quantitative Approach," *IEEE Software*, 18(2), 30–7.

Moreland, R. L. and Myaskovsky, L. (2000) "Exploring the Performance Benefits of Groups Training: Transactive Memory or Improved Communication?" *Organizational Behavior and Human Decision Processes*, 82(1), 117–33.

Murugesan, S. (1999) "Leverage Global Software Development and Distribution Using the Internet and Web," *Cutter IT Journal*, 12(3), 57–63.

Olin, J. G., Greis, N. P., and Kasarda, J. D. (1999) "Knowledge Management Across Multi-tier Enterprise: The Promise of Intelligent Software in the Auto Industry," *European Management Journal*, 17(4), 335–47.

Olson, J. S. and Olson, G. M. (2004) "Culture Surprises in Remote Software Development Teams," *Queue*, 1(9), 52–9.

Orlikowski, W. J. (2002) "Knowing in Practice: Enacting a Collective Capability in Distributed Organizing," *Organization Science*, 13(3), 249–73.

Oshri, I. and Newell, S. (2005) "Component Sharing in Complex Products and Systems: Challenges, Solutions and Practical Implications," *IEEE Transactions on Engineering Management*, 52(4), 509–21.

Peters, J. F. and Pedrycz, W. (2000) *Software Engineering: An Engineering Approach*, John Wiley, New York.

Rafii, F. (1995) "How Important Is Physical Collocation to Product Development Success?" *Business Horizons*, (January–February), 78–84.

Ravichandran, T. and Rothenberger, M. A. (2003) "Software Reuse Strategies and Component Markets," *Communications of the ACM*, 46(8), 109–14.

Repenning, A., Ioannidou, A., Payton, M., Ye, W., and Roschelle, J. (2001) "Using Components for Rapid Distributed Software Development," *IEEE Software*, 18(2), 38–45.

Sarker, S. and Sahay, S. (2003) "Understanding Virtual Team Development: An Interpretive Study," *Journal of the Association for Information Systems*, 4, 1–38.

Sarker, S. and Sahay, S. (2004) "Implications of Space and Time for Distributed Work: An Interpretive Study of US–Norwegian System Development Teams," *European Journal of Information Systems*, 13(1), 3–20.

Starr, M. K. (1965) "Modular Production: A New Concept," *Harvard Business Review*, 43 (November–December), 131–42.

Strauss, A. L. and Corbin, J. M. (1998) *Basics of Qualitative Research*, Sage, Thousand Oaks, CA.

Szyperski, C. (1998) *Component Software Beyond Object-Oriented Programming*, Addison-Wesley, New York.

Traas, V. and Hillegersberg, J. (2000) "The Software Component Market on the Internet: Current Status and Conditions for Growth," *ACM SIGSOFT*, 25(1), 114–17.

Turnlund, M. (2004) "Distributed Development Lessons Learned," *Queue*, 1(9), 26–31.

Ulrich, K. T. and Eppinger, S. D. (2000) *Product Design and Development*, McGraw-Hill, New York.

Vitharana, P. (2003) "Risks and Challenges of Component-Based Software Development," *Communications of the ACM*, 46(8), 67–72.

Walz, D. B., Elam, J. J., and Curtis, B. (1993) "Inside a Software Design Team: Knowledge Acquisition, Sharing, and Integration," *Communications of the ACM*, 36(10), 62–77.

Yenne, B. (2002) *Inside Boeing 777: Building The 777*, MBI Publishing Company, St Paul, Minnesota.

Yin, R. K. (1994) *Case Study Research: Design and Methods*, Sage, Newbury Park, CA.

CHAPTER 8

Developing congruent and actionable understandings in information systems development offshoring relations

Vinay Tiwari, Paul C. van Fenema, and Paul W. L. Vlaar

Introduction

The last decade has witnessed a sharp increase in offshore outsourcing activities (Hirschheim *et al.*, 2005), which Robinson and Kalakota (2004: 4) define as "the delegation or subcontracting of administrative, engineering, research, development, or technical support processes to a third-party vendor based in a low-cost location". Although such activities may entail numerous benefits, compared to conventional outsourcing, offshoring generally faces organizations with additional complications (Carmel and Tjia, 2005; King *et al.*, 2004).

Problems tend to be highest during requirements analysis, where incomplete representations of client demands and differences in perception and understanding among stakeholders are common (Newman and Robey, 1992; Corbin and Strauss, 1990). This is caused, amongst other factors, by differences in assumptions, backgrounds, and contexts (Kellogg *et al.*, 2006). Hitherto, little has been discovered about the resulting challenges: microlevel studies and empirical research on offshoring remain scarce. We therefore pose the following research question: *Which factors affect the development of congruent and actionable understandings in offshoring relations?*

A review of the literature on the construct of a congruent and actionable understanding and the means that can be used to advance such an understanding (see Sandberg and Targama, 2007; Vlaar *et al.*, 2007; Bechky, 2006, 2003; Carmel and Tjia, 2005; Cramton, 2001) suggests that the development of congruent and actionable understandings depends on at least five categories of factors: (1) social conditions; (2) social processes; (3) individual conditions; (4) individual processes; and (5) task and contextual characteristics.

We capture these categories in an integrative conceptual framework, which is illustrated by an exploratory case study involving a major US financial services firm and one of India's largest offshore IT outsourcing vendors. Although offshoring concerns a wide variety of tasks and projects (Couto *et al.*, 2006), we selected an outsourced ISD project. These projects are commonly known for their complexity and high risk of failure (Oza and Hall, 2005; King *et al.*, 2004; Sinha and Terdiman, 2002; Rajkumar and Dawley, 1997). By interviewing 18 vendor participants, both onsite and offshore, we solicited perceptions relating to requirements analysis procedures regarding four ISD modules.

The conceptual framework, which is supported by the results from our case study, addresses one of the main challenges involved with managing professional work in general (Sandberg and Targama, 2007) and ISD offshoring in particular (Vlaar *et al.*, 2007). It contributes to the literature by explicitly distinguishing five categories of factors influencing the development of congruent and actionable understandings among geographically dispersed stakeholders. Our framework distinguishes between the *social* and *individual* factors that may enable or inhibit the development of congruent and actionable understandings (e.g. see Sandberg and Targama, 2007). Furthermore, it complements some of the relatively static views on requirements analysis currently dominating the literature (see Cullen *et al.*, 2005), which focus on the *conditions* conducive to achieving congruent and actionable understandings, with an emphasis on the dynamic *processes* by which parties may improve their understandings over the course of ISD projects (consistent with Das and Teng, 2002; Doz, 1996). The results from the case study support our framework and suggest that researchers and practitioners should pay balanced attention to each of the factors influencing the development of understanding when engaging in or investigating global knowledge work, such as offshoring and new product development.

We first define the central concepts in our study: (i) requirements analysis, and (ii) congruent and actionable understandings. Subsequently, we elaborate on the effects that social, individual, task, and contextual factors have on these understandings. We then illustrate our conceptual framework with a rich and actual case study. In the discussion, we explore the theoretical and practical implications of our findings, and avenues for future research.

Conceptual background

In this section, we present the theoretical underpinnings of our study. After elaborating on requirements analysis and the importance of establishing congruent and actionable understandings in offshoring relationships, we develop a generic research model that captures the factors affecting the development of such understandings.

Requirements analysis in offshore ISD

We conceptualize requirements analysis as the framing of expectations among stakeholders related to the business value and technical properties of an information system (Davidson, 2002). It is considered the most important, yet most difficult, process in ISD. Requirements analysis may involve clients incapable of clarifying their needs, and analysts unable to elicit requirements (Salaway, 1987; Boland, 1978). Moreover, different stakeholders provide multiple perspectives with evolving interests and understandings that may result in deliverables that are incompatible with clients' expectations (Davidson, 2002). In addition, requirements analysis entails high levels of ambiguity, uncertainty, and anxiety, making it a critical and complex phase (Curtis *et al.*, 1988). In the context of offshoring, these problems tend to become more severe, as stakeholders are no longer co-located, reducing opportunities for face-to-face contact. Differences in culture, background, and experience aggravate issues of interaction and understanding (Kumar *et al.*, 2005; Carmel, 1999).

Compared to traditional outsourcing arrangements, offshoring is generally accompanied by a higher degree of insourcing, implying that part of the vendor staff is working at the client's office. Clients and vendors commonly seek to balance, on the one hand, the benefits from low offshore labour costs, while, on the other hand, recognizing the value of the onsite presence of vendor personnel to foster contacts with client representatives. This generally results in an indirect communication

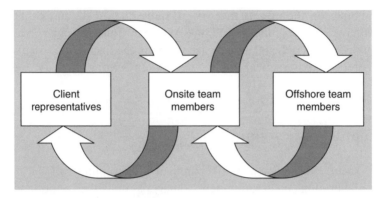

Figure 8.1   Communication flows in the client–onsite–offshore model

setup, as is reflected in Figure 8.1, which exacerbates the costs associated with coordination and control (García-Canal *et al.*, 2003; Herbsleb and Mockus, 2003; van Fenema, 2002; Carmel and Agarwal, 2002; Carmel, 1999). Due to these issues, the creation of congruent and actionable understandings becomes a fundamental issue for delivering requirements and developing systems in accordance with clients' expectations.

Congruent and actionable understandings

Understanding concerns an individual's imaginative capability (Spender, 1989, 1996). It implies that one focuses attention on a particular topic and invests mental efforts in developing meaningful and elaborate thoughts (Weick *et al.*, 2005; Bakhtin, 1986). This should reduce doubts and allow actors to understand *clearly* what needs to be done (Boland, 1978). In the context of ISD offshoring, understandings tend to assume a social character, as they involve joint accomplishments of onsite and offshore teams. In such cases, understandings should at least be congruent among different actors to enable organized action (Maitlis, 2005; Weick and Roberts, 1993; Donnellon *et al.*, 1986).

This does not imply that they need to be entirely the same: diverse interpretations and understandings among actors will always persist due to lasting differences in prior experience (Balogun and Johnson, 2004; Brown, 2004, 2000; Polanyi, 1958), bounded rationality (Simon, 1991), and differences in interests and objectives (Vlaar *et al.*, 2006). It rather means that several parties envision comparable work processes and outcomes. Along with congruence, understandings among clients and offshore and onsite vendor teams need to be actionable – they should enable orderly action in that they consist of "interpretations that are dissimilar but that have similar behavioral implications" (Donnellon *et al.*, 1986: 44). This enables stakeholders to act in a manner coherently tied to others' expectations (Maitlis, 2005; Weick, 1993).

Initially, requirements are usually elicited from clients by onsite vendor teams. Subsequently, they are communicated between onsite and offshore vendor teams in the form of documents and emails (Meadows, 1996; Krepchin, 1993). Based on the use of jargon, technical concepts, and generic conventions (Bowker and Star, 2002), recipients construct literal, "face-value" understandings of these texts (Boland, 1991: 453 as cited in Lee, 1994).

However, words and texts are also understood in terms of their contextuality (Kellogg *et al.*, 2006; Bechky, 2003; Cramton, 2001; Ngwenyama and Lee, 1997). As shown by Cramton (2001: 355), one of the problems inhibiting the development of mutual knowledge is "the failure to communicate and retain contextual information". Bechky (2003: 313) adds that "even when knowledge is made explicit in a codified routine, [and] when it is communicated across group boundaries, some organizational members may not understand it because they apply and interpret this knowledge within different contexts". The next section therefore explores how organizations deal with the challenge of developing congruent and actionable understandings.

Factors influencing the development of understandings

Based on the extant literature, (e.g. Felin and Hesterly, 2007; Hargadon and Bechky, 2006), we conceptualize five categories of factors influencing the development of congruent and actionable understandings: (1) social conditions; (2) social processes; (3) individual conditions; (4) individual processes; and (5) task and contextual characteristics (Figure 8.2). *Social conditions* pertain to, amongst other factors, the availability of resources, the division of work, cultural differences, and social group dynamics of power and peer pressure. *Social processes* may take the shape of sensegiving, sensemaking, sensedemanding, and sensebreaking. *Individual conditions* refer to, amongst other factors, one's accumulated experience, knowledge, and cognitive ability. *Individual processes* regard socio-cognitive mental processes such as representing, reflecting, and imagining. Finally, *task and context characteristics* include, for example, the complexity and ambiguity of a task, environmental change, and

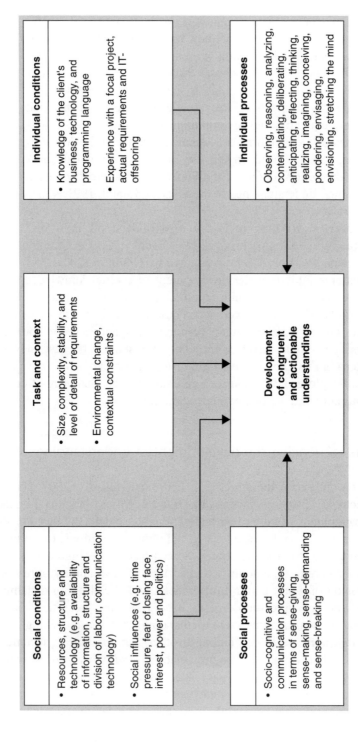

Figure 8.2 Factors affecting the development of congruent and actionable understandings

contextual constraints affecting the development of a person's under-standing. We now elaborate on these categories in more detail.

Social conditions and processes

Social conditions influence the development of congruent and actionable understandings, as they facilitate or constrain the interaction and comm-unication between stakeholders (Bhat *et al.*, 2006). These conditions include, amongst other factors, the availability of resources, the division of work among stakeholders, and the communication technologies that are used to exchange, create, and clarify requirements and deliverables by members of offshoring relationships. Social conditions affect the degree of information asymmetry among partners, the ease with which they communicate, and the availability, completeness, and ambiguity of information that is being shared among clients and vendor teams. Cultural differences among team members involved in a project introduce a range of interpretations and heterogeneous communication practices (e.g. Cramton, 2001).

The use of communicative technologies, such as messengers and video conferencing, for example, has been suggested to improve the interaction between distributed actors (Gasson, 2005). Social influence factors such as peer pressure, divergent interests, and power and politics, in contrast, have been argued to impede communication and the development of advanced understandings in ISD contexts (Wiegers, 2006).

Apart from social conditions, several authors have emphasized the importance of *social processes* for ISD projects (Ciborra and Lanzara, 1994; Walz *et al.*, 1993; Curtis *et al.*, 1988; Boland, 1978). In this respect, congruent and actionable understandings between different groups can be achieved by developing common ground and mutual knowledge (Bechky, 2003; Cramton, 2001). This may occur through the microlevel social processes of sensemaking, sensegiving, sensedemanding, and sensebreaking (Vlaar *et al.*, 2007). Sensemaking concerns the interactive processes by which participants construct accounts that constitute their comprehension of the world and enables them to act collectively (Maitlis, 2005; Rouleau, 2005; Weick *et al.*, 1993).

These efforts tend to be undertaken in concert with acts of sensegiving, which are aimed at influencing "the sensemaking and meaning construction of others towards a preferred redefinition of organizational reality" (Gioia and Chittipeddi, 1991: 442). Sensegiving may involve providing stakeholders with descriptions and explanations and creating opportunities for interaction that help others to make sense (Maitlis, 2005; Weick, 1995). This process is enabled by individual conditions, such as "the possession of discursive ability", as well as social conditions, such as the time and the opportunity that stakeholders have to engage in sensegiving (Maitlis and Lawrence, 2007).

Stakeholders in offshoring relationships may also try to arrive at more congruent and actionable understandings by demanding sense from other participants or by "breaking" (i.e. challenging) existing understandings held by others (see Vlaar *et al.*, 2007). Sensedemanding involves, for instance, cross-checking one's own perceptions and interpretations with those of participants from another team or organization (Maitlis and Lawrence, 2007; Weick, 2001; Roberts and Moore, 1993; Daft and Weick, 1984), actively eliciting information from counterparts (Quinn and Dutton, 2005; Ramirez *et al.*, 2002) and continuously requesting confirmation (Vlaar *et al.*, 2007).

In addition, sensebreaking implies an attempt to unsettle or problematize existing understandings that are incongruent with those of others or that are inactionable. This social process involves the destruction or breaking down of others' understandings, helping them to "question the bases on which they have been acting", and interrupting any undesirable courses of action they may have undertaken (Lawrence and Maitlis, 2005: 15). In the context of ISD offshoring, sensebreaking may assume the form of offering remote counterparts contradictory evidence, negatively evaluating work accomplishments, providing an "overall" or "big" picture, presenting alternative and radically different views, and openly questioning assumptions.

Individual conditions and processes

While social conditions and processes have received abundant attention in discussions on the development of advanced understandings in distributed work settings, the role of individual conditions and individual cognitive processes has remained relatively underexposed. Although we recognize that actors cannot arrive at understandings in a social vacuum, we follow Sandberg and Targama (2007) in contending that social as well as individual processes and conditions influence the construction of understanding (Figure 8.2).

In terms of *individual conditions*, several aspects play a role. First, the cognitive limitations of human beings, biases in their perception and thinking, myopia, mental rigidity, and autopoiesis may reduce the likelihood that congruent and actionable understandings emerge. Second, perception and attention may be directed by prior knowledge and experience as well as by people's interests, causing professionals to approach a situation from their particular point of view (Weick *et al.*, 2005). Knowledge and experience residing within the individual (Grant, 1996) not only determine the learning that takes place inside the head (Simon, 1991), but also the attention that is paid to cues in the environment. Third, individuals may differ in their cognitive abilities and level of cognitive complexity in a particular task domain and under particular work conditions (such as time pressure). Some people may be more likely than others to engage in stereotyping or the use of prejudices, applying rigid rules or heuristics for integrating information, exhibiting empathy, and replacing themselves in others' viewpoints (Dechesne *et al.*, 2007). Individuals further deploy different schema, frames, or mental models to help them orient themselves, to interpret cues from the environment, and to guide information seeking (Corner *et al.*, 1994; Harris, 1994).

As examples of individual conditions, a vendor's knowledge of the client's business, technology and programming language, as well as their experience with a focal project, actual requirements, and the phenomenon of IT-offshoring have been argued to influence the extent to which they are able to understand requirements (e.g. Vlaar *et al.*, 2007). Congruent and actionable understandings among participants in offshoring relationships are generally achieved more easily, for example when members have more knowledge about a variety of topics related to a requirement, as this increases their absorptive capacity concerning information communicated by counterparts (Lane and Lubatkin, 1998), and because it augments the likelihood that knowledge becomes "mutual" in nature, suggesting that collaborating parties share it in common and know that they share it (Bechky, 2003; Cramton, 2001; Weick, 1995). In this case, it is more likely that they have similar or overlapping knowledge bases, and that they interpret information in a similar vein (Davidson, 2002). Similarly, understandings among participants in offshoring relationships may be less congruent and less actionable due to differences in experience with a focal project, actual requirements, and IT-offshoring in general, something which tends to be more problematic when participants come from distinct backgrounds and when they work in different industries, with dissimilar belief systems (Lane and Lubatkin, 1998; Sutcliffe and Huber, 1998; Doz, 1996).

Next to these individual conditions, participants may engage in a complex apparatus of mental, *individual processes* (Nevo and Wand, 2005; Brandon and Hollingshead, 2004; Lambert and Shaw, 2002; Yoo and Kanawattanachai, 2001). The interactive, creative, and continuous constructing activities of the mind consist of individual processes that help to synthesize different pieces of information (Barnard, 1938). Such processes involve, amongst others, interpreting and representing (Crowston and Kammerer, 1998; Weick and Roberts, 1993), encoding and storing (Lewis *et al.*, 2005; Hollingshead, 1998), imagining (Bigley and Roberts, 2001; Spender and Grant, 1996), reflecting (Giddens, 1986), reasoning, abstracting, and constructing (Boland *et al.*, 1994).

Individuals represent their task environment and co-workers' communications and activities (Weick and Roberts, 1993). Fuelled by an individual's accumulated knowledge and experience, cognitive devices such as frames, mental models, schema, or scripts are used (Harris, 1994; Walsh, 1995) to construct an internal image (Endsley and Jones, 2001) or account of their reality (Maitlis and Lawrence, 2007). Bigley and Roberts (2001) offer the example of firefighters, who use the term "size-up" to describe the development of operational representations. As one of the engine-company captains in their study states: "We call it size up. What's going on? What's the time of day? What's the wind, weather like? What are the traffic conditions? What type of building are we going to? What type of engine? And then what is it when we get there? We have this picture of what's happening. We constantly evaluate that. We're supposed to constantly evaluate what is going on to see if we have to make any changes . . . It's an ongoing picture. It's an ongoing process" (*ibid.*: 1291).

Regarding encoding and storing, authors have noted that impressions are encoded and stored in an organized fashion (Lewis *et al.*, 2005). Individuals can retrieve these in collaboration with others and arrive at a common interpretation. Imagining, in turn, applies when individuals develop alternatives in an entrepreneurial fashion (Spender, 1996), by envisioning "what-if" scenarios, and by visualizing potential sequences of activities, task dependencies, and bottlenecks (Weick and Roberts, 1993; Arnheim, 1966). It occurs when individuals use cues to imagine, fantasize, empathize with others, or anticipate what a situation elsewhere or in the future might look like (Bigley and Roberts, 2001; Brown and Duguid, 2001; Cook and Brown, 1999).

Finally, individuals reason and theorize about, and they reflect upon, their experiences, including the texts they read and the systems they use (Lee, 1994; Boland, 1991). They attempt to explain and contextualize observations of situations and behaviours (Weick *et al.*, 2005), so as to synthesize information – pertaining to past, current, and future experiences – and move beyond primary representations in order to enrich their experience, anticipate future conditions, and develop relevant means–ends patterns (Bougon *et al.*, 1977). The extent to which individuals are capable of developing and synthesizing various interpretations of the same task environment (Dechesne *et al.*, 2007) affects the likelihood that congruent and actionable understanding emerge.

Task and context factors

Beyond social and individual conditions and processes, the development of congruent and actionable understandings is also contingent upon the task and contextual characteristics of offshore work (see Figure 8.2). Large and complex requirements, for example, may impose high cognitive demands on participants (Campbell, 1988), which hinders learning (Nidumolu, 1996) and may lead to a state where "common sense and everyday reasoning no longer provide adequate guides" (Simon, 1997: 246). Most ISD projects tend to escalate beyond initial expectations in terms of size and complexity (Keil, 1995), which may be due to various forms of distance and diversity among dispersed team members (Carmel and Agarwal, 2002; Carmel, 1999; Rajkumar and Dawley, 1997). This is likely to impede the development of congruent and actionable understandings.

Similarly, the level of abstraction and detail at which requirements are specified (e.g. product, feature, function, or component-level) may affect the development of understanding among stakeholders. In this respect, combinations of abstract and detailed requirements specifications are considered superior (Gorschek and Wohlin, 2006; Battin *et al.*, 2001). In a similar vein, environmental changes and constraints may make it more difficult to arrive at congruent and actionable understandings, as they imply that understandings need to be continuously adapted and incorporate constraints of which not all participants in offshoring relationships may be aware (see Jones and Hinds, 2002). In the following sections we will illustrate our model with the analysis of an actual offshore ISD relationship.

About this research

The research was carried out in a leading Indian IT vendor, Tata Consulting Services. Additional information about this vendor can be found in the Appendix. Three criteria were used for selecting an appropriate project for this research. First, we chose India as the offshore location, as one of the authors had worked for a major offshore organization and thus had intimate experience of working in an offshore team in various roles. Second, we selected a project involving a financial services client, because these clients are relatively mature in terms of working with Indian vendors. Third, the project that was chosen should be in a stable, relatively mature, state and it should include several instances of requirement sharing between onsite and offshore teams.

After initial discussions with each of the project managers, the FINANCE project was chosen to illustrate our framework, as it satisfied all conditions. This project consisted of four modules. Module A pertained to the development of tools for the analysis of programs in the Report Program Generation and FOCUS language. It involved two onsite and three offshore team members. Module B was created to respond to bugs and errors produced in the production system of the client. The requirements involved making minor changes to existing programmes and the module entailed work for one onsite and two offshore team members. Module C focused on migrating an application that ran on two separate systems to one system. It included three onsite and three offshore team members. Module D facilitated the representation of new partners in the client's information systems. The module involved two onsite and two offshore team members.

Data collection was done using semi-structured interviews and follow-up email exchanges to confirm, refine, modify, or reject our own construction of reality. In May, 2006, we conducted 18 semi-structured interviews with both onsite and offshore team members. These phone-based interviews were recorded with the permission of our informants, and one of the authors took extensive notes. Interviews lasted up to one hour and were conducted in either English or Hindi, which allowed informants to speak in their mother tongue, and increased their comfort with sharing views and ideas.

Data analysis was carried out in parallel to data collection. Interviews were transcribed and analysis was governed by qualitative data analysis techniques (Miles and Huberman, 1994; Corbin and Strauss, 1990). We went from citations to first-order concepts by using open-coding techniques (Strauss and Corbin, 1998) and we then proceeded towards second-order themes by organizing the first-order concepts into broader categories (van Maanen, 1979), based on the literature and our own, emergent understandings.

Insights from the finance project

We use the FINANCE project to examine whether it supports our distinction between social conditions and processes, individual conditions and processes, and task and contextual characteristics, as categories of factors affecting the development of congruent and actionable understandings as set out in Figure 8.2.

Congruent and actionable understandings

During our study, we found several instances of misunderstandings occurring between onsite and offshore teams. When offshore members received the requirements in the form of a requirements document and visual images, they tried to grasp their meaning, based on their comprehension of terminologies in IS development and their familiarity with the project. Since offshore members only received and processed the requirements document, they were unable to form a complete picture of the requirements as initiated by the client or onsite team. The following quotations illustrate this:

> Basically the thing is that they [onsite] have the knowledge about what they are going to do with the requirement so they have a certain expectation, and we don't know what they are going to do with it [requirements] and hence it is not very clear to us which results they expect. (Mr RK – offshore)

> The capability is not bad but they [offshore] don't have as much exposure as we get at onsite. Offshore cannot see and understand the parts that we see, such as how the system is working and how requirements are connected. That's why their understanding is generally at a modular level. (Mr NS – onsite)

Requirements documents are generally written in a technical language, and they tend to lack business or contextual information. This limits the offshore team in terms of developing optimal solutions and it leads to frequent queries. Onsite members expressed these concerns:

> Depending on the output sent by them [offshore] we had to explain over the phone or mail that this was not what was expected when we wrote the document. You have to do it in a different way. If something

was missing in the document we modified it and resent a new version of the document with more information. (Mr SK – onsite)

Though the business documents are there at offshore, most people don't read them. Even if they read them and have doubts, there is no one at offshore to explain or clarify these to them. (Mr GK – onsite)

Social conditions and processes

The first category in our research framework, social conditions, suggests that understandings are influenced by the structure of project teams, the availability of relevant resources, and information, turnover, cultural differences, and the division of work among project members. In at least one case, misunderstanding between onsite and offshore seemed to have been caused by a changing division of work offshore:

A report needed to be made and the fields in the report had to be aligned properly, but the alignment was not correctly done by the offshore team. They thought it is still okay to do [it] like this but the report is to be used by business user and he needs everything to be perfect. They didn't know this thing and neglected the case. I thought they would themselves take care of these things and I didn't have to tell them, because there were a few such requirements sent to them before and they handled it properly then, so I thought it will do the same. But the offshore team consisted of two people. Sometimes one of the guys does the job when he gets the requirement, but the other guy forgot to do it. This time, the mistake maybe occurred because they didn't consult between them; their "perception" was different. (Mr A – onsite)

The structure of the offshore team, which involved very few members who had onsite working experience, contributed to a lack of information sharing and learning across the teams:

Offshore doesn't get the picture of the business perspective. Whenever we send the design document we try to clear the business perspective, what needs to be tested, et cetera. The onsite guy who is sending [the document] has the global picture of what the design is and how it should be constructed in order to fulfil the requirement. Offshore only has a one-sided picture that you have to do these things and do this testing, so offshore is not aware of the business knowledge. (Mr N – onsite)

This asymmetrical distribution of knowledge (see Chapter 3 for an elaboration on knowledge bases) compelled offshore team members to send requests for clarifications on minor issues. At times, this frustrated onsite team members, and further increased incidences of misunderstandings among members:

> But in the present structure of offshore, they don't have anyone who has been to onsite for this project; they are all quite new people. They don't understand the technical languages or business processes. (Mr SK – onsite)

> The problem is that she [an offshore team member] cannot imagine anything. She needs all the input and does not try anything at her end. She used to call daily and I had to explain her everything. How to check out and how to run FOCUS. Now I avoid her calls. (Mr AB – onsite)

The division of labor among members within the project influenced the occurrence of misunderstandings. Due to repeated interactions, certain team members were better able to understand and deliver certain sets of requirements than others. Moreover, informants indicated that when labour was divided in such a way that task requirements became smaller in size and less complex, this led to fewer problems of understanding:

> Initially they will send a requirement bunch to us. And if the volume of requirements is high, you will not be able to grasp all of it in the initial days. What happens is that these people will call for teleconferencing and we get our views clarified via that, whereas if the requirement is pretty small, we do just certain main conversation, or we use instant messaging or emails with the US team. (Mr RK – offshore)

Along with the previously mentioned social conditions, there are social influences such as time pressure, fear of losing face, and interests, power, and politics that constrained the advancement of understandings. In several instances, offshore team members felt the need to engage in communication with onsite to provide clarifications, explain their approach, and avoid embarrassment in case of poor delivery. Moreover, both onsite and offshore members agreed that conflicts generated by the influence of power or politics were harmful to the collaborative efforts of the project:

> If a requirement was clear, we still used to ask [questions] before doing something, because we were a little bit scared that if we did something wrong, onsite would say something, as they are under pressure directly from the customer and they have the responsibility to finally deliver to the client. (Mr NK – offshore)

> I feel that whenever they [onsite] sent a mail to offshore, the language mattered. Generally people could tell the same thing in a normal way rather than blaming someone for the bug. It was always better to have soft language. Sometimes, when we send something, we write politely. Otherwise it strains the relationship in the longer run. (Mr NS – offshore)

Onsite and offshore team members also adopted social processes of sensegiving, sensemaking, sensedemanding, and sensebreaking processes to develop congruent and actionable understandings. Conference calls and email exchanges provided onsite with an opportunity to explain more to offshore about the background of the requirements, their origins, and their significance for the client and the client's systems:

> At the beginning, queries were very frequent because the offshore team had no technical capabilities of RPG/FOCUS. But when we began discussing these with them, they started understanding the things and queries became less and less. (Mr SK – onsite)

> They [onsite] first sent us the requirement document and then explained what exactly needed to be done. They asked us to use our own logic to come up with the solution to solve the problem that was being discussed. (Mr AB – offshore)

Onsite and offshore teams proceeded through the design process by sharing their knowledge of each others' domains with the intention of unearthing information gaps, misunderstandings, and incorrect assumptions. Both teams were aware of the importance of explicitly stating their assumptions and regularly checking whether these were in line with their counterparts' understandings. These social processes entailed mutual verification of one another's thinking by proceeding through feedback loops. Offshore participants continuously sought the approval of onsite to ensure that their actions were in line with client expectations:

> If we are stuck, we have to discuss within our team. It's because of them that the bigger picture is made clear to you. But if those people are not there, you have to constantly call onsite for every small issue. (Mr VM – onsite)

> I will prepare a document with regard to how I will proceed, and then I send that document to onsite for them to have a look and confirm my understanding. (Mr RM – offshore)

> Once onsite explained to us what the problem is and how we have to handle it, I read the requirements document and communicate my understanding and how I will proceed. (Mr YP – offshore)

The vendor teams engaged in continuous interaction to maintain congruent understandings. This increased team members' opportunities for sharing information and it reduced the likelihood that misunderstandings or faulty assumptions would surface later.

Individual conditions and processes

When an offshore team member received a requirement document, the knowledge bases of this member were used to identify and relate existing conceptions to the text. Offshore team members usually possess relatively little knowledge of a client's business – its systems, structures, processes, jargon, concepts, and models – which may lead to severe problems, as becomes evident from the following interview excerpt:

> There were many problems because the requirements mainly related to business knowledge. It was very important to have that for this requirement, to know whether transactions are being created, where they are supposed to go and so on. They [offshore] could not understand these things . . . . So, there were many such problems in the delivery. (Mr NS – onsite)

We found that differences in experience between onsite and offshore team members led to the presence of information asymmetry, which had to be bridged by increasing communication:

> Although the development work is done over there [at offshore], as far as the business knowledge is concerned, the competency at offshore is very low. They didn't have the entire business perspective, which makes it difficult to interpret the requirements. (Mr GK – onsite)

> Usually they [offshore] clarify their doubts on mail and phone. On phone, we sometimes skip a few things assuming that offshore must be aware of it. But if we feel that a point is important to convey to them explicitly, we do that. So, we ourselves call them sometimes to make sure that they have understood the point. (Mr NK – onsite)

Knowledge of technology is important to understand how software functions on different types of hardware. If people do not have sufficient knowledge of a technology, they will not understand the terminologies and technological jargon used in the requirement text. In this project, five languages were used: FOCUS, RPG, JCL, VPLUS, and Visual Basic. Programming language knowledge, acquired by training and learning on-the-job was critical for understanding requirements documents:

> People in Bangalore didn't have expertise of that particular technology. They had done AS 400 training or they had experience of AS 400 but they didn't have knowledge of the HP 3000 platform and the perspective needed for HP 3000. So, when we sent them the requirement document, they analyzed it, but for some part they analyzed it in AS 400 and for some part in HP 3000. Consequently, they couldn't come down to the actual thing. (Mr NS – onsite)

Team members differed in their experience with the focal project in terms of their awareness of the project's background, routines, and common practices, the quality and past performance of team members, and the demands and preferences of business users and clients. The interviewees indicated that only after a few years of experience with the onsite–offshore model do people understand the idiosyncrasies and "rules of thumb" of this setup:

> I can handle daily requests easily now, because I have been working in this project for the last 15 months. Compared to others, I have had more exposure to the different modules, and as I am one of the senior

people amongst the trainees, I have been handling *customer requirements* for some time now. Earlier, there used to be many bugs, but now this has decreased. (Mr GS – offshore)

Concerning individual processes, offshore team members studied the requirements document in depth, trying to develop an understanding of its implications for the behavior and outcomes that were expected from them. During this stage, they used cognitive processes of analyzing, thinking, and reasoning to advance their understanding of requirements. They connected the current state of the system with the changes that were needed, as shown by the excerpt below:

> They [the client's IT staff] don't have a specific way or standard way of coding. They have written codes in their own ways and their systems are 30 years old. We had first to understand the logic behind these codes and then apply the new changes. (Mr AR – offshore)

Before asking onsite for clarifications, offshore team members themselves contemplated and deliberated, trying to develop a better understanding of the requirements:

> When I get the requirement, I analyze it. If I think I know enough about the requirement, then I will start coding directly. I usually get my thinking checked by someone senior in the project, especially if the requirement has to be delivered by the end of the day. If it is for more than one day, I will prepare a document with regard to how I see the changes and how I will proceed and send that document to onsite for them to have a look and confirm my understanding. (Mr RP offshore)

> The last requirement that I did was somewhat ambiguous. I had to interpret it myself and it took me some time to understand it. At that time, it was a bit late to call onsite, so I finished the work according to my perspective. In the evening, I called onsite and told them how I was proceeding and which things were not clear to me. I also asked whether I was right in what I did. In this case, I was correct, because onsite wanted the same thing. (Mr RK – offshore)

Task and context characteristics

The characteristics of the task and the context from which a requirement originated and for which it is delivered also influenced the development of congruent and actionable understandings. If requirements were large in size, highly complex, novel, or ambiguous, for example, it became more difficult for onsite and offshore team members to achieve congruent and actionable understandings:

> If the volume of requirements is high you will not be able to grasp all of them in the initial days. So what happens is that these people will call for teleconferencing and we get our views clarified via that, whereas if the requirement is pretty small we just do certain main conversation or we use instant messaging or emails with the US team, because there is a time difference. (Mr YP – offshore)

Furthermore, continuous change in requirements increased the problems of the offshore team in developing a clear picture of requirements. As depicted by the quote below, change required reframing and reworking past accomplishments:

> We received the requirement document and they explained it to us. Later we started developing the tool. After one week, when we had completed the first part of the requirement, we came to know that output had to be presented in another format. Again after one week, they asked us to change the complete logic and to present output in some other format. At the end, there was a big slippage in the schedule and when we submitted [the output] there were lot of bugs. (Mr AR – offshore)

Discussion and implications

The conceptual framework that we have introduced contributes to the literature by explicitly distinguishing the categories of factors involved in the development of congruent and actionable understandings among geographically dispersed stakeholders in distributed work-settings. Our review of the literature suggested that advancing understanding involves five categories of factors: (1) social conditions; (2) social processes; (3) individual conditions; (4) individual processes; and (5) task and contextual characteristics. Based on these categories, we developed an integrative conceptual framework, which we illustrated with an actual ISD project involving a major US financial services firm and one of India's largest offshore outsourcing vendors.

Implications: Diminishing misunderstanding

Our research has strong implications for researchers and practitioners, because achieving congruent and actionable understandings appears fundamental in preventing misunderstandings from occurring and in reducing the likelihood that rework has to be performed (see also Hinds and Mortensen, 2005). First, our research suggests that the development of congruent and actionable understandings is contingent upon various, interrelated categories of factors. This implies that researchers and practitioners who only take into account one of the categories of factors that we presented may not be able to explain why congruent and actionable understandings arise, and that they may attribute their observations to single or inappropriate causes. Take, for example, cross-sectional studies on cultural differences and their impact on the delivery of ISD requirement. These studies tend to neglect the social processes used by participants in offshoring relationships that help to overcome these problems.

Second, following other studies on interorganizational collaboration (e.g. Das and Teng, 2002; Doz, 1996), we have distinguished conditions from processes influencing the evolution of collaborative relationships. Such a partitioning is warranted, because attempts at changing unfavourable conditions and attempts at changing detrimental processes may be of an entirely different nature. Reducing a lack of knowledge, for example, may require specific education and training programmes concerning programming languages, whereas a lack in one's ability to give or break sense may demand communication training sessions or improved relational skills. Moreover, conditions and processes may act as substitutes in creating congruent and actionable understandings. Consider, for example, an offshoring relationship in which time constraints preclude intensive communication. In such cases, more experienced personnel may be asked to perform the job, so as to make sure that understandings among stakeholders become congruent and actionable rapidly.

Practitioners could use the categories of factors introduced in our research framework to gauge the risks that misunderstandings occur in particular offshore ISD projects. Table 8.1 exhibits a brief questionnaire to determine the scores in the categories for a particular project. In the case that problems of understanding (Vlaar et al., 2006) are observed, mitigation measures can be used such as increasing the frequency of group/ project meetings, improving the quality of communicative acts among team members, reassessing resource availability and allocation, institutionalizing collaboration processes among team members, examining and discussing

Table 8.1 Questionnaire: Assessing the potential for misunderstandings

In relation to your project, please rate the following questions on a scale of 1 to 5 (1 = very low; 3 = neither low nor high; 5 = very high)					
Social Conditions and Processes	**1**	**2**	**3**	**4**	**5**
Availability of relevant resources in the project	☐	☐	☐	☐	☐
Availability of relevant information in the project	☐	☐	☐	☐	☐
Appropriateness of task division in the project	☐	☐	☐	☐	☐
Time pressure experienced by team members	☐	☐	☐	☐	☐
Power & politics experienced by team members	☐	☐	☐	☐	☐
Cultural differences among team members	☐	☐	☐	☐	☐
Frequency of communication among team members	☐	☐	☐	☐	☐
Continuous feedback among team members	☐	☐	☐	☐	☐
Supportive interaction among team members	☐	☐	☐	☐	☐
Team members engage in processes of sense giving	☐	☐	☐	☐	☐
Team members engage in processes of sense making	☐	☐	☐	☐	☐
Team members engage in processes of sense demanding	☐	☐	☐	☐	☐
Team members engage in processes of sense breaking	☐	☐	☐	☐	☐
Individual Conditions and Processes	**1**	**2**	**3**	**4**	**5**
Team member's knowledge of client's business	☐	☐	☐	☐	☐
Team member's knowledge of technology and programming language	☐	☐	☐	☐	☐
Team member's experience with the focal project	☐	☐	☐	☐	☐
Team member's experience with actual requirements	☐	☐	☐	☐	☐
Team Member's experience of IT offshoring	☐	☐	☐	☐	☐
Team member's cognitive abilities such as analyzing, imagining, anticipating	☐	☐	☐	☐	☐
Task and Context	**1**	**2**	**3**	**4**	**5**
Complexity of requirements in the project	☐	☐	☐	☐	☐
Novelty of requirements in the project	☐	☐	☐	☐	☐
Stability of requirements in the project	☐	☐	☐	☐	☐
Environmental/contextual constraints faced in the project	☐	☐	☐	☐	☐
Environmental/contextual change faced in the project	☐	☐	☐	☐	☐

team member interactions regularly, increasing training and learning on technology and business, promoting peer-to-peer learning through mentoring, organizing interproject best-practice sessions and cross-cultural training sessions, and improving individuals' cognitive abilities.

Our study challenges practitioners to rethink their decision-making process, their management of a project in progress, and the interventions they make during projects. Since understanding is fundamental to the performance of professional workers (Sandberg and Targama, 2007) and members of distributed workteams (e.g. Bechky, 2006, 2003; Cramton, 2003), we recommend practitioners to consider and manage each of these categories when developing training and education programmes, selecting team members, pricing services, and monitoring progress.

Future research

Avenues for future research on understanding in distributed work are abundant. First, researchers may explore more systematically how each of the categories of factors distinguished in this chapter relates to other categories and to what extent deficiencies regarding one condition or process may be compensated for by another, more favourable, condition or process. Second, inquiries may be directed at investigating the means that firms could use to solve problems emerging from unfavourable social and individual conditions and processes. Third, studies could be conducted in which the relative significance of different types of understanding is assessed. For example, to what extent should understandings be shared (Bechky, 2003; Bigley *et al.*, 2001), common (Davidson, 2002; Orlikowski and Gash, 1994), similar (Dougherty, 1992), mutual (Cramton, 2001), or congruent and actionable (Vlaar *et al.*, 2007) to make sure that client needs in offshoring relationships are met in an effective and efficient manner? Finally, researchers may explore how current trends in ISD such as cosourcing and alliances (Kaiser and Hawk, 2004), multivendor outsourcing (Rottman and Lacity, 2006), nearshoring (Carmel and Abbott, 2006), and (partial) backshoring (Schwartz, 2006) influence the development of congruent and actionable understandings in offshore IS projects.

References

Arnheim, R. (1966) *Toward a Psychology of Art*, University of California Press, Berkeley.

Bakhtin, M. (1986) *Speech Genres and Other Essays*, University of Texas Press, Austin, TX.

Balogun, J. and Johnson, G. (2004) "Organizational Restructuring and Middle Manager Sensemaking," *Academy of Management Journal*, 47(4), 523–49.

Barnard, C. I. (1938) *The Functions of the Executive*, Harvard University Press, Cambridge, MA.

Battin, R. D., Crocker, R., Kreidler, J., and Subramanian, K. (2001) "Leveraging Resources in Global Software Development," *IEEE Software*, 18(2), 70–7.

Bechky, B. A. (2003) "Sharing Meaning Across Occupational Communities: The Transformation of Understanding on a Production Floor," *Organization Science*, 14(3), 312–30.

Bechky, B. A. (2006) "Gaffers, Gofers, and Grips: Role-Based Coordination in Temporary Organizations," *Organization Science*, 17(1), 3–21.

Bhat, J. M., Gupta, M., and Murthy, S. N. (2006) "Overcoming Requirements Engineering Challenges: Lessons from Offshore Outsourcing," *IEEE Software*, 23(5), 38–44.

Bigley, G. A. and Roberts, K. H. (2001) "The Incident Command System: High Reliability Organizing for Complex and Volatile Task Environments," *Academy of Management Journal*, 44(6), 1281–99.

Boland, R. J. (1978) "The Process and Product of System Design," *Management Science*, 24(9), 887–98.

Boland, R. J. (1991) "Information Systems Use as a Hermeneutic Process," in *Information Systems Research: Contemporary Approaches & Emergent Traditions* (Eds, Nissen, H. E., Klein, H. H., and Hirschheim, R.) North-Holland, New York, NY, pp. 439–58.

Boland, R. J., Tenkasi, R. V., and Te'eni, D. (1994) "Designing Information Technology to Support Distributed Cognition," *Organization Science*, 5(3), 456–75.

Bougon, M., Weick, K., and Binkhorst, D. (1977) "Cognition in Organizations: An Analysis of the Utrecht Jazz Orchestra," *Administrative Science Quarterly*, 22(4), 606–39.

Bowker, G. C. and Star, S. L. (2002) *Sorting Things Out: Classification and its Consequences*, MIT Press, Cambridge, MA.

Brandon, D. P. and Hollingshead, A. B. (2004) "Transactive Memory Systems in Organizations: Matching Tasks, Expertise, and People," *Organization Science*, 15(6), 633–44.

Brown, A. D. (2000) "Making Sense of Inquiry Sensemaking," *Journal of Management Studies*, 37(1), 45–75.

Brown, A. D. (2004) "Authoritative Sensemaking in a Public Inquiry Report," *Organization Studies*, 25(1), 95–112.

Brown, J. S. and Duguid, P. (2001) "Knowledge and Organization," *Organization Science*, 12(2), 198–213.

Campbell, D. J. (1988) "Task Complexity: A Review and Analysis," *Academy of Management Review*, 13(1), 40–52.

Carmel, E. (1999) *Global Software Teams: Collaborating across Borders and Time Zones*, Prentice Hall, Englewood Cliffs, NJ.

Carmel, E. and Abbott, P. (2006) "Configurations of Global Software Development: Offshore versus Nearshore," Paper presented at the International Conference on Software Engineering (ICSE), Shanghai.

Carmel, E. and Agarwal, R. (2002) "The Maturation of Offshore Sourcing of IT Work," *MIS Quarterly Executive*, 1(2), 65–77.

Carmel, E. and Tjia, P. (2005) *Offshoring Information Technology Sourcing and Outsourcing to a Global Workforce*. Cambridge University Press, Cambridge.

Ciborra, C. U. and Lanzara, G. F. (1994) "Formative Contexts and Information Technology: Understanding the Dynamics of Innovation in Organizations," *Accounting, Management, and Information Technology*, 4(2), 103–18.

Cook, S. D. N. and Brown, J. S. (1999) "Bridging Epistemologies: The Generative Dance Between Organizational Knowledge and Organizational Knowing," *Organization Science*, 10(4), 381–400.

Corbin, J. and Strauss, A. L. (1990) "Grounded Theory Research: Procedures, Canons, and Evaluative Criteria," *Qualitative Sociology*, 13(1).

Corner, P. D., Kinicki, A. J., and Keats, B. W. (1994) "Integrating Organizational and Individual Information Processing Perspectives on Choice," *Organization Science*, 5(3), 294–308.

Couto, V., Mani, M., Lewin, A. Y., and Peeters, C. (2006) *The Globalization of White-Collar Work: The Facts and Fallout of Next-Generation Offshoring*, Booz/Allen/Hamilton and Offshoring Research Network, The Fuqua School of Business, http://offshoring.fuqua.duke.edu/.

Cramton, C. D. (2001) "The Mutual Knowledge Problem and its Consequences for Dispersed Collaboration," *Organization Science*, 12(3), 346–71.

Cramton, C. D. and Orvis, K. L. (2003) "Overcoming Barriers to Information Sharing in Virtual Teams," in *Virtual Teams that Work: Creating Conditions for Virtual Team Effectiveness* (Eds, Gibson, C. B. and Cohen, S. G.) Jossey-Bass, San Francisco, 214–30.

Crowston, K. and Kammerer, E. (1998) "Coordination and Collective Mind in Software Requirements Development," *IBM Systems Journal*, 37(2), 227–45.

Cullen, S., Seddon, P. B., and Willcocks, L. P. (2005) "Managing Outsourcing: The Process Imperative," MIS Quarterly Executive, 4(1), 229–46.

Curtis, B., Krasner, H., and Iscoe, N. (1988) "A Field Study of the Software Design Process for Large Systems," *Communications of the ACM*, 31(11), 1268–86.

Daft, R. L. and Weick, K. E. (1984) "Toward a Model of Organizations as Interpretation Systems," *Academy of Management Review*, 9(2), 284–95.

Das, T. K. and Teng, B. (2002) "The Dynamics of Alliance Conditions in the Alliance Development Process," *Journal of Management Studies*, 39(5), 725–46.

Davidson, E. J. (2002) "Technology Frames and Framing: A Socio-Cognitive Investigation of Requirements Determination," *MIS Quarterly*, 26(4), 329–58.

Dechesne, M., Van den Berg, C., and Soeters, J. L. L. M. (2007) "International Collaboration under Threat: A Field Study in Kabul," *Conflict Management and Peace Science*, 24, 25–36.

Donnellon, A., Gray, B., and Bougon, M. G. (1986) "Communication, Meaning, and Organized Action," *Administrative Science Quarterly*, 31(1), 43–55.

Dougherty, D. (1992) "Interpretive Barriers to Successful Product Innovation in Large Firms," *Organization Science*, 3(2), 179–202.

Doz, Y. L. (1996) "The Evolution of Cooperation in Strategic Alliances: Initial Conditions or Learning Processes?" *Strategic Management Journal*, 17, 55–83.

Endsley, M. R. and Jones, W. M. (2001) "A Model of Inter- and Intrateam Situation Awareness: Implications for Design, Training, and Measurement," in *New Trends in Cooperative Activities: Understanding System Dynamics in Complex Environments* (Eds, McNeese, M., Salas, E., and Endsley, M.) Human Factors and Ergonomics Society, Santa Monica, CA, pp. 46–67.

Felin, T. and Hesterly, W. S. (2007) "The Knowledge-Based View, Nested Heterogeneity, and New Value Creation: Philosophical Considerations on the Locus of Knowledge," *Academy of Management Review*, 32(1), 195–218.

García-Canal, E., Valdés-Llaneza, A., and Ariño, A. M. (2003) "Effectiveness of Dyadic and Multi-party Joint Ventures," *Organization Studies*, 24, 743–70.

Gasson, S. (2005) "The Dynamics of Sensemaking, Knowledge, and Expertise in Collaborative, Boundary-Spanning Design," *Journal of Computer-Mediated Communication*, 10(4), http://jcmc.indiana.edu/.

Giddens, A. (1986) *The Constitution of Society: Outline of the Theory of Structuration*, University of California Press, Berkeley, CA.

Gioia, D. A. and Chittipeddi, K. (1991) "Sensemaking and Sensegiving in Strategic Change Initiation," *Strategic Management Journal*, 12(6), 433–48.

Gorschek, T. and Wohlin, C. (2006) "Requirements Abstraction Model," *Requirements Engineering*, 11(1), 79–101.

Grant, R. M. (1996) "Toward a Knowledge-Based Theory of the Firm," *Strategic Management Journal*, 17(Winter), 109–22.

Hargadon, A. B. and Bechky, B. A. (2006) "When Collections of Creatives Become Creative Collectives: A Field Study of Problem Solving at Work," *Organization Science*, 17(4), 484–500.

Harris, S. G. (1994) "Organizational Culture and Individual Sensemaking: A Schema-Based Perspective," *Organization Science*, 5(3), 309–21.

Herbsleb, J. D. and Mockus, A. (2003) "An Empirical Study of Speed and Communication in Globally-Distributed Software Development," *IEEE Transactions on Software Engineering*, 29(3), 481–94.

Hinds, P. and Mortensen, M. (2005) "Understanding Conflict in Geographically Distributed Teams: The Moderating Effects of Shared Identity, Shared Context, and Spontaneous Communication," *Organization Science*, 16(3), 290–307.

Hirschheim, R., Löbbecke, C., Newman, M., and Valor, J. (2005) "Offshoring and Its Implications for the Information Systems Discipline," Paper presented at the International Conference on Information Systems (ICIS), Las Vegas.

Hollingshead, A. B. (1998) "Communication, Learning, and Retrieval in Transactive Memory Systems," *Journal of Experimental Social Psychology*, 34, 423–42.

Jones, H. L. and Hinds, P. (2002) "Extreme Work Teams: Using SWAT Teams as a Model for Coordinating Distributed Robots," Paper presented at the CSCW 2002, New Orleans.

Kaiser, K. M. and Hawk, S. (2004) "Evolution of an Offshore Software Development: From Outsourcing to Cosourcing," *MIS Quarterly Executive*, 3(2), 69–81.

Keil, M. (1995) "Pulling the Plug: Software Project Management and the Problem of Project Escalation," *MIS Quarterly*, 19(4), 421–47.

Kellogg, K., Orlikowski, W. J., and Yates, J. (2006) "Life in the Trading Zone: Structuring Coordination Across Boundaries in Postbureaucratic Organizations," *Organization Science*, 17(1), 22–44.

King, W. R., Davis, G., Ein-dor, P., and Torkzadeh, R. (2004) *IT Offshoring: Prospects, Challenges, Educational Requirements and Curriculum Implications*, Paper presented at the International Conference on Information Systems (ICIS), Senior Scholars Paper, Washington, DC.

Krepchin, F. (1993) "When Offshore Programming Works," *Datamation*, 39(14), 55–6.

Kumar, K., van Fenema, P. C., and Von Glinow, M. A. (2005) "Intense Collaboration in Globally Distributed Work Teams: Evolving Patterns of Dependencies and Coordination," in *Managing Multinational Teams: Global Perspectives* (Eds, Shapiro, D. L., Von Glinow, M. A., and Cheng, J. L. C.) Elsevier/ JAI, Oxford, pp. 127–54.

Lambert, M. H. and Shaw, B. (2002) *Transactive Memory and Exception Handling in High-Performance Project Teams*, Standford University, Center for Integrated Facility Engineering, Technical Report #137.

Lane, P. J. and Lubatkin, M. (1998) "Relative Absorptive Capacity and Interorganizational Learning," *Strategic Management Journal*, 19(5), 461–77.

Lawrence, T. B. and Maitlis, S. (2005) *The Disruption of Accounts: Sensebreaking in Organizations*, Paper presented at the Academy of Management Annual Meeting, Honolulu, HA.

Lee, A. S. (1994) "Electronic Mail as a Medium for Rich Communication: An Empirical Investigation Using Hermeneutic Interpretation," *MIS Quarterly*, 18(2), 143–57.

Lewis, K., Lange, D., and Gillis, L. (2005) "Transactive Memory Systems, Learning, and Learning Transfer," *Organization Science*, 16(6).

Maitlis, S. (2005) "The Social Processes of Organizational Sensemaking," *Academy of Management Journal*, 48, 21–49.

Maitlis, S. and Lawrence, T. B. (2007) "Triggers and Enablers of Sensegiving in Organizations," *Academy of Management Journal*, 50(1), 21–49.

Meadows, C. J. (1996) "Globework: Creating Technology with International Teams," PhD Thesis, Harvard University, Boston, MA.

Miles, M. B. and Huberman, A. M. (1994) *Qualitative Data Analysis: An Expanded Sourcebook* (2nd ed.), Sage Publications, Thousand Oaks, CA.

Nevo, D. and Wand, Y. (2005) "Organizational Memory Information Systems: A Transactive Memory Approach," *Decision Support Systems*, 39, 549–62.

Newman, M. and Robey, D. (1992) "A Social Process Model of User–analyst Relationships," *MIS Quarterly*, 16(2), 249–66.

Ngwenyama, O. K. and Lee, A. S. (1997) "Communication Richness in Electronic Mail: A Critical Social Theory and the Contextuality of Meaning," *MIS Quarterly*, 21(2), 145–67.

Nidumolu, S. R. (1996) "Standardization, Requirements Uncertainty, and Software Project Performance," *Information and Management*, 31(3), 136–50.

Orlikowski, W. J. and Gash, D. C. (1994) "Technological Frames: Making Sense of Information Technology in Organizations," *ACM Transactions on Information Systems*, 12(2), 174–207.

Oza, N. V. and Hall, T. (2005) "Difficulties in Managing Offshore Software Outsourcing Relationships: An Empirical Analysis of 18 High Maturity Indian Software Companies," *Journal of Information Technology Case and Application Research*, 7(3), 25–41.

Polanyi, M. (1958) *Personal Knowledge: Towards a Post-Critical Philosophy*, University of Chicago Press, Chicago, IL.

Quinn, R. W. and Dutton, J. E. (2005) "Coordination as Energy-in-Conversation," *Academy of Management Review*, 30(1).

Rajkumar, T. and Dawley, D. (1997) "Problems and Issues in Offshore Development of Software," in *Information Systems Sourcing: Theory and Practice* (Eds, Willcocks, L. P. and Lacity, M. C.) Oxford University Press, Oxford.

Ramirez Jr., A., Walther, J. B., Burgoon, J. K., and Sunnafrank, M. (2002) "Information-Seeking Strategies, Uncertainty, and Computer-Mediated Communication: Toward a Conceptual Model," *Human Communication Research*, 28(2), 213–28.

Roberts, K. H. and Moore, W. H. (1993) "Bligh Reef Dead Ahead: The Grounding of the Exxon Valdez," in *New Challenges to Understanding Organizations* (Ed., Roberts, K. H.) Macmillan, New York, pp. 157–67.

Robinson, M. and Kalakota, R. (2004) *Offshore Outsourcing: Business Models, ROL, Best Practices*, Mivar Press, www.mivarpress.com, Alpharetta, GA.

Rottman, J. W. and Lacity, M. C. (2006) "Proven Practices for Effectively Offshoring IT Work," *Sloan Management Review*, 47(3), 56–63.

Rouleau, L. (2005) "Micro-Practices of Strategic Sensemaking and Sensegiving: How Middle Managers Interpret and Sell Change Every Day," *Journal of Management Studies*, 42(7), 1413–41.

Salaway, G. (1987) "An Organizational Learning Approach to Information Systems Development," *MIS Quarterly*, 12(2), 245–64.

Sandberg, J. and Targama, A. (2007) *Managing Understanding in Organizations*, Sage, London.

Schwartz, E. (2006) "Bringing Software Development Back In-house," http://www.infoworld.com/article/06/02/07/74958_07OPreality_1. html?OUTSOURCING%20SERVICES), accessed February 7.

Simon, H. A. (1991) "Bounded Rationality and Organizational Learning," *Organization Science*, 2(1), 125–34.

Simon, H. A. (1997) *Administrative Behavior*, The Free Press, New York.

Spender, J. C. (1989) *Industry Recipes*, Blackwell, Oxford.

Spender, J. C. (1996) "Making Knowledge the Basis of a Dynamic Theory of the Firm," *Strategic Management Journal*, 17(Winter), 77–91.

Spender, J. C. and Grant, R. M. (1996) "Knowledge and the Firm: Overview," *Strategic Management Journal*, 17(Winter), 77–91.

Strauss, A. and Corbin, J. (1998) *Basics of Qualitative Research*. Sage Publications, Thousand Oaks, CA.

Sutcliffe, K. M. and Huber, G. P. (1998) "Firm and Industry as Determinants of Executive Perceptions of the Environment," *Strategic Management Journal*, 19(8), 793–807.

van Fenema, P. C. (2002) *Coordination and Control of Globally Distributed Software Projects*. Unpublished doctoral dissertation, Erasmus University, Rotterdam, http://hdl.handle.net/1765/360.

van Maanen, J. (1979) "The Fact of Fiction in Organizational Ethnography," *Administrative Science Quarterly*, 24, 539–50.

Vlaar, P. W. L., Fenema, P. C. V., and Tiwari, V. (2007) "Achieving Congruent and Actionable Understandings of ISD Requirements among Onsite and Offshore Vendor Teams," Working paper, Free University, Amsterdam.

Vlaar, P. W. L., van den Bosch, F. A. J., and Volberda, H. W. (2006) "Coping with Problems of Understanding in Interorganizational Relationships: Using Formalization as a Means to Make Sense," *Organization Studies*, 27(11), 1617–38.

Walsh, J. P. (1995) "Managerial and Organizational Cognition: Notes from a Trip Down Memory Lane," *Organization Science*, 6(3), 280–321.

Walz, D. B., Elam, J. J., and Curtis, B. (1993) "Inside a Software Design Team: Knowledge Acquisition, Sharing, and Integration," *Communications of the ACM*, 36(10), 62–77.

Weick, K. E. (1993) "The Collapse of Sensemaking in Organizations: The Mann Gulch Disaster," *Administrative Science Quarterly*, 38, 628–52.

Weick, K. E. (1995) *Sensemaking in Organizations*, Sage, Thousand Oaks, CA.

Weick, K. E. (2001) "Friendly Fire: The Accidental Shootdown of U.S. Black Hawks over Northern Iraq," (book review), *Administrative Science Quarterly*, (March), 158.

Weick, K. E. and Roberts, K. (1993) "Collective Mind in Organizations: Heedful Interrelating on Flight Decks," *Administrative Science Quarterly*, 38, 357–81.

Weick, K. E., Sutcliffe, K. M., and Obstfeld, D. (2005) "Organizing and the Process of Sensemaking," *Organization Science*, 16(4), 409–21.

Wiegers, K. E. (2006) *More about Software Requirements*, Microsoft Press, Redmond, WA.

Yoo, Y. and Kanawattanachai, P. (2001) "Development of Transactive Memory Systems and Collective Mind in Virtual Teams," *International Journal of Organizational Analysis*, 9(2), 187–208.

CHAPTER 9

Information technology for personal, impersonal, and automated e-coordination modes

Paul C. van Fenema and Julia Kotlarsky

Introduction

Coordination can be defined as the process of achieving concerted action (Thompson, 1967) in situations of task dependence (Crowston, 1997). Electronic coordination (further referred to as e-coordination) refers to the situations when a coordination process relies on electronic media and Information Technology (IT). Electronic media and IT play an indispensable role in advanced societies as (partial) substitutes for human coordination practices and thereby they enable the global knowledge-based workplace (Majchrzak *et al.*, 2000; Argyres, 1999; Ciborra *et al.*, 1996b). Knowledge workers depend on advanced technologies for coordinating work processes with colleagues, clients, and vendors. Advanced technologies for collaboration (e.g. web-based project management software and Groupware), coordination (e.g. CATIA product development software), simulation, and visualization (collaborative CAD/CAM software products) reinforce multiple categories of knowledge processes (see Chapter 4). However, these new technologies – designed and used for coordination processes – usually result in a complex mixture of positive and negative impacts on individual lives, organizations, and society (Zuboff, 1988). With the technologies used for e-coordination, various instances have been reported where organizations were confused about the way they could deploy them in their daily operations. In virtual teams,[1] individuals have been struggling with Groupware functionality that formalizes tasks previously accomplished in a more personal manner (Ciborra and Patriotta, 1996). New technologies require learning: for example, a rocket components product development team had to adapt its initial e-coordination strategy. They decided to let technology play a more supportive rather than central role as a coordinator of collaboration processes (Majchrzak *et al.*, 2000). In its supportive role, technology enables interpersonal coordination; in its central role, it coordinates activities independently (e.g. a traffic light). Pilots have misunderstood advanced cockpit automation computer technology in aviation (Marriott, 1999a, 1999b; Sweet, 1995; Sandza, 1989). Air traffic controllers have been confused about the role of advanced collision warning systems in causing fatal accidents (BFU, 2004). Similarly, global software teams struggle to make effective and efficient use of technologies for coordinating the distributed professionals constituting a team (Herbsleb and Mockus, 2003; Carmel, 1999; Rajkumar and Dawley, 1997; Meadows, 1996).

Examples such as these illustrate the multiple roles and meanings of technologies (Orlikowski, 2000). Technology designed for the same context can lead to different organizational implementations (Barley, 1986) and thereby coordination practices. We focus in this chapter on technology in use. Contributing to the confusion about the role of technology in coordinating work processes is the potential of Information and Communication Technology (ICT) to both *informate* and *automate* (Zuboff, 1988). Each option changes the role of technology in relation to individuals and the relation between technologies.

Confusion about the role of technologies used for e-coordination (further referred to as e-coordination technologies) increases project risks, costs, and cycle times. This is likely to increase as ever more intelligent and automated devices and software tools enter the workplace. These artifacts can fulfil different roles and blur the distinction between human-based and artifact–based contributions to work processes. Resolving this confusion is becoming imperative, as current business is operating in a network-centric manner that relies heavily on technologies (Walsh and Maloney, 2002).

Studies relevant to understanding e-coordination usually focus on specific technologies such as virtual product development environments, Groupware, and distributed learning environments (Majchrzak *et al.*, 2000; Goodman and Darr, 1998; Kunz *et al.*, 1998; Adams and Adams, 1997; Sabbagh, 1996). These studies commonly are less strong in terms of developing typologies for comparing technologies at an abstract level, and they offer limited insight into the relationship between technology-based coordination and task (properties). Many studies focus on dispersed student teams (i.e. not professionals) using basic technology such as email and chat for assignments (Sarker and Sahay, 2004; Cramton, 2001; Jarvenpaa *et al.*, 1998). However, these results may not suffice for understanding teams consisting of professionals working with advanced software and media tools on complex projects. Consequently, the lack of solid typologies of e-coordination modes makes it difficult to categorize and analyze e-coordination technologies in relation to the work context in which these are deployed.

To fill this gap, the objective of this chapter is to develop a typology of e-coordination modes that distinguishes between (i) different types of e-coordination and (ii) different roles of e-coordination technologies, and that clarifies (iii) the changing role of technology versus humans. Through empirical research we examine the usefulness of this typology for identifying and analyzing e-coordination practices in a particular work context.

Conceptual background: E-coordination modes

Coordination theory

Coordination is necessary for dealing with dependencies that emerge from work division (Crowston, 1997; Gulick, 1937; Smith, 1793). Dependencies may refer to situations in which activities should not interfere with each other (interference dependence, e.g. a crossroads), or situations in which contributions are supposed to add up in a meaningful manner (contributive dependence, e.g. restaurant staff responsible for a large dinner). Work division is inevitable when humans undertake large-scale, long-term projects exceeding individuals' capacities in multiple areas. First, mentally, human comprehension and knowledge bases are limited (Tsoukas, 1996; Simon, 1991). Second, physically, humans cannot work non-stop as they need a minimal amount of rest. Also of importance for global projects is the fact that particular humans cannot be physically at two sites at the same time (unlike items of information). Thus, the goal of coordination is to join together contributions from different actors working within their constraints at possibly different sites and times.

Traditionally, researchers have suggested two modes[2] of coordination (Goodhue and Thompson, 1995; van de Ven *et al.*, 1976; March and Simon, 1958): *personal coordination* and *impersonal coordination*. *Personal coordination*, commonly referred to as *mutual adjustment*, such as meetings and informal conversations (Goodhue *et al.*, 1995; Mintzberg, 1979; van de Ven *et al.*, 1976), is achieved by individuals exchanging information about themselves and the task (context). These communications result in the development of shared understanding (Weick and Roberts, 1993; Donnellon *et al.*, 1986). *Impersonal coordination* relies on the use of plans, standards, design guidelines, and procedures (Sanchez and Mahoney, 1996; Scott, 1990). This coordination mode implies that individuals coordinate their perceptions and intended actions by outlining how they or others will and should behave, or they report how they have operated, without interpersonal interaction. During the actual work, individuals draw on these impersonal structures and artifacts to shape their behaviors (Bechky, 2003; Adler and Borys, 1996), resulting in coordinated action.

A typology of e-coordination modes

For the development of a typology of e-coordination modes we follow a stream of research that investigates the use of technology for coordination, in particular in software projects (Neuwirth *et al.*, 2001; Faraj and Sproull, 2000; Crowston and Kammerer, 1998; Failla, 1996; Nidumolu, 1996), NPD (Hoegl *et al.*, 2004), and dispersed software teams (Carmel, 1999, Kotlarsky *et al.*, 2006). Most of this research focuses on a particular relationship between technology and coordination. In our study we combine and extend these views by allowing for various combinations of technology and e-coordination modes.

Coordination theory was first developed in an era of limited development of ICT (in the 1950s and 1960s). With the proliferation of sophisticated IT, we can reinterpret coordination from a technological perspective. We suggest that technology supports three coordination modes – personal, impersonal, and automated and thus enables what we call e-coordination. A key dimension for comparing the modes is the *enabling* and *unloading*[3] (Crick and Mitchison, 1995) impact of technology on coordination processes:

- *Enabling* refers to the idea that structures – such as procedures or technology – enhance the quality, duration, and scope of human performance (Adler and Borys, 1996).
- *Unloading* means here that coordination is achieved without individuals having to perform information processing activities, i.e. they can reduce their efforts. For instance, coordinating structures – such as a plan – substitute for interaction processes under stable work conditions. People know what to do and how to coordinate without having to consult others (Gabarro, 1990; Bryman *et al.*, 1987; Simon, 1950).

We now elaborate on each mode in more detail.

Personal e-coordination. This mode could be characterized as a personal loop. E-coordination technologies support personal coordination by means of computer-mediated communications, such as email, phone, videoconferencing, and chatting (Fulk *et al.*, 1992). Technology changes the time-space configurations of personal contact (Boland and Citurs, 2001 Maznevski and Chudoba, 2000; DeSanctis and Gallupe, 1987). Individuals connect from dispersed sites, and choose between real-time and asynchronous communications (e.g. videoconferencing versus email). This *enabling* role of technology is essential in virtual team environments where individuals usually cannot meet face-to-face because of distance, or cannot meet in real time because of time differences (Adams *et al.*, 1997; Meadows, 1996). In this mode, technology does not unload (substitute for interpersonal coordination) but rather facilitates these meetings.

Impersonal e-coordination. E-coordination technologies enhance the role of the impersonal coordination mode. Individuals share externalized knowledge (Nonaka and Konno, 1998) and representations of their work, such as project plans, methods (Ciborra and Patriotta, 1996), and design sketches (Majchrzak *et al.*, 2000; Venkatraman and Henderson, 1998). They check standards and procedures online without contacting anyone else. Impersonal e-coordination represents a more indirect form of coordination compared to the first mode. Instead of talking directly to others, individuals use technology-supported coordination mechanisms, such as standards, representations, and plans, to shape their behaviours (Adler and Borys, 1996). E-coordination technologies in this category support the capturing and sharing of information with virtually no limitations in terms of capacity, and support the spatial-temporal availability of information. Technology plays an *enabling* role by making impersonal mechanisms available that present individuals with explicit (externalized) know-how (Nonaka and Konno, 1998; Adler and Borys, 1996). Technology thus becomes a knowledge management vehicle for coordination. Furthermore, technology *unloads* individuals by informing individuals about "who-does-what," and about task expectations, project plans, and the status of a project (Moreland, 1999).

Automated e-coordination. With the advance of new technologies, we introduce a coordination mode that extends impersonal coordination: *automated coordination*. Conceptually speaking, *automation* means an artifact that functions autonomously (Zuboff, 1988). Autonomous technology takes steps which constitute a coordination process (Crowston, 1997). It senses the task environment, processes cues, synthesizes information, and responds. This active role differentiates automation from traditional impersonal coordination mechanisms such as plans or standards. Coordination can be achieved by autonomously operating technologies such as Artificial Intelligence (AI), Automated Guided Vehicles (AGVs), active agents, and soft bots (Neuwirth *et al.*, 2001). For example, the Boeing 777 team adopted CAD/CAM software that identified the dependencies of design tasks and notified the teams involved (Argyres, 1999; Sabbagh, 1996). Distributed software development increasingly relies on automation in the form of automated CASE tools, configuration, and version management tools, and notification services (Cheng *et al.*, 2004). These tools automate certain aspects of the software development process, such as coding, and version and configuration management. Automated coordination relies on intelligent information systems that operate autonomously (Neuwirth *et al.*, 2001; Argyres, 1999; Zuboff, 1988), i.e. without the need for human effort. These systems on the one hand coordinate task accomplishment in an active manner, and, on the other hand, they perform some tasks themselves. Technology enacts a coordinating role when it controls task dependencies, handles schedule conflicts, and controls versions and configurations of products and components. These technologies are designed for autonomously sensing their environment (inputs), deciding (based on sets of algorithms), and generating outputs that include acting, providing information, or warning. Moreover, technology sometimes performs the task being coordinated, e.g. moving physical artifacts in a factory (e.g. AGVs), or manufacturing cars. Technology – as a coordinating and work performing device – thus moves beyond enabling. It *unloads* individuals and reduces their role from active participation towards controlling (Burnes and Fitter, 1987). Autonomous technology coordinates and performs tasks often faster and in a more continuous fashion than humans could, i.e. without human constraints (Simon, 1991a).

To conclude, we distinguish personal, impersonal, and automated e-coordination modes. These modes do *not* refer to the embedded properties of technologies (DeSanctis and Gallupe, 1987), i.e. their designed use, but to the way technologies are used for coordination (Orlikowski, 1992). Given the various options for enacting e-coordination technology, confusion may arise with respect to the mode in which technologies are used for e-coordination (Collins and Kusch, 1999). The boundary between humans and machines in terms of task performance and coordination may become diffuse and evolve dynamically. We therefore use this typology for empirically categorizing and understanding the use of various technologies in e-coordination processes.

About this research

We examine e-coordination in globally distributed software development teams, because these teams have to rely heavily on tools and technologies for communication and software development processes (e.g. CASE tools, configuration and version management tools). We conducted an in-depth qualitative case study to illustrate our typology in practice, and to examine the implications of each mode for e-coordination processes. Linkages between types of tasks and e-coordination modes are explored. We conducted an in-depth study of a globally distributed software development project at the global software development group of LeCroy Corporation. Additional information about LeCroy can be found in the Appendix. Interviews were conducted at two remote sites with Maui team members based in Switzerland and in the US.

Insights from the LeCroy Maui project

The global software team had a long history of working together developing software for oscilloscopes. When this study was carried out it had already developed strategies for working together across distance. However, the Maui project introduced new challenges to the global software team at LeCroy. The project involved switching from embedded programming to component-based development using Microsoft COM (Component Object Model) technology, which was very different from the approaches LeCroy software engineers had used to develop embedded software for earlier products. Therefore, one of the dilemmas LeCroy faced while developing the Windows-based Maui platform was how to train programmers used to embedded programming but being located at different sites, while ensuring that this transition would not trigger disruptive communication problems and breakdowns.

To give an overview of the coordination activities that take place on a regular basis at the LeCroy global software team, we summarize coordination activities we identified during data collection (Table 9.1). The table also presents technologies and tools used in different e-coordination modes. (A)synchronicity refers to the distinction between coordination involving remote counterparts communicating in real time (synchronous), versus coordination where individuals work at different times, often

Table 9.1   E-coordination between LeCroy New York and Geneva

E-coordination mode	Coordination activities	Technology used for e-coordination
1. Personal e-coordination		
Synchronous	• Solving short and urgent questions, e.g. clarifications • Helping in fixing bugs (e.g. show conditions of failure) • Transferring knowledge (e.g. showing slides during presentation) • Conducting design reviews • Joint product design • Conducting progress team meetings • Conducting major design reviews	• On line chat • Application sharing and internet conferencing • Videoconferencing
Synchronous or asynchronous	• Solving urgent complex issues • Conducting update and progress meetings between managers • Resolving misunderstandings and conflicts	• Phone (teleconferencing) and email
Asynchronous	• Solving non-urgent (low priority) issues, and clarifications • Distributing information (PUSH mode), e.g. sending information to a specific person/group of people • Bug fixing (accelerating development process by passing bug fixing between teams in different time zones)	• Email
2. Impersonal e-coordination		
Synchronous or asynchronous	• Ensuring consistency and integratability of software components being developed at remote locations • Ensuring that remote team members have access to the most updated information	• Standardization of software development tools and methods used across dispersed sites; standard component interfaces • Single development environment, replicated databases

(Continued)

Table 9.1   (Continued)

E-coordination mode	Coordination activities	Technology used for e-coordination
	(product files and project documents) through constant replication of databases over the Web	• Centralized tools, central project repository and Web access
Asynchronous	• Providing guidelines for the use of software development methods and tools (accessible through the Web to ensure remote counterparts can access the same documents)	• Standard project documents, templates, guides • Web access
	• Informing about project status (project plans and progress) • Informing about updated product status (e.g. new components, roadmap)	• Intranet/central project repository (where standard project documents are posted, templates and guidelines)
3. Automated e-coordination		
Synchronous	• Informing team members about availability of their remote counterparts	• Online chat (seeing who is online and their status)
Synchronous or asynchronous	• Managing interdependencies between components and related files • Rapidly updating changes in product files and project documents	• ComProjMgr (internal tool of LeCroy) • Automated "building" of components that have changed • Automated replication of databases

because of time-zone differences. (New York is located in UTC −5, Geneva in UTC +1, so there is a six hours' time gap. For instance, 9 a.m. New York time corresponds with 3 p.m. Geneva time.) Next, we discuss the findings presented in the table for each e-coordination mode. The coordination activities shown involve co-located and remote team members. However, given our focus on the use of technologies for e-coordination, we were particularly interested in coordination activities between remote counterparts.

Personal e-coordination

At LeCroy, many coordination activities were conducted through interpersonal loops that took place in a *one-to-one* configuration (someone asks his remote counterpart to clarify a product specification), a *one-to-many* configuration (during a knowledge transfer session when someone explains to his local and remote counterparts the principles of Maui design), and a *many-to-many* configuration (during progress meetings managers from different geographical locations update each other about progress and issues via a teleconference). In the personal e-coordination mode, technology *enabled* interaction between remote counterparts. From the empirical data we identified the following technologies as contributing to this role: online chat, phone (teleconferencing), videoconference, email, and application sharing (often combined with simultaneously talking by phone or voicechat). These technologies enabled dispersed team members to get in touch to coordinate their activities despite geographical distance. And they enabled synchronous and asynchronous communications, so that remote counterparts could coordinate their activities regardless of (and sometimes benefiting from (Carmel, 1999)) time-zone differences.

Next, we describe the major coordination activities mentioned in Table 9.1, illustrated by quotes from our study, and we discuss the technology used for e-coordination.

Solving urgent problems and issues was typically done by online chat (for short queries) or a combination of phone, email, and chat (for complex issues that usually involved email or chat message followed by a phone call). At LeCroy every member of the software development group appears on the list of an Instant Messenger application. This tool enabled real-time remote contact:

> For having a chat with someone, wherever they may be in the world in the given time, you just need to double click on their name and start typing a line. During the day if you have a question or you need somebody's help you largely use online chat. It is immediate, it does not matter where they are in the world – whether they are in the next cubicle or whether they are in the next country, they use that system. (Anthony)

However, if an issue is complex or requires more than a couple of lines of response, team members tended to pick up the phone and talk to each other.

For **design reviews** software engineers typically used an Application/Desk-top Sharing Tool[4] (AST): it allowed developers to observe the screen of a remote computer, and to share and take over control. Software developers made extensive use of this tool for code reviews. Larry explained:

> I have even seen it within this building, you see two guys in almost the next cubicle to each other – they do a code review: sitting next to each other, but they are sitting at their desks and looking at their own screen working through the code. So, it is actually an interesting tool, and individuals are used to doing code reviews across the ocean or up to Maine.[5]

For **joint product design** (e.g. when designing a new feature or user interface) Larry and Anthony frequently used AST: "We have been working in Visual Studio when laying out a dialog for a product via AST when Anthony will be in Geneva and I'll be here [in New York]" (Larry).

Joint product design refers to a complex, collaborative task involving team interdependence and therefore high information processing needs (van de Ven *et al.*, 1976). When someone needed **help with debugging**, AST was commonly used for taking control of a computer. Gilles gave an example:

> If someone has problem in Geneva, he finds where the code is failing and he wants to show me the code and the condition under which it is failing. Then we use AST to show the code. So I control his computer to see what goes wrong, and I get results right on my screen.

Typically in such situations, developers used AST to see what was happening on the computer, and at the same time they used the phone or voicechat capability of AST to discuss the problem.

About one year before launching the Aladdin system (from early 2001), software managers started using videoconferencing (VC) for **progress meetings** at least once a week. Furthermore, VC was used for **updating a remote team** (e.g. when Anthony was in New York he was holding progress meetings with his team in Geneva), or updating developers from both locations:

> When the majority of the individuals started coming on board of Maui, we started having this almost every week. And every once in a while, more recently, as NY guys also started working with Maui, we have transatlantic videoconferences with all the software guys in NY and Geneva. (Anthony)

Some coordination activities took place asynchronously. These concerned mainly **non-urgent, low priority, tasks**, and tasks that could not be completed in real time because of time-zone differences. Most of these tasks were accomplished through email. For example: "Stuff that doesn't need an immediate answer or things that happen outside of the overlapping time period, that all happens by email" (Anthony). Furthermore, the LeCroy team used opportunities for asynchronous coordination to accelerate the development process through utilizing time-zone differences: "We use the fact that we are not working together to allow us to work around-the-clock" (Gilles). Anthony explained:

> I would not say that time differences are a disadvantage, and close to a release or big milestone they can be a big advantage. Because problems, bugs fixes, can be passed on from time zone to time zone.

Compared to co-located work environments, the combination of time-zone differences and coordination technologies thus accelerates the process of coordinating tasks.

Impersonal e-coordination

This e-coordination focuses more on indirect coordination mechanisms. The "e-"aspect of this mode refers to the use of ICT for mediating loops that coordinate individuals' work practices. This technology enhances the role of impersonal coordination modes such as plans, procedures, and documents. From the empirical data we identified the following main types of impersonal e-coordination tools (Table 9.1):

- Standardized software development tools and methods. These were available for dispersed team members on a central server and through a single development environment.
- Standard project documents which informed team members about project status and product specifications, templates, and guides. These were available in a central project repository on the Intranet and accessible through the Web.

In the impersonal coordination mode, technology, first, *enabled* dispersed team members to use coordination mechanisms by making them available for all members of the team, regardless of their geographical location (e.g. through Web access and a single development environment). Second, the technology *unloaded* individuals by informing them about the progress of a project and product (product features and specifications), the division of work between remote counterparts, and other aspects that constitute the coordination necessary for ensuring consistency and integratability of components developed at different sites. Technology provided synchronous and asynchronous support for impersonal coordination (Table 9.1). Below we describe impersonal coordination activities observed at LeCroy, and we discuss the technology used for this type of e-coordination.

To **ensure consistency of software components** being developed at remote locations, the LeCroy team standardized software development tools and methods across dispersed locations:

> All are identical, absolutely identical. We have one Version Control System [VCS], at least for Maui, which is located in Geneva: it is on the network, so everyone can get to it. The Lotus Notes system we use is on servers in NY and in Geneva. And they are replicated, so they are identical essentially. Everything is the same. Everyone working with Maui uses the same tools. (Anthony)

The main tools the software team used were COMProjMgr (COM Project Manager) for managing interdependencies between components, Perforce for version and configuration management, BugBase for managing bugs, and SoftwareTestHarness for testing components. (Of the four main tools, Perforce is a commercial tool, and COMProjMgr, SoftwareTestHarness, and BugBase are all tools developed by the LeCroy software team.) Team members used these tools synchronously from their dispersed locations.

Integratability of components was ensured by adopting standard interfaces that are part of the Maui architecture:

> The interfaces describe how these components talk to each other. If you want to make a component for Maui – whether it will be something to display waveforms, to control the front panel, an acquisition system, any of these things – in order to integrate them into the system and to attach them to the rest of the system, they have to implement or use one of the Maui interfaces. It is a bunch of standards, and it is a tool kit. (Anthony)

In order to **ensure that remote team members have access to the most updated files** in real time, the LeCroy team had one central database accessible over WAN from remote locations, and a repository/database for each project accessible via the Web. Remote counterparts had thus access to the latest versions of files and components. For example, LeCroy used a Lotus Notes-based tool called BugBase for tracking bugs. This tool was accessible and constantly replicated over the Web. Every LeCroy office had access to BugBase and used it for coordination purposes:

> Also all our sales offices – in Japan for instance, they have a copy of it. In sales offices employees can enter bugs and monitor the status, but they cannot change anything. The person who has entered a bug gets notified when it has been fixed. (Larry)

Impersonal mechanisms for asynchronous coordination included *guidelines that explain how to use software development methods and tools*. This involved documents such as standard project templates and guides accessible through the Web which enabled access to all remote counterparts. Maui tools and methods were described in the Maui Software Developer's Guide. It listed the tools used and explained how to create and debug components in Maui:

> [The Guide] describes the complete software-development process for the Maui Software Platform. Developers new to Maui can follow the directions in this guide to configure a "virgin" workstation for Maui development, create Maui Components, debug them, and evaluate their performance. (extract from the Maui Software Developer's Guide)

This guide was considered invaluable for making individuals familiar with Maui. Working with identical tools and resources made it easier for individuals at remote locations to understand and help each other.

Furthermore, asynchronous impersonal coordination concerned *informing team members about project status* (progress and updated project plans) *and evolving products* (e.g. new components, roadmap). These asynchronous e-coordination mechanisms allowed team members to access the required information from any location, at any time. The LeCroy team had access to its own Intranet environment where internal documents and other relevant information were posted. For example: "Project plans are accessible via the Web [Intranet]. This provides marketing and team members at all locations with updated information on the status of a project" (Larry). Technology used for impersonal coordination thus enabled and unloaded team members in the performance of their tasks.

Automated e-coordination

According to the proposed typology, this e-coordination mode could be characterized as an automated loop in which (i) coordination activities are programmed and (ii) some project activities are performed by the technology. Therefore, humans play a limited role: they mainly control and maintain an overview of the project work while technology performs the coordination activities automatically, based on the programmed rules, and executes some tasks independently. Compared to the previous mode, technology is an active system that, virtually independent of human intervention, performs and enforces coordination. It does not enable humans to act in a coordinated fashion, but acting autonomously it unloads humans.

From the empirical data we identified the following tools and methods that were used for automated e-coordination: online chat, standard component interfaces, and tools for automated management of interdependencies between components, automated "building" of components, and automated replication of databases. These tools and technologies *unloaded* team members from the need to complete some activities manually. Team members could concentrate on activities and roles that could not be automated. Furthermore, tools and technologies used for automated e-coordination unloaded team members from mental pressure by completing repetitive and routine (coordination) tasks that would take ages for a human to perform because of physical or mental constraints (Simon, 1991b).

We now describe the automated e-coordination activities observed at LeCroy, and discuss the technology used for this type of e-coordination.

To **inform team members about availability of their remote counterparts** in real time LeCroy team used online chat: "We use MSN Messenger from Microsoft – every member of the software development group, they appear on the list" (Anthony). When an employee logs into the system, MSN Messenger opens automatically. This way, team members could see who of their remote counterparts was in the office and, by looking at their status, they could gauge whether a counterpart might be available to help or answer a question.

Managing interdependencies between components and related files is a key issue in component-based development. Components and files are tightly interrelated, so every modification and new component requires changes in the whole development environment. Managing these interdependencies is not a problem as long as the number of components is small, because in such a case the dependencies can be modelled and understood visually by project members. However, when the number of components becomes (extremely) high, visual understanding is no longer an option. As Anthony explained:

> Imagine building one DLL in one project under Visual Studio. It is very easy to do. Building two or three project DLLs that depend on each other is also fairly easy to do. Building 300 or 500 of these things is impossible.

To manage interdependencies between a high number of components, LeCroy developed an in-house tool (COMProjMgr). Anthony explained how the tool works:

> COMProjMgr basically is a dependency scanner; it will scan through all source and header files looking for dependencies from other files. And it will tell us about these dependencies.

Having a globally distributed team working on the project imposed additional challenges related to ensuring that remote team members have access to updated files. To deal with these challenges LeCroy team used Lotus Notes databases that were programmed to replicate automatically:

> Because we are working at separate locations and Lotus Notes replicates databases, it is very good for us. The big databases are local to Geneva and here [New York], and they get replicated constantly over the Web. (Larry)

Automated replication unloaded individuals from the task of checking with others the status of documents. It reduced intersite communications, and thereby contributed to the efficiency of the virtual team.

Furthermore, to support **rapid updating of changes**, the LeCroy software team programmed four times a day a components "build":

> Most individuals leave their computer running at night and they can set it to import the latest components from the Version Control System at 5 o'clock in the morning. We have a server that builds four times a day all the components, and produces "release binaries". So I don't have to build every component locally. If someone changes the hardcopy component and they put it back, it will be rebuilt on the server and then in the morning I can import that component and just use it. (Larry)

Automated building ensured that components – including changes after the last "build" – could interact coherently. This tool enabled the LeCroy team to leverage time-zone differences.

Discussion

In this chapter we have developed a typology of e-coordination modes that distinguishes between (i) different types of e-coordination and (ii) different roles of e-coordination technologies, and (iii) clarifies the changing role of technology versus humans. Our conceptual study resulted in a framework consisting of three types of e-coordination modes: personal, impersonal, and automated.

The three e-coordination modes in practice

The empirical results suggest that the three e-coordination modes provide a useful framework for clarifying the contributions of technology to different ways of e-coordination in various task contexts:

Personal e-coordination is supported by multiple types of communication tools at LeCroy, such as online chat, email, phone, application sharing, and videoconferencing. These technologies helped to reduce the perception of distance between remote counterparts. They *enabled* interaction between dispersed team members, sharing information, and solving problems across sites in real time and asynchronously.

Impersonal e-coordination is supported by creating a homogeneous work environment across remote sites. LeCroy deployed a single development environment, standard tools, and enabled Web access to synchronize multisite operations without extensive interpersonal communications. Furthermore, LeCroy utilized knowledge that the company had accumulated: resources such as the Maui Guide, which explains how to use methods and tools. This enabled team members to facilitate knowledge sharing (as the Guide made explicit): the knowledge of individuals who initially developed the basics of the Maui platform. The use of standard tools and technologies across locations and the centralization of tools also *unloaded* LeCroy engineers from the task of ensuring consistency and integratability of components developed at different sites.

Automated e-coordination tools coordinate tasks by informing team members about availability, managing interdependencies between components, and rapidly updating changes. ICT used in this mode *unloads* team members from the need to complete some activities manually, thus enabling them to concentrate on other activities and roles that cannot be automated. Furthermore, tools and technologies used for automated e-coordination *unload* team members from mental pressure by completing repetitive and routine coordination tasks that would take ages for a human to perform because of mental constraints (for example technically it is possible to manage interdependencies between components manually; however, in practice this would be inefficient). Technology also accomplishes tasks humans could not possibly perform because of their physical constraints. For instance, at LeCroy the software is working for 24 hours a day, compared to individuals' 8–9 hour working days. What we can learn from LeCroy work practices is that automation of specific tasks, such as daily software building and replicating databases, can increase coordination efficiency since software can work non-stop. We know therefore more about the task context and scope for ICT deployment.

Same technology, different e-coordination modes

The same technology can be used for e-coordination in different modes, while in each mode it is used in a different manner. For example, the LeCroy team uses online chat for personal e-coordination (e.g. to solve urgent issues that require short replies online, in this situation chat is used on a one-to-one basis), as well as for automated e-coordination (e.g. to inform team members about their availability online, in this situation chat is used to inform anybody who might need to know whether a person is in the office and available). Therefore, decisions about the e-coordination mechanisms must acknowledge the multiple uses of e-coordination technologies, and the multiple ways to perform a coordination activity, rather than finding and institutionalizing a "perfect match" between technology and the e-coordination mode. For example, providing detailed "awareness" information about what is going on at remote sites is an important part of coordination between globally distributed teams. However, the choice of technology to be used to provide such information depends on the type of "awareness" information one wants to provide to remote counterparts. "Awareness" information may be distributed to the entire team, for instance by LeCroy using online chat to distribute information about who is available at remote locations. "Awareness" information may also include the log of a project file activity that team members would see upon each login instance (e.g. who downloaded what file, who uploaded what file, who commented on what file, and so forth). The idea would then be that making team members more aware of others' activities would help overcome some of the information inadequacies of dispersed teams observed by Cramton (1997). She had noted that lack of communication between teammates, often as a result of simple errors or timing problems, gave others the impression that remote teammates were disinterested or were not actively working on the project. Hence the intention could be to "fill in the blanks" by automatically logging any team activity in a shared file directory. However, such tool, while being helpful for some teams and providing remote counterparts with "awareness" information, might have some negative effects. For example, imagine a situation when software engineers from remote locations schedule a teleconference to complete a design review, and agree that design documents should be sent one day in advance so that all parties will have enough time to read through the documents and comment. Then, on the day of the teleconference, team members who uploaded the design documents notice that their documents have been downloaded only 20 minutes before the meeting. Such "awareness" information would give the impression that remote counterparts were not reading the work the team uploaded to the server well before their scheduled meeting, despite the fact that the other team purposely placed the work on the system a day beforehand to give time for review. This is likely to create a sense of distrust and a rather dysfunctional working pattern, and may affect the quality of a joint collaborative outcome. This hypothetical situation highlights how providing "awareness" information can have counter-productive effects if the wrong type of technology is chosen for coordination between the teams. With personal e-coordination this over-transparency problem would not occur, but the literature contains few studies that suggest that impersonal and automated coordination provides information that individuals would prefer to hide. The reasons for such non-informing could be shame over incomplete designs, mistakes common to human work processes (Ciborra et al., 1996), or political tensions in interorganizational collaboration (Loebbecke and van Fenema, 2000). Organizations could therefore revert under such conditions to personal e-coordination, which leaves individuals with more control over information sharing. Individuals could email (one-to-many) or upload the document to a central repository that shows when the document was created or modified (and not when and by whom it was downloaded).

E-coordination modes and tasks

The literature suggests that e-coordination often leads to confusion, tensions, and mistakes, (e.g. BFU, 2004; Cramton, 2001). Our conceptual work and the LeCroy case study offers pointers for improving our understanding of and capability to deploy e-coordination technologies. We extend the framework by mapping e-coordination modes against the three categories of tasks (in Figure 9.1, see vertical "match" linkages).[6]

Personal e-coordination is associated with tasks like building mutual understanding, sharing knowledge, and socialization. Impersonal e-coordination is suitable for routine, large-scale coordination, and for synchronized planning and information sharing. Automated e-coordination should be used for clearly specified tasks that are simple (e.g. replicating databases), that require limited variation, and/or that demand non-stop processing.

Mismatches occur for instance when complex tasks are coordinated impersonally (Malhotra *et al.*, 2001); when personal e-coordination is used for tasks that could be accomplished more efficiently using automated technology; or situations where advanced automation is deployed when individuals prefer to coordinate personally (Sweet, 1995; Sandza, 1989).

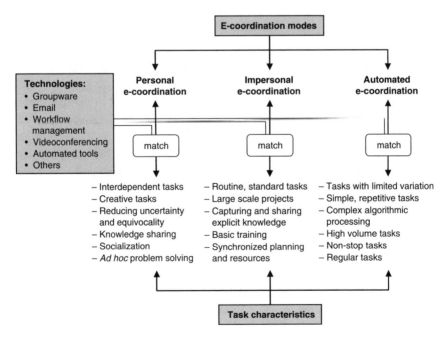

Figure 9.1 E-coordination modes and task characteristics

Mismatches may occur unknowingly, for instance when a technology is introduced without specifying its use, or when the use of technology shifts across the modes over time. The framework and our findings clarify appropriate opportunities for deploying e-coordination technologies, as well as the boundaries between them. In the following section we explore the implications of this study for research and practice.

Implications for practice and research

The typology provides practitioners with frameworks (Figure 9.1) for evaluating e-coordination activities and selecting, designing, and modifying appropriate e-coordination technologies. If e-coordination activities are interactive, highly interdependent, and urgent, managers should opt for personal e-coordination. For large-scale, complex tasks, impersonal e-coordination is essential for reducing uncertainty over plans and work progress. Finally, organizations may want to automate specific tasks that can be characterized as routine (automated e-coordination). Automated e-coordination makes it possible to use time-zone differences advantageously. Technology can work non-stop "around-the-clock", and unload individuals such that they can focus on more interesting work which only humans can perform.

Practitioners should realize the risks associated with each mode, and the danger of confusing the modes. The first mode should not be used for tasks that can be reutilized and automated. This burdens professionals unnecessarily. The second mode cannot be used for highly adaptive tasks (Majchrzak *et al.*, 2000; Ciborra *et al.*, 1996). These tasks require mode 1 and possibly face-to-face meetings. The third mode can be used for high volume, well-defined tasks. In this mode demarcations of responsibilities between individuals and systems should be precise and *ex ante* communicated to those involved (BFU, 2004). Awareness of each e-coordination mode is compulsory for effective technology deployment. If we suppose that tasks change, more research is needed to understand practices for switching between e-coordination modes, i.e. a dynamic cross-modal view. Recurrent discussions on the mode in which technology is used helps to build shared knowledge bases and deal with the constraints of distributed collaboration, as explained in Chapter 3. Usually, this mode changes over time as tasks evolve and teams become more experienced working at (global) distances (Malhotra *et al.*, 2001; Majchrzak *et al.*, 2000).

From an academic point of view, the framework presents a typology that can be used for analyzing the role of e-coordination tools in various task contexts. The framework can support analysis of problems and accidents that are (partially) caused by the inappropriate use of e-coordination tools. Furthermore, researchers can refine and extend the typology by exploring ties to theories in areas such as social cognition, (electronic) communications, organizational behavior, and Computer Supported Collaborative Work.

To conclude, the typology categorizes technologies along three generic dimensions (the e-coordination modes). This has the advantage that even advanced e-coordination technologies that may emerge in the (near) future can be analyzed for their usefulness, and can be mapped to specific work contexts. As suggested in Figure 9.1, matching e-coordination modes, technologies, tasks, personnel selection, and training will enhance the likelihood of e-coordination success.

Notes

1. We use the terms "virtual team" and "globally distributed team" interchangeably. These groups are defined as internationally dispersed professionals who rely almost exclusively on technologies to accomplish their work.
2. A coordination mode means a coherent category of practices aimed at integrating contributions from multiple individuals.
3. *Unloading* is a concept originally developed in the cognitive and brain sciences. It refers to the reduction of attention and mental effort associated with a task.
4. The name of the actual tool cannot be used for reasons of confidentiality.
5. A chief engineer is working for LeCroy from his home-office in Maine.
6. The "technologies" box is included to suggest that the same technology could be used for different e-coordination modes. The figure focuses however on the (mis)match between e-coordination modes and tasks.

References

Adams, J. R. and Adams, L. L. (1997) "The Virtual Project: Managing Tomorrow's Team Today," *PM Network*, 11(1), 37–42.
Adler, P. S. and Borys, B. (1996) "Two Types of Bureaucracies: Enabling and Coercive," *Administrative Science Quarterly*, 41, 61–89.

Argyres, N. S. (1999) "The Impact of Information Technology on Coordination: Evidence from the B-2 'Stealth' Bomber," *Organization Science*, 10(2), 162–80.

Barley, S. R. (1986) "Technology as an Occasion for Structuring: Evidence from Observations of CT Scanners and the Social Order of Radiology Departments," *Administrative Science Quarterly*, 31, 78–108.

Bechky, B. A. (2003) "Sharing Meaning Across Occupational Communities: The Transformation of Understanding on a Production Floor," *Organization Science*, 14(3), 312–30.

BFU (2004) *Investigation Report*, German Federal Bureau of Aircraft Accidents Investigation (Bundesstelle für Flugunfalluntersuchung (BFU)), Braunschweig (Germany), document # AX001-1/-2/02 (English version), http://www.bfu-web.de.

Boland, R. J. and Citurs, A. (2001) *Work as the Making of Time and Space*, vol. 2, Winter, Sprouts: Working Papers on Information Environments, Systems and Organizations, http://weatherhead.cwru.edu/sprouts/2002/020101.pdf

Bryman, A., Bresnen, M., Beardsworth, A. D., Ford, J., and Keil, E. T. (1987) "The Concept of the Temporary System: The Case of the Construction Project," in *Research in the Sociology of Organizations* (Eds, Bacharach, S. B. and Ditomaso, N.) vol. 5, JAI, Greenwich CT, pp. 73–104.

Burnes, B. and Fitter, M. (1987) "Control of Advanced Manufacturing Technology: Supervision Without Supervisors?" in *The Human Side of Advanced Manufacturing Technology* (Eds, Wall, T. D., Clegg, C. W., and Kemp, N. J.) John Wiley, Chichester.

Carmel, E. (1999) *Global Software Teams: Collaborating across Borders and Time Zones*, Prentice Hall, Englewood Cliffs, NJ.

Cheng, L., DeSouza, C. R. B., Hupfer, S., Patterson, J., and Ross, S. (2004) "Building Collaboration into IDEs," *Queue*, 1(9), 156–62.

Ciborra, C. U., Orlikowski, W. J., Failla, A., Patriotta, G., Bikson, T. K., Suetens, N. T., and Wynn, E. (1996). *Groupware & Teamwork: Invisible Aid or Technical Hindrance?* John Wiley, Chichester.

Collins, H. and Kusch, M. (1999) *The Shape of Actions: What Humans and Machines Can Do*, MIT Press, Boston, MA.

Cramton, C. D. (1997) "Information Problems in Dispersed Teams," *Proceedings of the Annual Meeting of the Academy of Management Best Papers Proceedings*, Boston, MA.

Cramton, C. D. (2001) "The Mutual Knowledge Problem and Its Consequences for Dispersed Collaboration," *Organization Science*, 12(3), 346–71.

Crick, F. and Mitchison, G. (1995) "REM Sleep and Neural Nets," *Behavioral Brain Research*, 69(1–2), 147–55.

Crowston, K. (1997) "A Coordination Theory Approach to Organizational Process Design," *Organization Science*, 8(2), 157–75.

Crowston, K. and Kammerer, E. E. (1998) "Coordination and Collective Mind in Software Requirements Development," *IBM Systems Journal*, 37(2), 227–45.

DeSanctis, G. and Gallupe, R. B. (1987) "A Foundation for the Study of Group Decision Support Systems," *Management Science*, 33(5), 589–609.

Donnellon, A., Gray, B., and Bougon, M. G. (1986) "Communication, Meaning, and Organized Action," *Administrative Science Quarterly*, 31(1), 43–55.

Failla, A. (1996). "Technologies for Co-ordination in a Software Factory," in *Groupware & Teamwork: Invisible Aid or Technical Hindrance?* (Eds, Ciborra, C. U., Orlikowski, W. K., Failla, A., Patriotta, G., Bikson, T. K., Suetens, N. T., and Wynn, E.) John Wiley, Chichester.

Faraj, S. and Sproull, L. (2000) "Coordinating Expertise in Software Development Teams," *Management Science*, 46(12), 1554–68.

Fulk, J., Steinfield, C., and Burkhardt, M. E. (1992) "Organizations and Communication Technology," *Administrative Science Quarterly* (September), 492–4.

Gabarro, J. J. (1990) "The Development of Working Relationships," in *Intellectual Teamwork: Social and Technological Foundations of Cooperative Work* (Eds, Galegher, J., Kraut, R. E., and Edigo, C.) Lawrence Erlbaum, Hillsdale, NJ, pp. 70–110.

Goodhue, D. L. and Thompson, R. L. (1995) "Task-Technology Fit and Individual Performance," *MIS Quarterly*, 19(4), 213–35.

Goodman, P. S. and Darr, E. D. (1998) "Computer-Aided Systems and Communities: Mechanisms for Organizational Learning in Distributed Environments," *MIS Quarterly*, 22(4), 417–40.

Gulick, L. (1937) "Notes on the Theory of Organization," in *Papers on the Science of Administration* (Eds, Gulick, L. and Urwick, L.) Institute of Public Administration, New York.

Herbsleb, J. D. and Mockus, A. (2003) "An Empirical Study of Speed and Communication in Globally-Distributed Software Development," *IEEE Transactions on Software Engineering*, 29(3), 481–94.

Hoegl, M., Weinkauf, K., and Gemuenden, H. G. (2004) "Interteam Coordination, Project Commitment, and Teamwork in Multiteam R&D Projects: A Longitudinal Study," *Organization Science*, 15(1).

Jarvenpaa, S. L., Knoll, K., and Leidner, D. E. (1998) "Is Anybody out There? Antecedents of Trust in Global Virtual Teams," *Journal of MIS*, 14(4), 29–64.

Kotlarsky, J., van Fenema, P. C. and Willcocks, L. P. (2006) "Case Research in Global Software Projects: Coordinating through Knowledge," *Proceedings of the International Conference of Information Systems*, Milwaukee, WI, US, Association for Information Systems.

Kunz, J. C., Christiansen, T. R., Cohen, G. P., Jin, Y., and Levitt, R. E. (1998) "The Virtual Design Team," *Communications of the ACM*, 41(11), 84–91.

Loebbecke, C. and van Fenema, P. C. (2000) "Virtual Organizations That Cooperate and Compete: Managing the Risks of Knowledge Exchange," *Knowledge Management and Virtual Organizations* (Ed., Malhotra, Y.) Idea Group Publishing, Hershey, PA, pp. 162–80.

Majchrzak, A., Rice, R. E., King, N., Malhotra, A., and Ba, S. (2000) "Technology Adaptation: The Case of a Computer-supported Inter-organizational Virtual Team," *MIS Quarterly*, 24(4), 569–600.

Malhotra, A., Majchrzak, A., Carman, R., and Lott, V. (2001) "Radical Innovation Without Collocation: A Case Study at Boeing-Rocketdyne," *MIS Quarterly*, 25(2), 229–49.

March, J. G. and Simon, H. A. (1958) *Organizations*, Wiley, New York.

Marriott, L. (1999a) "Charkhi-Dadri, India, 1996 Saudi Arabian Airlines Boeing 747-168B and Kazakhstan Airlines Ilyushin Il-76TD," in *Air Disasters* (Eds, Marriott, L. L., Stewart, S., and Sharpe, M.) PRC Publishing/Barnes and Noble Books, London.

Marriott, L. (1999b) "Straits of Hormuz, Persian Gulf, 1988 Iran Air Airbus A300B2," in *Air Disasters* (Eds, Marriott, L., Stewart, S., and Sharpe, M.) PRC Publishing/Barnes and Noble Books, London.

Maznevski, M. L. and Chudoba, K. M. (2000) "Bridging Space over Time: Global Virtual Team Dynamics and Effectiveness," *Organization Science*, 11(5), 473–92.

Meadows, C. J. (1996) "Globalizing Software Development," *Journal of Global Information Development*, 4(1), 5–14.

Mintzberg, H. (1979) *The Structuring of Organizations*, Prentice Hall, Englewood Cliffs, NJ.

Moreland, R. L. (1999) "Transactive Memory: Learning Who Knows What in Work Groups and Organizations," in *Shared Cognition in Organizations: The Management of Knowledge* (Eds, Thompson, L., Messick, D., and Levine, J.) Lawrence Erlbaum, Mahwah, NJ.

Neuwirth, C. M., Kaufer, D. S., Chandhok, R., and Morris, J. H. (2001) "Computer Support for Distributed Collaborative Writing: A

Coordination Science Perspective," in *Coordination Theory and Collaboration Technology* (Eds, Olson, G. M., Malone, T. W., and Smith, J. B.) Lawrence Erlbaum, Mahwah, NJ.

Nidumolu, S. R. (1996) "A Comparison of the Structural Contingency and Risk-Based Perspectives on Coordination in Software-Development Projects," *Journal of Management Information Systems*, 13(2), 77–113.

Nonaka, I. and Konno, N. (1998) "The Concept of 'Ba': Building a Foundation for Knowledge Creation," *California Management Review*, 40(3), 40–54.

Orlikowski, W. J. (1992) "The Duality of Technology: Rethinking the Concept of Technology in Organizations," *Organization Science*, 3(3), 398–427.

Orlikowski, W. J. (2000) "Using Technology and Constituting Structures: A Practical Lens for Studying Technology in Organizations," *Organization Science*, 11(4), 404–28.

Rajkumar, T. and Dawley, D. (1997) "Problems and Issues in Offshore Development of Software," in *Information Systems Sourcing: Theory and Practice* (Eds, Willcocks, L. and Lacity, M.) Oxford University Press, Oxford.

Sabbagh, K. (1996) *Twenty-First Century Jet: The Making and Marketing of the Boeing 777*, Scribner, New York.

Sanchez, R. and Mahoney, J. T. (1996) "Modularity, Flexibility, and Knowledge Management in Product and Organization Design," *Strategic Management Journal*, 17(Winter), 77–91.

Sandza, R. (1989) "Phantom of the Cockpit," *Newsweek*, 114(3), 61.

Sarker, S. and Sahay, S. (2004) "Implications of Space and Time for Distributed Work: An Interpretive Study of US–Norwegian System Development Teams," *European Journal of Information Systems*, 13(1), 3–20.

Scott, W. R. (1990) "Technology and Structure: An Organizational Level Perspective," in *Technology and Organizations* (Eds, Goodman, P. S. and Sproull, L. S.) Jossey-Bass, San Fransisco.

Simon, H. A. (1950) *Administrative Behavior*, The Free Press, New York.

Simon, H. A. (1991) "Bounded Rationality and Organizational Learning," *Organization Science*, 2, 125–34.

Smith, A. (1793) *An Inquiry into the Nature and Causes of the Wealth of Nations* (7th edn), Straham and Cadell, London.

Sweet, W. (1995) "The Glass Cockpit," *IEEE Spectrum*, 32(9), 30–9.

Thompson, J. D. (1967) *Organizations in Action*, McGraw-Hill, New York.

Tsoukas, H. (1996) "The Firm as a Distributed Knowledge System: A Constructionist Approach," *Strategic Management Journal*, 17 (Winter), 77–91.

van de Ven, A. H., Delbecq, A. L., and Koenig Jr, R. (1976) "Determinants of Coordination Modes Within Organizations," *American Sociological Review*, 41(April), 322–38.

Venkatraman, N. and Henderson, J. C. (1998) "Real Strategies for Virtual Organizing, *Sloan Management Review*, 40(1), 33–48.

Walsh, J. P. and Maloney, N. G. (2002) "Computer Network Use, Collaboration Structures, and Productivity, in *Distributed Work: New Ways of Working across Distance Using Technology* (Eds, Hinds, P. and Kiesler, S.) MIT Press, Cambridge, MA.

Weick, K. E. and Roberts, K. (1993) "Collective Mind in Organizations: Heedful Interrelating on Flight Decks," *Administrative Science Quarterly*, 38, 357–81.

Zuboff, S. (1988) *In the Age of the Smart Machine: The Future of Work and Power*, Basic Books, New York.

About the companies

1 LeCroy: Background

Cases relating to LeCroy are described in Chapters 1, 3, 7, and 9. Founded in 1964 by Walter LeCroy, a physicist, LeCroy Research Systems (in 1980 the name was changed to LeCroy Corporation) was quickly recognized as an innovator in instrumentation. In 1972 the company established an instrument design and production facility in Geneva, Switzerland. In 1976 the corporate headquarters moved to its present location in Chestnut Ridge, New York.

Initially, LeCroy developed technology to capture, measure, and analyze sophisticated electronic signals in a stringent scientific environment. In 1985, the company began transferring this technology to a popular line of general-purpose instruments. Growth in the commercial test and measurement market really took off when the company introduced its first digital storage oscilloscope products. Since that time the core business of LeCroy has been the design and production of oscilloscopes and oscilloscope-like instruments – signal analyzers, signals generators, and others.

During the last 20 years, LeCroy has opened a number of sales offices in Europe (in France, Italy, Germany, Switzerland, and the UK). There are also offices in Japan, South Korea, China, and Singapore. LeCroy now employs more than 400 people worldwide. In 2004 the company reported annual revenues of more than USD 150 million.

The case described in this book is about the development of an oscilloscope family. Three teams – software, hardware, and manufacturing – were involved in the production of these oscilloscopes. Initially, all three teams were located in New York and Geneva and worked together from these two locations. In 1999 manufacturing and hardware were consolidated in New York. Software development stayed as it initially was, distributed between New York and Geneva. In this book we focused on the Maui project, which concerned the development of a software platform for new generations of oscilloscopes and oscilloscope-like instruments based on the Windows operating system. There were about 10–15 people in the Geneva team and the same amount in New York.

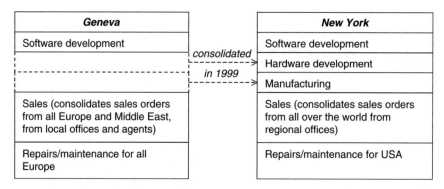

Figure A.1   Division of responsibilities between New York and Geneva offices

Table A.1   LeCroy – Interviewees' details

Name	Role	Location
Larry*	Director of Software Engineering	New York
Anthony*	Chief Software Architect	Geneva
Gilles	Software engineer	Geneva
Adrian	Web-master	New York
Corey	Vice President, Information Systems	New York
Dave	Vice President, Chief Technology Officer	New York

* These individuals were interviewed twice.
Note: Interviews were carried out between November, 2001 and January, 2003 in Geneva and New York sites. Roles are correct for 2002.

Figure A.1 illustrates the division of responsibilities between the New York and Geneva offices.

2 SAP: Background

Cases relating to SAP are described in Chapters 1 and 4. Founded in 1972, SAP is a recognized leader in software solutions. The company employs nearly 40,000 people in more than 50 countries, with software sales of EUR 9 billion in 2006. In this book, the cases focus on the Knowledge Management (KM) Collaboration Unit/Group, which is part of the Enterprise Portal Division. The KM Collaboration Group has developed a collaborative platform to foster teamwork. The goal of the SAP Collaboration tools project was to develop a comprehensive collaborative platform that would enable both individuals and teams in different

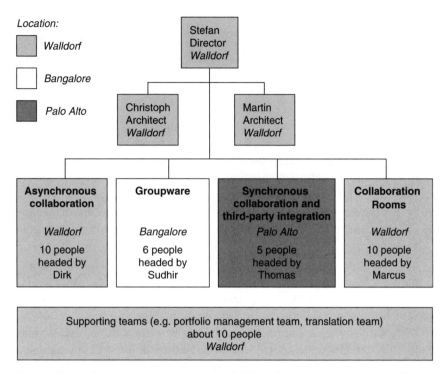

Location:

Walldorf

Bangalore

Palo Alto

Stefan
Director
Walldorf

Christoph
Architect
Walldorf

Martin
Architect
Walldorf

Asynchronous collaboration	**Groupware**	**Synchronous collaboration and third-party integration**	**Collaboration Rooms**
Walldorf	*Bangalore*	*Palo Alto*	*Walldorf*
10 people headed by Dirk	6 people headed by Sudhir	5 people headed by Thomas	10 people headed by Marcus

Supporting teams (e.g. portfolio management team, translation team)
about 10 people
Walldorf

Figure A.2   Organizational structure of KM Collaboration group (as of June 2002)

locations to communicate in real time and asynchronously, and to support the teamwork of any distributed project teams. The SAP Collaboration tools were developed to be part of the next generation application and integration platform (that is, SAP NetWeaver), and to allow integration with various tools of different providers. This Group consisted of four teams (see Figure A.2): two teams in Walldorf, Germany (ten people in each team), one team in Bangalore, India (6 people) and one team in Palo Alto, USA (5 people). Each team worked on a different part of the Collaboration project.

The development of SAP Collaboration tools started in September 2001. By June 2002, the first version of SAP Collaboration tools was released and the group was working on the second release.

3 TCS: Background

As part of the TATA Group, TCS was founded in 1968 as a consulting service firm for the emerging IT industry. Since than, TCS has expanded to become a global player with revenues of over USD 2 billion in 2006.

With over 74,000 associates and 50 service delivery centres, TCS has established a presence in 34 countries providing various services including business process outsourcing (BPO) and IT maintenance and development, to hundreds of clients across the globe. The company has developed a global delivery model in which the execution of projects has been achieved mainly through the support of teams located remotely from the client.

The case in Chapter 4 concerns the development and implementation of Quartz, an integrated financial platform aimed at providing solutions for financial institutions such as traditional and internet banks, brokerage/ securities houses, and asset managers. Quartz consists of a collection of architectural and business components that can be integrated with third party components to provide a solution according to the requirements of a specific customer. The Quartz group (a unit within TCS) is running several Quartz implementations simultaneously, for different clients. A typical Quartz implementation included the integration of Quartz with a customer's system and its customization to suit the needs of a specific customer.

The project organization of a Quartz implementation consists of an *onsite* team at the customer location and *offshore* teams at the development centres of TCS for system development and front-end design (Figure A.2). The majority of the Quartz team resided in one location throughout the project, either onsite or offshore, while only a small number of individuals travelled between remote locations for short visits. Teams at each site are headed by project leaders who report back to the project manager and ultimately the Quartz programme manager. The following Quartz implementation projects are investigated: (1) Skandia bank in Zurich, and (2) Dresdner bank in San Francisco. Both projects are concerned with the implementation of Quartz, therefore they are analyzed together as one "embedded" case study (Yin, 1994): the two projects are subunits of analysis. In terms of global distribution, the Skandia development team was distributed across three geographical locations: two *offshore* teams in Gurgaon and Bombay (India), and an *onsite* team at the customer location in Zurich (Switzerland). Furthermore, vendors of third-party components were located in different countries (more than 25 vendors in total). The Dresdner development team involved an *offshore* team in Gurgaon and an *onsite* team at the customer site in San Francisco (Figure A.3).

TCS and the ABN AMRO deal: Background information

The case in Chapter 5 concerns the ABN AMRO bank – TCS outsourcing programme which was announced in late 2005. In this EUR 1.8 billion

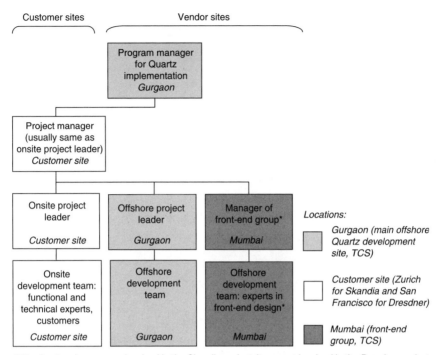

Figure A.3 Organizational structure of TCS Quartz projects

contract, the Netherlands-based bank contracted five vendors, among them Tata Consultancy Services (TCS), to provide support and application enhancement services. TCS will provide these services in cooperation with the other Indian company, Patni Computers, and Accenture as the preferred partner for application development. Facilities from TCS involved in the contract are located in Mumbai, Amsterdam, Luxemburg, and Sao Paulo.

The outsourcing project organization of the ABN AMRO-TCS deal consists of *onsite* teams at the customer locations in Amsterdam, Luxembourg, and Sao Paolo, and *offshore* or *nearshore* teams at the global delivery centres of TCS in Mumbai, Hungary, and Sao Paolo. The offshore team organizational structure is a mirror image of the onsite team organization structure (apart from some minor variations in role names). Typically, team members reside in one location throughout the project, either onsite or offshore, while only a small number of individuals travel between remote locations for short visits. The entire onsite team is made up of project members, project leaders, portfolio managers, programme

Table A.2 TCS – Interviewees' details

Name	Role	Location
Sanjay*	Executive manager for Quartz	Gurgaon
Sanjay*	Delivery manager for Quartz	Gurgaon
Sunil*	Offshore project leader for Dresdner	Gurgaon
Sandeep	Project manager and onsite project leader of Dresdner	San Francisco
Bala	Software engineer (team of Sunil)	Gurgaon
Pankaj*	Offshore project leader for Skandia	Gurgaon
Sourin	Software engineer (team of Pankaj)	Gurgaon
Nitin*	Technical consultant (former technical architect for Skandia)	Gurgaon
N. G. S	Vice President	Gurgaon
Ashvini	Technical architect and team leader for Skandia	Zurich
Tuhin	Software engineer (team of Ashvini)	Zurich
Krishna	Manager of front-end team (head of team in Mumbai)	Zurich
Rik	Executive for TCS-Skandia Relationships (IS)	Zurich
Rajan	Project manager and onsite project leader for Skandia	Zurich

* These individuals were interviewed twice
Note: Interviews were carried out in March 2002 in Gurgaon and Zurich sites. Roles are correct for 2002.

managers, a transition head, relationship manager, and other functions such as quality assurance, human resource, and organization development personnel. In terms of the expertise development, team members located either onsite or offshore needed to learn and develop expertise about clients' systems and markets in order to ensure that clients' applications are well-maintained offshore and that their applications are further developed. Expertise and know-how within the onsite and offshore teams have been ramped-up during two phases, Transition and Steady State. In the Transition phase, the onsite team learned about ABN AMRO's systems and transferred this knowledge to the offshore team. In the Steady State phase, mainly the offshore team, but also the onsite team, supported these systems as well as engaging in application development activities.

4 ALPHA: Background

The case in Chapter 6 concerns a supplier network that Alpha (a pseudonym) is part of. The firm, Alpha, is a global power systems company.

Their principally served markets include the civil aerospace, defence, marine, and energy markets. A worldwide network of offices, manufacturing, and service facilities supports this market. They have a broad customer base including airlines, corporate and utility aircraft, and helicopter operators.

The focus of this study is limited to the aerospace sector. Process innovations are being sought through investment in, and development of, an emerging-market supply network, which represents a significant evolution of Alpha's current supply network. Previous to this initiative, all design functions were carried out in-house at Alpha. As they seek to cut costs and focus internal resources on the development of core competences, Alpha has identified a limited number of design tasks that, they believe, can be outsourced without compromising the organization's core competences. Because of the nature of the task, Alpha was keen to move away from their traditional, transactional approach to outsourcing and develop long-term relationships with suppliers. Furthermore, their awareness of the cost advantages associated with emerging market economies has led them to explore strategic sourcing opportunities in the Far East. Alpha's lack of experience in sourcing design services has led them to arrange a contract with a home-based service provider ("Bravo"). However, this contract was carefully conceived to present significant incentives for a percentage of the contracted work to be subcontracted to an Alpha-approved, second-tier supplier ("Charlie") in the emerging market economy. We explore how learning capabilities were developed within this network in an attempt to improve network success.

5 Baan: Background

The Baan Corporation was created in 1978 by Jan Baan to provide financial and administrative consultancy services. A few years later his brother, Paul Baan, joined the company. Baan started to develop software packages, and in the mid 1990s, with the emergence of the Enterprise Resource Planning (ERP) industry, Baan became one of the market leaders and biggest vendors of ERP software, competing with SAP, PeopleSoft, and Oracle. In the mid 1990s Baan opened several development centres in different countries: the main sites were in Hyderabad (India), Quebec (Canada), and the headquarters in Barneveld (The Netherlands). In 2000 Baan was acquired for about USD 700 million by Invensys, a global automation, controls and process solutions group that offers products and services to improve resource productivity.

Three years later, in 2003, Invensys sold Baan Corporation for USD 135 million to two American private equity firms.

This case study in Chapter 4 concerns one Baan globally distributed project. This project was involved in the development of an E-Enterprise Suite. The case study was conducted in early 2002, when two globally distributed locations, Hyderabad (India) and Barneveld (The Netherlands), were working together on the E-Enterprise Suite. The E-Enterprise Suite was designed to let users extend their Baan manufacturing, financial, and distribution software on the Web to allow them to collaborate better with customers, suppliers, and partners. In March, 2002 the E-Enterprise Suite consisted of seven products that were all based on one platform called E-Enterprise Server. Products included in the E-Enterprise Suite were developed to be stand-alone as well as to be integrated with the ERP package developed by Baan.

Development of the E-Enterprise suite was organized by feature/ product function. From a geographical perspective, the E-Enterprise

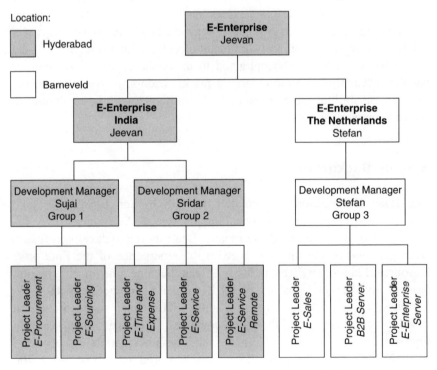

Figure A.4 Organizational structure of E-Enterprise development group (as of March 2002)

group was distributed between two locations: Hyderabad (about 60 people working on five products of the E-Enterprise Suite) and Barneveld (about 35 people working on two products and the common platform of the E-Enterprise Suite) (see Figure A.4).

In addition to the E-Enterprise group, the Marketing and Alliances group and the Project and Process office were involved in the management of the E-Enterprise suite.

Reference

Yin, R. K. (1994) *Case Study Research: Design and Methods*, Sage Publications, Newbury Park, CA.

NAME INDEX

Achrol, R. S.   134
Akgun, A. E.   76, 101
Araujo, L.   136–7

Baan, J.   249
Baan, P.   249
Battin, R. D.   18, 20
Bechky, B. A.   186, 189, 207
Bigley, G. A.   194
Blackler, F.   27–8
Blanck, E. L.   4
Boland, R. J.   71, 79
Brown, J.   45
Byrne, J.   49, 101

Cake, A.   63
Carlson, J. R.   57–8, 79
Child, J.   4
Citurs, A.   71
Cramton, C.D.   24, 186, 189, 191, 207, 234, 235
Crnkovic, I.   171
Crocker, R.   20
Cullen, S.   186, 210
Currie, W   49
Cutler, R.S.   26

Darr, E.D.   5
Das, T.K.   186, 205
Davenport, T.H.   79
Davis, G.   212
Davis, J.C.   154
Dawley, D.   186
De Neve, P.   18
DeSouza, K.   28
Doz, Y.L.   186, 205
Drucker, P.   xi
Dubois, A.   139
Dyer, J.H.   138, 148, 156

Ebert, C.   18
Ein-dor, P.   212
Evaristo, J.R.   28

Faraj, S.   5–6, 76, 79
Felin, T.   189
Fenema, P.C., van   x, 49, 186–7, 196, 214, 219
Fisher Gardial, S.   154

Fitzpatrick, G.   108
Flint, D.J.   137, 147
Flint, D.J.   137, 154
Ford, D.   135–6
Fredriksson, P.   136, 137
Frizelle, G.   156

Gadde, L.E.   135, 139
Gallivan, M.J.   7
Gassenheimer, J.B.   136, 154
Gemuenden, H.G.   7
Goodman, P.S.   5
Grant, R.M.   6, 74, 79

Håkansson, H.   135–6, 155
Hall, T.   186
Handfield, R.B.   132
Hansen, M.T.   27–8, 50
Hargadon, A.B.   189
Hendricks, P.   5
Herbsleb, J.D.   4, 5
Hesterly, W.S.   189
Hillegersberg, J. van   ix
Hinds, P.   195, 205
Hoegl, M.   7
Holbrook, M.B.   136
Holmen, E.   139, 155
Houston, F.S.   154

Jarvenpaa, S.L.   8
Jones, D.T.   134
Jones, H.L.   195

Kalakota, R.   185
Kanawattanachai, P.   25, 42
Keskin, H.   49, 101
King, W.R.   186, 212
Kotlarsky, J.   ix, 24, 219
Kreidler, J.   20
Kumar, K.   ix–x

Lai, A.W.   136
Langlois, R.N.   147
Larsson, M.   171
Lave, J.   43, 107, 108–9, 126
LeCroy, C.   170, 244
LeCroy, W.   243
Leidner, D.E.   8